THE AMERICAN REVOLUTION
AND RELIGION

THE AMERICAN REVOLUTION AND RELIGION

Maryland 1770-1800

BY

THOMAS O'BRIEN HANLEY

THE CATHOLIC UNIVERSITY OF AMERICA PRESS
CONSORTIUM PRESS
WASHINGTON, D.C.

Library of Congress Cataloging in Publication Data

Hanley, Thomas O'Brien.
 The American Revolution and religion; Maryland
1770-1800.

 Bibliography: p.
 1. Maryland--Church history. 2. United States--
History--Revolution--Religious aspects. I. Title.
BR555.M3H28   277.3   72-4742
ISBN 0-8132-0524-7

for

Kathleen M. O'Brien

CONTENTS

PREFACE

It is a happy thought to write of religion in the American Revolution at this time when the bicentennial celebrations of that event have been announced by the President of the United States. In the present case, the endeavor was begun ten years ago. This was fortunate for any results that the author hopes to attain in this volume. At its initiation then I became fully aware that the subject undertaken without any further restriction on the topic would be entirely unsatisfactory. There have been too many studies too broadly conceived, not in the mind of the author, but within the limits of a book's covers. There have been few instances of depth-testing by regional or other breakdowns of such highly generalized works. Their conception has also often lacked an incisive and detailed research of some significant element of the whole.

The present study has been an attempt at improving upon this methodology. From the first I was fortunately led into the field of study with proper respect for depth and detail within a feasible scope. A descriptive case for the improvement of religion was made from manuscripts in religious and other archives touching Maryland from 1770 to 1800.

What remained to be done was more difficult. How explain the nature of the improvement, its causes, and the relation of these to the previous years before the Revolution? Could responses to these questions be cast in any meaningful interpretation? Particularly with this last problem, a period of further study led to such a defensible interpretation and explanation.

Related to this more specific study were others that were broader in the period and general topic of American religious and cultural history. All of this, I believe, prepared me to accept the central fact of an emerging Christian state as extremely important to those times, uncomfortable though it seems to us today. For having done this, I shall be most pleased if controversy ensues. We have been entirely too compliant with our own times in postponing a dialogue on church and state with eighteenth century gentlemen less acceptable to us than is

Mr. Madison. I would also hope that the methodology employed here or some other would be applied to other regions, so that some day, perhaps at the 250th anniversary of the War, we might have a book title, "Religion in the American Revolution."

To Professor Richard Walsh of Georgetown University I am greatly indebted for the initiation of this study and its first formulations. Professors Frederick A. Norwood of Garrett Theological Seminary and Douglas R. Chandler of Wesley Seminary made helpful suggestions from their readings of portions of this work; so too, the Reverend Dr. Nelson Waite Rightmyer, Historian of the Diocese of Maryland of the Protestant Episcopal Church. I express my gratitude to them and to the staffs of the several archives who so kindly assisted me with my research and whose institutions are noted in the bibliography. I wish to thank Mrs. Vada I. Hummell for editing the final manuscript.

Washington, D. C.
July 31, 1971.

I

CONFINEMENT OF RELIGION

Contrary to what is generally said, the American Revolutionary War brought an era of religious growth and vitality in Maryland. A broad view of religious life, based on descriptive source material, shows that it improved over what was previously the case in the province. In general the new Constitution of 1776 put an end to the established Church of England in Maryland. The religious constraint found in a union of church and state was removed. The way was cleared for the many religious achievements which marked the period from 1776-1800.

Much more than this must be said. Religious life did not merely improve as an accidental by-product of a political revolution. There was a positive aspiration to a Christian state stirring simultaneously with the political ferment, both movements ultimately fusing in the Revolutionary War and the era which it created. This study, therefore, will not merely provide descriptive evidence that religious life was better. Account must be taken of how this aspiration to a Christian state brought improvements; of how the aspiration was generated and progressed. This dynamic process consequently justifies regarding the Christian state as a revolutionary emergence, propelled by forces within religious life itself.

In formulating these conclusions, it must be kept in mind that religion as understood here has a broad meaning. Something far more than denominational health is estimated, for the quality of religious life must be judged in primitive dimensions. Man's thoughts, purposes, and zealous efforts in universal history have reached out to objects beyond the immediate. A cosmic order of things and a deity at its center command his thoughts in quest of meaning. Both awaken his devotion as they are discovered. This devotion, as religion thus broadly defined, is both leaven and cohesive of his society. The state as the instrument of the society gave institutional force to religion of this dimension. So too the sect, denomination, or church became their more exact representation of religion on a social basis. In all of this, Maryland in the eighteenth century was generically Christian, whatever the diversity of institutional expression. The provincials and citizens of the new state became increasingly aware of this generic experience of religion.

The values of the current historian and the people of the period themselves affect the appraisal of religious growth that is attempted in this study. In the first case, some minimal standards are essential and beyond question in judging improvement and deterioration of religious life. The expansion of human freedom in the form of toleration seems such a value. Its growth in consequence of the Revolution marks the event as religiously significant. Did the religious impulse more effectively reach out to worthy objects which were meaningful then as now? With all of their religious differences, Marylanders had some common measures of the worth of their life and its religious objects. The Revolution's idealism greatly clarified them. It is possible to judge religious improvement by reference to eighteenth century values, as well as by more general ones of current times. Revolutionary Marylanders thought that the short-comings of existing political conditions and the church-state arrangement were confining the potential growth of religion broadly conceived. The revolution brought release from the confinement and opened the door to a further clarification of the aspiration to a better religious life. The new order that resulted favored achievement of religious objects.

It is important, therefore, thus to consider the meaning attached to religion and to estimate the exact nature of the religious improvement found in this period.

A final preliminary clarification can be made by examining what some important writers have said. Because they have not agreed with the conclusion of this study, their views should be stated. It should be noted, however, that the scope of their consideration has been quite different from the present one, which generalizes only about a specific area not heretofore examined in detail.

There is considerable confusion in the prevailing literature which takes a dim view of religion during and after the Revolution. It would appear that a Baptist preacher of that era stated the myth which was taken up by the twentieth century historians: "God sent them liberty," he wrote, "but with it leanness of soul". William Warren Sweet used this remark to sum up his own view of the material he had seen.[1] Writing ten years later, Nelson R. Burr came to the same conclusion with his bibliographical survey: "The quarter of a century after the Declaration of Independence was unfavorable to evangelical religion," he concluded. "The prevalent condition of religion was torpid." Organizational problems, it seemed to many historians, absorbed efforts, leaving little for the cultivation of vital religion.[2]

On the face of it, all of this seemed in conflict with J. Franklin

Jameson's seminal essay of 1924 on the Revolution as a social movement. The Revolution, according to him, cast the denominations in the
ecclesiastical forms long familiar thereafter, implying that this was good
for religion. Jameson, unaware of contradictions in his statements,
repeated the previous view that religion declined after the Revolution. [3]
Perhaps in the second instance he referred to religion in a broader sense
than ecclesiastical transformation. A recent reassessment of Jameson did
not take this consideration into account. Research subsequent to Jameson's essay, it was noted, merely filled out his thesis. These studies did
so only in reference to his dominantly ecclesiastical sketch. [4] The general
religious condition has not been the object of any systematic inquiry
which could establish that religion declined after the Revolution even
in the face of ecclesiastical transformation. This ambivalence of optimistic
and pessimistic statement had been overlooked by Jameson himself as well
as historians working in reference to him. The purpose here is to remove
such ambivalence, to show the general improvement in religious life,
and to indicate how a changed ecclesiastical structure in the Christian
state contributed to such improvement. For this, depth research on regions is essential. To see religion generally and the churches in a specific State is a necessary logical, inductive approach. [4]

One dramatic and provocative insight of Jameson was stated but
not explored with this kind of historical detail. He spoke of the Revolution as a great stream "spread broad upon the land." "Many aspirations were seat free." Yet the religious aspiration was not studied in its
origin nor its impulse to religious experience in the Revolutionary Era. [5]
Jameson had no tentative suggestions about these matters. It is the
purpose of the present study to do so in one region. The result will show
that something far more than the transformation of ecclesiastical structure
took place during these years. The religious vitality which historians
have not previously noted will appear. So, too, its connection with
ecclesiastical realignment, notably as a Christian state replaced a confessional state. The era was thus not a mere prelude to the well-proven
revivalism after 1800 but a part of it, and even its very source in the
case of Maryland.

To understand the revolutionary emergence of the Christian state
in Maryland, it is necessary to appreciate the sense of confinement felt
before 1770. The establishment of religion was the root cause of this
condition, which bred a spirit of religious rebellion along side of its political counter-part.

Historians do not always accurately gauge the churchstate arrangement in Maryland before 1776 in this context. It is often imprecisely called a union of church and state seen from the twentieth-century point of view. Statesmen of the young republic termed it a case of establishment of religion. This was their theoretical category for the established Church of England as an adjunct of the state. All of these formulations are inadequate in representing the condition which confined the Marylander's religious spirit and the particular church he espoused.

The confessional state as a radical term reveals much more in defining the Maryland arrangement. Its generic meaning encompasses all of the terms indicated above and goes to the underlying point of view that justified them as well as made them a source of aggravation to religious freedom. In essence the confessional state was defined in the dictum of the Peace of Augsburg in 1555, *cuius regio eius religio* (the religion of the prince is the religion of the realm). So important did religion become for national unity in England in that century, that citizens had to profess a confession of faith to be in good standing. While Elizabeth sought some accommodation with Lutherans and Puritans, she still defended the requirement of the Thirty-nine Articles of Belief and the Book of Common Prayer as the object of conformity. Archbishop Laud's harsh enforcement later drove the Puritans to New England during the reign of the Stuarts.

The rise of religious libertarian movements created further problems for the advocates of strict conformity to the Church of England. Presbyterians, Congregationalists, and other sects put conditions on the nature of their conformity to the official church. They could even be classified under the term *dissenter*. Radical Protestant separatists, Catholics, and Jews were legally outside of the conformist category and the benefits it held. The Toleration Act of 1699 under William and Mary sought to alleviate the more rigorous demands in conformity in the case of dissenters. Remnants of the confessional state, however, were still a source of confinement to dissenters in the decades before the Revolution. Conformity to the Thirty-nine Articles was still required. Freedom in the formation and preaching of dissenter congregations was confined. The indirect coercion of taxation by the confessional state was calculated to favor adherents to pure belief and to the Church of England structure, which was expected to foster it. The Marylander who stood wholly or partially outside the pale of the Established Church viewed the state, the colonial governor, and the bishop of London no differently than the first New England Puritans did Elizabeth and Archbishop Laud.

Even within the Church of England in the remote colony of Mary-

land, prominent members had developed fundamental disagreements
with the prevailing structure of church authority. They had made innovations which on the eve of the Revolution the clergy and authorities in
the mother country threatened to remove. The bishop of London, who
had jurisdiction over the province, was sympathetic to the churchmen
who wished to strengthen a more traditional application of their authority in the parishes. In their secular aim the proprietor and governor
were inclined to support such a move. In the eyes of lay vestrymen and
others, this all stood as a threat. If carried out, it would confine religious life, which they thought could be best maintained without such
pressure. This intensification of the confessional state they therefore
regarded as a confinement of the religious spirit itself, a feeling which
they shared with dissenters.

The historian is inclined to go back into the seventeenth century to
account for this sense of confinement within a confessional state. This
seems sound in view of the fact that following the establishment of the
Church of England in 1707 Marylanders did so themselves. The Maryland Charter and Toleration Acts before 1640 were often recalled with
authority in questions of religious dissent since the founding of the
colony. It was on these foundations that a separation of church and state
existed in Maryland prior to the revolution of 1688. Their force was
seen by many eighteenth-century Marylanders as a support to personal
freedom. By implication, however, they passed on to consideration of the
confessional state, its function, and even of its worth. On the eve of the
Revolution, the charter and toleration acts when recalled generated further restlessness with remaining constraints of the confessional state.

It is important to see how a sense of confinement manifested itself
within the particular religious elements in Maryland. An examination
of this will also bring out the inferior condition of religious life prior
to the Revolution, explaining it to a great extent.

Consider the official church in Maryland as an essential of the confessional state. Its membership more than equalled that of all other religious groups together. The Anglican parishes, as the more than forty
local units of church life were called, revealed telling weaknesses prevailing in the forty years before the war. The first parishes had begun
with considerable strength in the lay-vestry, which was responsible for
promoting parish welfare. Instances of effective leadership showed the
potential of this feature of church life. By and large, however, few parishioners appeared for voting and attendance of vestrymen at sessions
was generally not good. Even where conditions were better than this

the position of the minister, the Anglican priest, was beset with countless difficulties, which frustrated the vital ministry of the church to the people. This was especially true of the minister as an Anglican priest, officially installed as rector of the parish and principal vestryman. [6]

While a case can be made against the quality of ministers in Maryland, the lack of permanence in their appointment was greatly responsible for the slowness of religious growth. A strong vestry might seek out good appointments, but final designation of a rector was in the hands of the governor under the guidance of the lord proprietor. The long wait for permanent appointment under this arrangement left many temporary ministers awaiting decision on who the official rector of the parish would ultimately be. The most desirable appointees shopped around, creating more delay. The vestries, furthermore, were often presented with minister friends of the governor and proprietor, who were far from the stature the office required. The appointment made, it was beyond the vestry power to remove the rector. At the same time, there was no commissary (a supervising minister representing the bishop of London), as had been the case in the first few decades of the century. In the whole scheme, the governor and proprietor stood between the parish appointment and the bishop, who often only gave ecclesiastical validity to what the secular officials arranged. [7]

Thus it is not surprising that the number of parishes did not grow in proportion to the population prior to the war. Some vestry records reflect the deterioration of religious life under the defective structure. [8] In one small parish the vestry cited thirteen persons in one month as guilty of fornication or adultery. It is questionable, of course, whether the very practice of vestry censorship of public morals on a quasi-civil basis placed the religious institution in the best light with parishioners. By 1770, however, there was a clamor in the vestries for some kind of control at least over the removal of delinquent ministers. Although the power recently given to the assembly for this purpose was not exercised, this maneuver manifested a coming fervor in the church. Superior vestrymen involved in provincial assembly politics accounted for it. From the other side, clergy who favored a resident bishop as a means of reform, in their way represented the same concern and judgment on the sad condition of religious affairs. In the minds of such vestrymen, however, a bishop would only extend the stifling effect of the confessional state. An end of the confessional state would make a resident bishop acceptable and effective in creating the reality of a Christian state. This the Revolution accomplished. [9]

In addition to the Anglican element before the Revolution, another broad force in Maryland religious life must be taken into account. The movement known as the Great Awakening tells of an object toward which society was reaching. Any object of aspiration has to be at least tasted; so, too, discontent is present when society is deprived of what one has tasted. This was the case with regard to evangelical religion, which in 1740 the Great Awakening stirred up and fostered through its revivals. In essence it was a movement away from the formalistic confinements of church doctrine and ritual. Rather than religion as instruction received, the preachers of the awakening convinced vast numbers that religion was to be experienced upon hearing the word of God. Emotional appeal and response were external manifestations of the inner vitality of the Christian life.

Theological change accounted for the emergence of evangelical religion in the awakening episode. John Calvin's theology of salvation was re-examined. The Dutch theologian Jacobus Arminius rejected his restrictions on man's free will. Jonathan Edwards, on the other hand, reinterpreted the Calvinistic notion of God's sovereignty, which was so essential to the spirit of the Great Awakening as a divine experience. German pietism, a reform movement within Lutheranism, had a pervading influence on all groups. Their emphasis on the simplicity of scriptural piety and devotion to the Redeemer transcended theological subtleties. John Wesley, outside of the Calvinistic tradition to a great extent, drew from this source. He himself stood, however, within the Anglican tradition of the Church of England. His followers in America understandably entered upon the awakening preaching. The Wesleyan development, known as Methodism, thus took form within the Church of England both in Europe and America. [10]

Of these facets of the Great Awakening, Maryland was affected more clearly by the Methodists. While Presbyterians had a rich experience of it and next to the Church of England constituted the largest sect in the province, the movement among them was restricted. Their ranks divided regarding enthusiastic preaching. Their influence, however modified, was added to the Methodist impact, so that evangelical religion took root in Maryland. The awakening did not reach the proportions found elsewhere and declined from the fervor of 1740. What then followed was a period of adjustment rather than a removal of evangelical Christianity. Although confined, the aspiration to such piety remained on the eve of the Revolution. [11]

This religious spirit reached out toward the state as an instrument of revival, which it had not been before the Revolution. The state could be sensitive to religious needs and, in this respect, could be said to have a conscience. Torpor characterized its current condition.

Another element of the religious background of the Revolution must be seen in dissenters from the established church, both Protestant and Catholic. The confinement of the confessional state in general upon them has already been noted, but it is in place here to mention a few specific conditions that adversely affected their religious life.

In decades past, it was true, the provincial government had mitigated some of the harshness which the confessional state brought down on Protestant dissenters and Roman Catholics. The Revolutionary debate following 1770 showed that a new spirit of understanding toward dissenters was moving among the Anglican citizens of Maryland, particularly its younger gentlemen. These were men of talent and leadership, the future patriots of the Revolution. The tax on Presbyterians, Quakers, Baptists, Lutherans and other Protestant communities for the support of the Anglican clergy and parishes of the Established Church, they now saw, had too long been taken for granted by the proprietary party and even by the assembly. In another case, a double tax had been imposed on Roman Catholics because of their identity in faith with the French enemy in the French and Indian War. Catholics *qua* Catholic were susceptible of sedition, it had been said from Elizabethan days, and Marylanders acted out the fiction again. This lack of sensitivity, then, constituted an evil condition in the old regime and caused bad spirit among dissenters. Reform-minded Anglican patriots were determined to revitalize the conscience of the state in all of these cases. The Revolution became an instrument for doing so.

There was a latent potential to transform society and the state with greater Christian harmony if the tax were removed. The Anglican and dissenter traditions of the faith could then come together on an equal footing where the official organisms of the state and society operated. Dissenters aspired to this condition.

Catholics, too, had their own special problem which the Revolution resolved, thus fulfilling their particular aspiration. The ecclesiastical structure of the ministry depended upon the Jesuit Order for its stability. The Jesuit superior of the Maryland mission had quasi-episcopal power and moved among his fellow priests as one of them, engaged in an active ministry. On the eve of the Revolution suppression of the Order threatened collapse of their increasingly fruitful apostolate. Somewhat analogously to the Anglican need of a bishop, Catholics now desperately needed a strong symbol of their ecclesiastical power in Maryland in the person of a bishop or one approximating this status. Only then could the former stability be maintained and commitment to the mission by former Jesuits won. The Revolution substantially met this demand in the favorable conditions for an independent American Church that resulted. There would be growth in numbers and a return to Catholic practices by many when the Revolution ended discriminatory legislation.

Within the Church of England in Maryland, there were those who had an answer to the complaints of dissenters and others. They constituted another element in the background of the Revolution. While the established church and the unsatisfactory condition of the Anglican community has been already discussed, it is in place here to take note of Anglicans who defended the old order and others who questioned it. The case for the latter group became more forceful after 1760 and was increasingly supported.

Loyal adherents of the Established Church dreaded sectarianism. Lack of full conformity in dissenters, they believed, sapped the capacity of the people in creating a Christian society and destroyed the charity which should characterize a Christian people. By keeping sectarianism down and within the Established Church as much as possible, these evils could be averted. To other Anglicans, however, this reasoning implied too little esteem for religious freedom as held by a growing number after 1760. Religion itself was more favorably affected by the enlargement of freedom than by increasing authoritarian structures in the Church of England as a device against bitter sectarianism.

The events after 1760 and the accompanying debate by eminent young Anglicans supported this contention. A confessional state did not create a Christian state. Many felt that the appointment of a colonial bishop, for example, would frustrate the aspiration toward a Christian state. This was due largely to the political context of a resident bishop and his appointment in the conditions of a confessional state. If the colony could somehow bring the different sects and denominations to equality before the law, the free condition would open the door to any authentic growth of which they were capable. The denominations would stand as natural facets of expression for a generally religious and Christian people. In such a setting an Anglican bishop would be acceptable. Unity and collaboration among such groups would result, something which the confessional state had failed to produce. Not until there was hope of political emancipation would a Christian state emerge in fidelity to this prevailing aspiration developed after 1760.

To these young Anglicans the social mission of Christianity was also confined by the confessional state. Care of orphans, the poor, and education was undoubtedly taken up by the Anglican vestries. The official church was related to the government and had the force of governmental law behind it. The records show significant instances in fulfilling this role of social service. At the same time, the broad base of society and its religious conscience went untapped under an arrangement of exclusive Church responsibility. The revolutionary era saw a reversal of this condition. All of the churches and society in general under the Christian impulse to charity took up this burden of general welfare. A religious vision of the secular was discovered. It drew upon Anglican and other traditions of Christian gentility, which urged the Christian destiny of society and the gentleman's role in fulfilling it.

The Christian vision, of course, extends to wider horizons than the welfare work of the vestries. There is the zealous hope that the whole of society be permeated with the spirit of the Gospel. Young Anglican gentlemen sensed this. The Established Church as the state's symbol of its Christianity rested too heavily upon the consciences of too many citizens who felt that a symbol was not enough. Perhaps there was a better way in which the state could play its Christian role. Significant numbers of this Christian people, for example, were uninvolved in the care of the young in schools. A truly Christian people demanded a broader commitment from the citizenry in the work of improving society in the image of the Gospel. There was a union of church and state, but was there a union of Christianity and society?

Young Anglicans and other Marylanders bristled under the increasing burden of the old political regime in Maryland; they understandably questioned the religious benefits which were supposed to be officially assured by that regime. There was indeed a delicate balance in what revolutionary Marylanders wanted. They were calling for more religion and less church at the state's hands. They hoped to gain a Christian society as a result of the change in state policy. Such a society, not an established church, would see to the reality of a Christian state. [12]

These then were, negatively speaking, the ingredients of unrest in Maryland before 1770: the confessional state, an inferior quality of its church and ministry, the tax on non-conformists. Positively, an aspiration grew up, initiated by the Great Awakening recalled and taken up by the young Anglican leaders of the American Revolution in Maryland. These opened the door to those of other Christian traditions. They were inspired by the common cause to create a Christian state and society.

The whole dynamic of evolution involved in this aspiration thus confined, rose dramatically to the surface beginning in 1770. It began with the attack of the strong vestry-minded leaders Samuel Chase and William Paca on the per poll (on each legally taxable person) tobacco tax for support of the clergy of the Church of England in Maryland. They also intended to scotch an attempt by the Reverend Jonathan Boucher to bring an Anglican bishop to Maryland. Thomas Johnson and Charles Carroll of Carrollton, supported by Chase and Paca, attacked Governor Robert Eden's proclamation of fees, as part of a general action to deter proprietary power. The unravelling of this debate became intertwined with the clergy tax and the episcopacy controversies. Ultimately, the whole justification of an established church and the resulting discrimination against religious minorities came into public controversy. [13]

The immediate forces that brought on the conflict at this time were quite evident. The lay vestries of the Anglican parishes fought to hold control of ecclesiastical government. The governor and the lord proprietor asserted the power of church government along the lines of the confessional state. They held fast to the power of appointing rectors of the parishes, whom they did not want under assembly supervision. Anglican ministers hoped to strengthen this proprietary policy by a move to bring an Anglican bishop to America. Usurpation of authority by the vestries would also be weakened by a resident bishop. The opponents of the proprietary party had their attack ready. They could point to Richard Browne, an Anglican minister, who had fled to Virginia under suspicion of having murdered a slave. The Reverend Bennet Allen, in another scandal, had leisurely proceeded to Philadelphia, there to enjoy its good life as a crony of Lord Baltimore, living on a £ 1300 annual income from a Maryland parish. Two curates did his work for him at All Saint's parish in Frederick County. [14] Would there ever be a Christian society under such official leadership? Acid critics raised the problem in this form. In 1770 William Paca and Samuel Chase did so with greater moderation and in their responsible roles as lower house assemblymen. The message of both groups was clear enough. The confessional state and the provincial establishment were confining the religious spirit and religion itself.

The Reverend Jonathan Boucher was one of those Anglicans who had long advocated a fully developed form of the Established Church as a means of vitalizing religious life in the province. He addressed his initial request for a bishop to Governor Horatio Sharpe, Robert Eden's predecessor, who took the matter under advisement. Sharpe understood that supervision of the clergy was one of the chief needs to be met by a resident bishop. His adviser, Hammersley, explained that the assembly had recently given itself this power. As yet it had not been employed. The vestry desired and, on occasion, attempted supervision indirectly. Hammersley pointed out that the Maryland Charter of 1632 gave no foundation for the appointment of a bishop in the province. [15] To do so now would be a violation of the charter. The Reverend Hugh Neill wrote to the Bishop of London, who had jurisdiction over all clergy in America, in response to Hammersley's reasoning. By the same token of the charter, Neill said, the governor's adviser would have to deny the validity of the assembly supervision of the church. This practice plainly violated the clause protecting "Holy Mother Church's rights and privileges". All discussion in terms of the charter thus implicitly added up to a denial by both parties of full establishment in the province. The door seemed to those who wanted a full-blown established church, bishop and all. [16]

More immediately and at the surface of public debate was the pending question of clergy salaries and the manner of computing them. The assembly had jurisdiction over such a temporality. The payment of this tax had always been in the form of tobacco. Recent fluctuations in its market value had caused a decline in the amount of salary actually received by the clergy, who now called for a reimbursement for losses of the recent period. Already annoyed by the drive for a bishop, the lower house became intransigent in the face of the clergy request for a 40 per poll tax. This question was in heated debate at the very time that Sharpe and Hammersley were consulting about Boucher's request for a bishop.

When the word was out that there was such a discussion of the validity of establishment in whole or part, several citizens made public statements. Argument shifted away from the charter and led to an examination of the laws which William and Mary had approved for the establishment of the Church of England in Maryland. Sounder legal evidence for the legitimacy of a Maryland bishop was found here. "Church of England Planter," however, noted in a handbill of September 1770, that King William had died before the governor of Maryland had received his instructions on the formation of the Established Church. He advocated vestry power to remove unsatisfactory ministers and opposed the amount of compensation requested by the clergy for their salaries during the tobacco price depression. [17]

Before the end of the year "A Constitutionalist" published a pamphlet, *Reply to Planter...*, which dealt with the technicality of William's death. It became evident that precise legal reasoning would bring no clearer conclusions than had been the case with Hammersley's argument from the charter. But obviously some basis in law accounted for the existing structure of the Established Church in Maryland. [18] Others now attacked "Church of England Planter" and his denial of the legality of establishment. He was labelled an "Advocate of Anarchy," a "Gentleman of the New Regulation," who had no law, even one conceivably invalid by a technicality, upon which to base his own ideas of church authority. The clergy now understandably elicited considerable sympathy for themselves, and their church. More than sixty years after the official enabling of an establishment, essential details of the church —such as a bishop—, were still wanting. The legal basis of even the restricted structure was also being called into question. Pseudonyms attached to letters in the *Maryland Gazette* did not conceal the identity of the "Gentleman of the New Regulation." Eminent men of the assembly were known to be in the ranks of Boucher's critics. Their skill in law and public persuasion menaced the set establishment and its clergy.

Seeing this ominous thundercloud, the clergy on October 5, 1771, addressed a petition to Governor Robert Eden, recently arrived successor to Sharpe. The burden of their message was quite simple, seen in the context of the confessional state theory. [19] The attack that now fell on themselves, they said, was directed at the lord proprietor himself and his governor as proprietary agent in the province. The governor's chief advisers, some of them members of the upper house, should have been part of the same structure of defense. They had now defected to the lower house, which opposed the clergy view of the per poll tobacco tax. Not only had the upper house abdicated their role as defensive screen of the clergy, it now appeared that the Governor was about to imitate them. The upper house could thus be blamed for unfavorable clergy legislation as well as failures previously to curb the power of the vestry. "Former Gov[erno]rs used to Place ye Council as a Screen between themselves & ye People," Charles Carroll of Carrollton's father slyly remarked, "Ye case is Reversed, if ye Gov[erno]r acknowledges instructions not to Clip ye 40 per Poll tax." [20] Boucher, recalling the episode in his later *Reminiscences*, said the same thing. The governor lined up the clergy to take the blows directed at himself. He did not see that he should be a martyr for the church's cause of higher salaries and a bishop. Let the clergy fight it out with the people. There was obviously little heart in those who wielded the secular arm of the confessional state. The plain fact was that the Governor was already engaged in a running battle with the clergy' opponents over customs, tobacco and other fees, which he had imprudently fixed by proclamation. He was trying to save his skin by using the upper house as a screen against the opposition of the lower house. Let the clergy play its role alone, thus leaving the Governor safe under any eventuality. [21]

With the stage thus set, distinguished "Gentlemen of the New Regulation" came into public controversy with Boucher and his partisans. Using no pseudonyms, they were willing to let the discussion run the gamut from the clergy salary bill to the constitutional basis for establishment in the colony. Samuel Chase was among the first to enter the newspaper controversy. He was the son of Reverend Thomas Chase, Rector of St. Paul's Parish, Baltimore, who had educated his son in the classics. Young Chase received his legal training in the law of offices of Hammond and Hall at Annapolis and served in the St. Mary's County Court as magistrate in 1761. He was a member of lower house when the clergy bill controversy came to a head. Politically he was in league with William Paca, distinguished member of the lower house and educated at Inner Temple, London. [22] Both men were associated under the leadership of Thomas Johnson in a group now dubbed "The Independent Whigs," because of their opposition to Parliament and the governor's recent arbitrary proclamation of fees. They were not only "Gentlemen of the New Regulation," but their liberalism had even brought into their circle Charles Carroll of Carrollton, a Jesuit educated Catholic. Through his wife. Johnson was identified with the congregational spirit of Protestantism in New England from which her family came. He had been educated in law at the offices of Stephen Bordley, long a power in lower house politics. He did legal work for the wealthy Carrolls and other important provincials. His public leadership against the Stamp Act in 1765 won him great popularity. [23]

The "Independent Whigs" and "Gentlemen of the New Regulation" embodied all of the elements which were hostile to a full establishment and to the basic assumptions of the confessional state. It was distressing to the clergy that they spoke with such great popular support. That they did so with great learning and statesmanship made their entry into the controversy doubly menacing to the supporters of establishment. William Eddis, the customs collector, recalled that their public life was characterized by "eloquence and force of reason... and the utmost regularity and propriety..." They were believed to be zealous for the improvement of religion. [24] Their strategy was for Johnson and Carroll to resist the Governor over fees by proclamation. Chase and Paca were to attack Boucher on the question of a bishop and the clergy per poll tobacco tax.

Chase reasoned that English Common Law justified prevailing practices within the Established Church in Maryland. Charter provision and the legislation by William and Mary were thus bypassed, or at least subordinated. Chase defender "Church of England Planter's" case against establishment, but he also noted that common law provided grounds for the development of vestry government in the province. [25] In January, 1773 a "Freeholder of St. Anne's" sought to use this basis of reasoning, but to refute Chase's claims for vestry power. The laws of 1640 and 1649, based on religious liberty provisions in the charter, he said, actually excluded the notion of vestries. Custom and common law could not change, the force of this law. [26] Following the same tack, Boucher, a month later argued that vestries could not stand since, as the "Gentlemen of the New Regulation" had claimed, the law of 1702 was void and with it any foundation for the existence of vestries. [27]

Thomas Johnson came to the rescue of Chase about a week after Boucher's attack. Customs originating in the province should be distinguished from those brought from the mother country, where vestries existed by custom. While vestries were not found in seventeenth-century Maryland, this did not prevent adoption of them by Maryland on the authority of their prior existence in the mother country. [28] William Paca also answered Boucher and Robert Goldsborough, a leader of the lower house supported by Boucher: [29] "Amicus Patriae" wrote another letter approving Paca. On March 18, 1773, Chase and Paca put their names to a fully developed presentation of their case. They related common law to the principle that church as well as state authority derives from the people. The people elected both the vestry and the assembly. Both are a source of regulation in the Church. "The law of right founded on reason," as they called this practice, is "a system of jurisprudence adored by Englishmen..." [30]

The appeal of this message extended beyond Anglicans long attached to the authority of the vestry. Presbyterians, Boucher believed, found in the statement a common religious bond which would protect dissenters against the appointment of a bishop. In view of the strong congregationalism feature of Chase's writings, the bond was not artificial. [31] "Presbyterian Patuxent" wrote in support of Chase as did "A True Patriot" a week later, showing the accuracy of Boucher's analysis. These writings show how great was the discontent with the recommendations of the clergy and an establishment system full of contradictions in their eyes. "Presbyterian Patuxent" gave lyrical expression to this feeling:

> "I could heartily wish as a mercy to these infant colonies, and to the nation in general, that all the religious differences which have so long subsisted and rent the church of the peaceful redeemer, were ever banished from human society, and that all who name the name of Christ, might be with one heart and one mouth, and would cease to oppress and rent one another, [after] the example of the prince of darkness" [32]

At this very time Paca and Chase published the formal petition of the clergy for a bishop, in order to further alert the public. It significantly contained the reasoning that only the appointment of a bishop could arrest the Presbyterian trend of the Established Church and its emphasis upon vestry power. All of the language of justification traditional with confessional states was used. "The growth of Sectaries has been so amazingly rapid", they noted with alarm, "and their conduct so daring and vexatious." The sectarians even dared to question the right of the lord proprietor to present Anglican rectors for appointment in parishes. This, the petition declared, "can only be put a stop to, by the admission of an American Bishop." In May Boucher again appealed to old confessional state structures. In the *Maryland Gazette* he noted that England had granted a complete Catholic Church establishment under Bishop Briand in Quebec. Maryland will grant no such toleration to the Anglican establishment in Maryland. "Dissenters, quaker, catholicks, all are completely tolerated: the Church of England only wants toleration." [33]

The device of revealing the petition for a bishop had the effects calculated by Paca and Chase. "A Consistent Protestant" in August wrote that the whole system of support for the clergy should be revised. "If, after all," he explained, "our legislators should judge it necessary or expedient, that every man should be under obligation to contribute to the support of some publick teacher of religion; all that I would ask of them is, let it be left to my option, whom I shall encourage as such." In this candid, if naive, expression is found an authentic aspiration for a Christian state. "I can truly say," he continued regarding clergy salary grants, "my choice would be determined, without any regard to sect or denomination, solely by appearances of the greatest capacity and the strongest inclinations to inculcate doctrines, unquestionably, beneficial to all men, viz doing justly, loving mercy, and walking humbly with God." Dissolution of the confessional state and the Established Church would set such a citizen free, yet without public authority ceasing positively to aid religion. "A Consistent Protestant" clearly spoke as herald of the Christian state. [34]

Popular response surprised the established clergy and provincial officials. In one area of public sentiment in which they felt more certain, they again misread the popular mind. It had long been taken for granted in eighteenth century Maryland that no apologies were needed for excluding a Catholic from voting, holding public office and public worship. As a corollary, it seemed to Boucher and his chief supporter in the upper house, Daniel Dulany the Younger, that a Catholic should not have a voice in public questions. In 1773 Dulany debated in the pages of the *Maryland Gazette* the question of fees by proclamation. A Catholic, Charles Carroll of Carrollton, entered the debate against Dulany. When Dulany began to lose this argument, he reasonably supposed he coul question the propriety of a Catholic influencing public law in this fashion. The public responded to Dulany with hostility. Its highly liberal reasoning in support of Carroll showed the discontent with a confessional state as it affected the free speech of certain Marylanders. Dulany's attack on Carroll's faith and exercise of free speech led a large number of citizens to examine their notions of church-state relations and personal freedom in the Maryland context. Again aspirations were expressed which revealed the confinement under which society labored. [35]

In the course of the debate Dulany reminded Carroll that such brash conduct by his father during the French and Indian War nearly brought further disabilities on Catholics. "Do these disabilities," Carroll responded in reference to his own case, "extend so far, as to preclude them from thinking and writing on matters merely of a political nature?" It was indeed a sore point with a confessional state to suggest such a notion of separation of church and state. In May "Protestant Planter" came to his defense in the *Maryland Gazette*. The public, he said, did not believe that Carroll would subvert church and state as his enemies said. [36] "He was a friend to public liberty." Paca and others said in their public letters of commendation. [37] Others re-stated the view of Boucher and Dulany, "Clericus" charged Carroll and his fellow Whigs with "rooting out the protestant establishment of this priest-ridden province." [38] Boucher used Carroll's tolerant references to establishment and the penal laws against the Independent Whigs who were critical of both of these conditions. The people were clearly becoming less tolerant of establishment. "Protestant Planter" said that the present repressive environment was foreign to the spirit of colonization that created Maryland.

A respondent to this point of view revealed the uneasiness of those who would be totally loyal to the old understandings of the confessional state. He felt that there was no choice in the matter of a Protestant establishment, unless it be a Catholic establishment. Tolerance, he felt, had gone too far for the good of the country. "There has hardly ever been a period since this country has been under a protestant government, when conduct, like his [Carroll's] wou'd have met with such a reception, as it now has. What this may forebode, I care not to inquire—the real friends of their country will think of it." These friends had indeed thought of it and in company with Carroll. The writer described it well as "the liberal spirit of the age we live in with respect to religious differences." "God forbid, that I shou'd wish it otherwise," he said, "I still am so tinctured with the old spirit of our constitution, as to think we go rather too far, when we encourage a professed Romanist to intermeddle in a dispute concerning a protestant establishment." [39]

This was indeed the portrait of a hesitant man gazing at the high ground of the revolutionary generation. The events that followed the debate of 1773 constituted a grand movement. The confinement of the old confessional state was oppressive. Once Marylanders came to the high ground of 1773 which led to independence, "the liberal spirit of the age" would generate the necessary leadership. In such leaders the religious aspiration of the people took tangible form and led to the creation of a Christian state.

By the fall of 1773, public support overwhelmingly favored the case which Paca and Chase had made to lower clergy fees. This pressure, rather than conviction, led the governor and the upper house to concur in a new tax bill. They agreed to a thirty pound tobacco levy, or the alternative of four shillings, imposed on each taxable person of the province (per poll) by the assembly. Had the bill been sponsored by more orthodox Anglicans, rather than the prebyterizers and "Gentlemen of the New Regulation" like Chase and Paca, Boucher could have bowed in defeat with some grace. As it was, he was embittered at the Governor and the upper house for the betrayal. Rather than move the Church closer to its true form, the year was closing with different results. Chase and Paca clearly interpreted reform in terms of ecclesiastical change: a further entrenching of vestry and assembly power over the church. Boucher had hoped for reform with a bishop and his opponents had frustrated his efforts. [40]

The "Independent Whigs" were shrewd enough to see that the compromising action of the governor and the assembly did not mean abandonment of Boucher and the more orthodox view of the Church of England. Still they sincerely felt that the good of religion did not safely rest in the hands of their opponents. This conviction rather than a specific ecclesiastical policy had prompted their political responses. Boucher and the proprietary party were now seen in the same light, as obstacles to progress. Both stood for the confessional state and firm political rule from London. In 1774 the "Independent Whigs" turned to the latter menace, putting aside the establishment question where it stood. Obviously general religious reform could not be accomplished by the recent clergy and other church legislation. The release of religious life from this modified confessional state was still to be attained. Very shortly it became evident that this could be accomplished only in conjunction with the political movement for independence.

Religious unrest was tied to the anti-proprietary movement as it broadened into the Revolutionary War. "Such a frame of thinking," Charles A. Barker correctly states in reference to the Church and related controversies, "was a powerful influence; it gave political and economic liberalism a friendly climate, and it had great vitality apart from public issues, the strength of consistency, of vision, of detachment, and of moral force." This is part of Barker's answer to the question, "What gave force to the politics of discontent?" Religious liberalism fused with a political liberalism in the tradition of English radical idealism, which had taken root in the seventeenth century. To this interpretation has been added here the notion of early Maryland law as a foundation for colonial radicalism, which was perhaps best expressed in Charles Carroll of Carrollton. [41]

At the very time when the clergy salary question was settled in October, 1773, the Lower House created a standing Committee of Correspondence and Inquiry. Its purpose was to collaborate with Massachusetts, Rhode Island, Connecticut and Virginia in defense of colonial rights. Chase, Paca and Johnson were among the eleven members of the committee. While there was little correspondence during the ensuing month, this condition changed in the spring of 1774. On June 1, crown authorities closed the Port of Boston as a reprisal for the Tea Party. Maryland and several other colonies intensified their involvement in dramatic patriot efforts in Massachusetts. The committee formed the previous year stated that all of the colonies stood in grave danger from the tyranny of the mother country. Maryland committed itself to the Continental Agreement of May, 31, 1774.[42]

The Maryland revolutionary leadership was substantially those men who had opposed the proprietary party's religious position. They initiated the first steps toward the formation of a new government. Congresses of county deputies were called. On June 22, ninety-two delegates from the counties gathered at Annapolis. In the course of the coming year this convention functioned as a revolutionary government, even though it was part of the traditional Lower House of the Assembly. The Committee of Correspondence was now enlarged, so that a body representative of the whole province entered into collaboration with the Continental Congress, which assembled in Philadelphia on September 2, 1774. Delegates from Maryland were present. In December the Maryland revolutionary body showed its intention to engage in mutual defense of the colonies. Able-bodied men from the ages of sixteen to fifty were called for military drill.[43]

While Maryland leaders were proceeding with prudence and moderation, they could not ignore the increasing danger of reprisal for the steps which they were taking. They had the immediate case of Virginia to warn them. There the royal governor had seized the province arsenal Without violence, the Maryland revolutionary assembly now forced Governor Robert Eden to yield the arsenal to his own provincial military forces, who were sympathetic to the patriots. By the end of 1775 Maryland thus stood in preparedness. Patriots had command of a revolutionary government, even though complete severance from the mother country had not yet taken place.[44]

Maryland was no less active through its delegates in the Continental Congress. Samuel Chase especially won the attention of such eminent members as John Adams. Adams had developed a diplomatic plan to support Benedict Arnold's bold attack on Quebec. He turned to Chase as a man suited to accompanying Benjamin Franklin to Montreal in the wake of successful military campaigns in Lake George and Lake Champlain. Adams wanted a commission appointed by the Congress to proceed into the northern theatre, so that it might advise on military policy. Secret investigation among the French peasants *(habitants)*, favored the plan of recruiting militiamen from their ranks. It was felt that they were disaffected to the recently imposed British regime. Through Chase, Adams gained insight into the religious situation with these prospective French patriots The Archbishop of Quebec, Jean Briand, had placed under the Church censure of *ex communication* anyone who collaborated with the American revolutionary efforts. To relieve such adherents to the patriot cause, Adams and Chase sought the efforts of Father John Carroll, kinsman of Chase's revolutionary associate, Charles Carroll of Carrollton. Both Carrolls were then named members of the Commission. In the liberal religious atmosphere emerging in Maryland, the plan was accepted by all parties. John Carroll believed he had the powers needed for removing *ex communication* of *habitants*. The Commission labored at its mission through April, May and June of 1776. [45]

During this period of confrontation with the mother country, Maryland moved with the more moderate colonies and their delegates in the Continental Congress. In April of 1776 it was clear to many that England offered no honorable adjustment of American grievances. In that month North Carolina instructed its delegates to declare for independence. Chase and the other Maryland delegates concurred in the general decision to set America free and create the state republic to which they aspired. The decision of July 4, 1776 also set Maryland free of the confinements of the confessional state. In the fall Marylanders addressed themselves to the task of drafting a constitution which expressed their religious as well as their republican idealism. Even before this systematic formulation of the Christian state with a written constitution, Marylanders were conducting a revolutionary government. Indeed, in the months before and after the Declaration of Independence and prior to the constitutional convention in the fall of 1776, the Christian spirit of Marylanders was on trial. It can also be said that while the war went on they employed a revolutionary government. Did a Christian conscience guide the government in these years?

REFERENCES

[1]William W. Sweet, *Religion in the Development of American Culture* (New York, 1952, pp. 53, 91-92, 95-96.

[2]Nelson R. Burr, *A Critical Bibliography of Religion in America* (2 vols.; Princeton, N. J., 1961), I, p. 155.

[3]Franklin Jameson, *The American Revolution Considered as a Social Movement* (Princeton, N. J., 1926).

[4]See Frederick B. Tolles, "The American Revolution Considered as a Social Movement: A Re-Evaluation," *American Historical Review*, LX (1954), 10-12.

[5]*Ibid.*

[6]Harold E. Hartdgen, "The Anglican Vestry in Colonial Maryland" (Ph. D. Diss., Dept. of History, Northwestern Univ., 1965). The outspoken remarks of Thomas Cradock significantly supports the interpretation given here and throughout the chapter on the Church and the bishop's role. See David Curtis Skaggs, "Thomas Cradock's Sermon on the Governance of Maryland's Established Church," *The William and Mary Quarterly*. Third Series, XXVII (Oct., 1970), 630-53.

[7]*Ibid.,* pp. 244, 43, 149-50.

[8]Charles A. Barker, *The Background of the Revolution in Maryland* (New Haven, 1940), p. 8.

[9]Hartdagen, pp. 234, 38-39; and Skaggs, p. 341, for Cradock on a bishop.

[10]Richard M. Cameron, ed., *The Rise of Methodism, a Source Book* (New York, 1954), pp. 83-88.

[11]*Ibid.,* pp. 89-93.

[12]Burr, I, 153-55.

[13]Thomas O'Brien Hanley, *Charles Carroll of Carrollton: The Making of a Revolutionary Gentleman* (Washington, D. C., 1970), ch. 13.

[14]David C. Skaggs, "Maryland's Impulse Toward Social Revolution: 1750-1776," *The Journal of American History,* LIV (Mar., 1968), 778-79.

[15]William H. Browne, *et al.* (eds.), *Archives of Maryland* (68 vols.; Baltimore, Md., 1883-   ), XIV, 394-95, 401, 431; and Barker, p. 360.

[16]Hugh Neill to the Bishop of London, Sep. 20, 1768, in Barker, p. 360.

[17]"Church of England Planter," *Maryland Gazette,* Sep. 28, 1770, and Barker, pp. 360-61.

[18]*Maryland Gazette,* June 27, 1771.

[19]"Address to Eden," Oct. 5, 1771 (Md. Diocesan Library, Md. Historical Society); Barker, p. 361.

[20]To son, Nov. 8, 1771 (*ibid.,* MS 206).

[21]Barker, p. 362.

[22]Hanley, *Charles Carroll,* pp. 224-225.

[23]Charles Carroll from his father, May 7, 1771 (Md. Historical Society, MS 206); Edward S. Delaplaine, "The Life of Thomas Johnson." *Maryland Historical Magazine,* XIV (Mar., 1919), 33-56.

[24]*Ibid.*

[25]*Maryland Gazette,* Aug. 6, Sep. 10, 1772.

[26]*Ibid.,* Mar. 18, and Jan. 28, 1773.

[27]*Ibid.,* Feb. 4, 1773.

[28]*Ibid.,* Feb. 11, 1773.

[29]*Ibid.,* Feb. 15, 1773.

[30]*Ibid.,* Mar. 18, 1773.

[31]*Ibid.,* Apr. 8, 1773.

[32]*Ibid.,* Mar. 25, 1773.

[33]*Ibid.,* May 27, 1773.

[34]*Ibid.,* Aug. 19, 1773.

[35]Hanley, *Charles Carroll,* ch. 14.

[36]Elihu S. Riley (ed.),*Correspondence of "First Citizen" — Charles Carroll of Carrollton, and "Antilon" — Daniel Dulany Jr., 1773, With a History of Governor Eden's Administration in Maryland 1769-1776* (Baltimore, 1902), pp. 59, 230-31.

[37]*Maryland Gazette,* May 13, July 29, and Sep. 9, 1773.

[38]*Ibid.,* Mar. 25, 1773.

[39]*Ibid.,* Oct. 21, 1773.

[40]Barker, pp. 359-68.

[41]*Ibid.,* pp. 377, 374.

[42]*Ibid.,* p. 370.

[43]*Ibid.,* pp. 367-69; and Allan Nevins, *The American States During and After the Revolution* (New York, 1924), pp. 40-41, 73.

[44]*Ibid.*

[45]John R. Alden, *The American Revolution, 1775-1783* (New York, 1954), pp. 42-58; and John Carroll, Memorandum (Baltimore, Md., Catholic Archdiocesan Archives, Special C-F). Carroll undoubtedly was shown that remonstrances by Canadians to the mother country would be fruitless, so that independence would be justified in the face of considerations noted in his memorandum.

II

CONSCIENTIOUS REBELLION

The revolutionary government showed that it had a Christian conscience. In doing so it revealed that it was giving birth to a Christian
state and an improvement in religious life. The government dealt
conscientiously with the delicate religious convictions of Marylanders as
they affected loyalties to the mother country or to the emerging independent state. There were inevitable conflicts within the spirit of many
Marylanders. Dedication to a church might also be involved—in some
cases regarding its beliefs about the morality of war and rebellion. In
being true to its own obligations, the revolutionary government had
somehow to be true to the free consciences of its citizens. In succeeding
with both demands, Maryland revealed the temper of the emerging
Christian state and a progressively improving religious life. Several situations of inviduals and groups in the revolutionary experiences establish
this conclusion.

The majority of Marylanders, and the largest body of clergymen,
belonged to the Established Church of England at the beginning of the
War. If one examines the ties which this religion had to the king and
Parliament, it will be evident that the Revolution brought great distress
to the conscience of its adherents, particularly those most aware of Anglican theology.[1] Perhaps no one better describes and analyzes this plight
of Marylanders than William White, who as one of the first three bishops
of the Protestant Episcopal Church in America led the old Church of
England into its new form. The laity and clergy were in time brought
into new "understandings" and "settlements" found in that Church.
William Smith, first organizer of the clergy of the Church of Eng·and
in Maryland during the Revolution, was his close collaborator.[2] White
observed the general situation of the old Established Church in 1782.
"Unhappily", he wrote in *The Case of the Episcopal Churches in the
United States Considered*, "there are some, in whose ideas the existence
of their church is connected with that of the civil government of Britain,
as to preclude their concurrence in any system formed on a presumed
final separation of the two countries.[3] In this year, when the War was
drawing to a close, there were still many in whom the conflict between
religious loyalty and civil loyalty remained unresolved. Their number
and condition at the beginning of the process of separation during the
preceding years was large and important.

Church-state connections were very real. The king was the head of the Church, so Maryland subjects owed him both civil and religious obedience. At the ordination of Anglican clergymen, an oath of loyalty to Parliament was taken. This tie brought a major crisis for both clergy and laity. The discerning layman would inevitably question the authority and sacramental power of his clergyman, whom he regarded as priest, when such a minister swore a Maryland revolutionary oath disavowing ties with England. The clergyman of the Established Church was the first to struggle with the problem of conscience in his oath to Parliament. The revolutionary government and soon the new constitutional government of Maryland demanded from all citizens a disclaimer of any loyalty to the king and Parliament. Many of the Anglican clergy could see no way out of their obligation to Parliament. Their ranks in Maryland were quickly decimated. Nine went to England, eight to other states; two or three took up teaching for a livelihood and five returned to some other form of private life.[4]

These men who refrained from the Maryland civil oath of disclaimer were not all of the same mind and conscience. Those who were thorough loyalists, in a political as well as a religious sense, could hope for compensations from the mother country. Any clergymen who had emigrated recently from England were thus only returning home. But there were others who were born in Maryland, whose ties were to flesh and blood and native soil. As the revolt advanced toward permanent proportions, their anxiety mounted in the face of the widening moral dilemma. Weighty considerations encouraged members of the Anglican clergy to remain in their ministry. They even took the revolutionary civil oath, hoping that some theological settlement would come about and allow them to meet the spiritual needs of their people. Immediately, there was the possibility of winning a dispensation from their tie to Parliament through authority of the Bishop of London. Acquisition of a bishop for America, one taken from among their own clergy and free from any dependence on Parliament, seemed likely. He would be divested of the temporal power assigned the office of bishop in the Church of England. This would remove any conflict with the new revolutionary civil authority.

As Maryland clergymen turned their minds toward the idea of a bishop, they were aware of many disturbing aspects in such a solution. Parliament would have to authorize the arrangement initially. White accurately formulated these difficulties with a native episcopacy. "What the people would have thought of measures," he wrote, "which must have required an act of that body [Parliament] to render them harmless, no person formerly acquainted with their temper and sentiments need be told ..." The American bishop and clergy would be in a position of dependence upon Parliament for its initial status.[5] "How far the prerogative of a king as head of the church," White continued, "might be construed to extend over the colonies, whether a bishop would bring with him that part of the law which respects ecclesiastical matters, and whether the civil powers vested in bishops in England would accompany that order to America, were questions which for aught they [Americans] knew would include principles and produce consequences, dangerous and destructive of their civil rights."[6]

William Eddis, a provincial official and an astute observer of these times in Maryland, agreed with White's description. "They [Marylanders] have" he wrote, "rooted prejudices against the higher orders of the church ..." He gave a reason for this. It was his belief that an episcopacy in Maryland would have led Maryland "to cherish ... monarchial principles; and have more strongly riveted the attachment of the colonies to the parent state."[7] A bishop would be just one more agent of unwelcome control from England, and of anti-republicanism. Some prominent clergymen of the Church of England, to make matters worse, had before the Revolution and again in its early stages enunciated a philosophy in conflict with the Spirit of Seventy-Six. William Smith, later organizer of the first Maryland conventions of the Episcopal Church, was an example. As late as 1776 he wrote on the advantages of perpetual union between Great Britain and the American Colonies.[8] In that same year he took issue with those who held that their own government was a natural right of the American colonies. "Unfortunatley for mankind," said Smith, "those are fine sounding words, which seldom or ever influence human affairs." He cleverly suggested that the ultimate application of such a liberal principle would be to turn the colonial domain back to the Indians.[9]

While these were conservative positions, there was a progression of thought toward acceptance of the Revolution in men like Smith. Few American at the beginning of strained relations with the mother country espoused that independence which eventually resulted. Smith illustrates the very real moral stress and strain in this progression within the Church of England in America.[10] Even when a separate status for the descendant of the Established Church of England —the Protestant Episcopal Church in America— had been settled, an anxious probing of the adjustment of theology with the new philosophy, particularly in the realm of the separation of church and state, went on. William Duke revealed this ad-

justment to the impact of the Revolution.[11] Discussion of separation
from the mother country led to an examination of the union of church
and state in England, since this affected the founding an independent
Church in America. This purified thinking in American Anglicans in
preparation for the emerging Christian State in Maryland.

The quest for episcopal consecration by Samuel Seabury of Connecticut during the Revolution throws light on the Maryland problem.
He ultimately was consecrated by a bishop in Scotland, who rejected the
power of Parliament over the office. In that country there had been
nonjuring bishops who were loyal to the House of Stuart in the seventeenth century and opposed to an oath to Parliament. Their tradition continued into Revolutionary times. Seabury received episcopal consecration from a Scottish bishop in this tradition and understood that he was
receiving powers that derived from Apostles of the early Church. Another line of reasoning had developed which would dissolve the tie to
Parliament more simply. The oath always had the reservation, *to Parliament or its lawful successors.* This interpretation provided for the new
governments in America to whom Anglicans were transferring their loyalty and which they believed were legitimate temporal authorities. The
Anglican priest thus need have no qualms about his ordination oath in
England, nor need a future bishop refrain from consecration there by
an English juring bishop. He might even take the oath on such an occasion, in the unlikely event that it would later be demanded in America after Independence, at which time one could say he had already given
allegiance to England's successor in America.[12]

The progression of this adjustment clearly moved toward an emphasis on the spiritual nature of the Church. Such an understanding was
not new in the Church of England. In the Elizabethan period, Richard
Hooker had called attention to the two-power distinction of authority,
even while the state was drafting spiritual creeds and imposing penalties
for their violations. If the Church was essentially spiritual, it was now
said, the Americans were not spiritually bound by the temporal identification with the king and Parliament. As for untangling this tie to
the temporal order, to the enemy government, White appealed to the
English theologian, Bishop Sherlock: "Stand clear of all disputes about
the rights of princes and subjects; so that such disputes must be left
to be decided by principles of natural equity and the constitution of the
country."[13] This was middle ground. It was accessible to the doctri-
naires of right and left without assuming the liabilities of their conclusions.[14]

This progression toward middle ground between the Tory minister and patriot preacher throws light on the conscience problem of the Episcopal laity. Obviously laymen were less concerned with theological adjustment. Their attention was more directed to the justice of the American cause as a civil matter which stood within the framework of the British Constitution. As they found their cause to be righteous in these terms at the various stages of the Revolution, they inevitably wanted assurance that religion was on their side. The popular preacher attacked by Jonathan Boucher was responding to this revolutionary mentality. Such clergymen assured Anglicans of the morality of their resistance. The more moderate laymen caused no problem since they left matters "to be decided by principles of natural equity and the constitution of the country."

"It may reasonably be presumed," concluded White, "that, in general, the members of the Episcopal churches are friendly to the principles, on which the present government[s] were formed; a fact particularly obvious in the southern states, where the Episcopalians, who are a majority of the citizens, have engaged and persevered in the war, with as much ardor and constancy as their neighbors." [15] Yet, in all of this, commitment to a civil philosophy only increased lay awareness of the precariousness of their religious connection with England. The departure of half of their clergy for reason of conscience must have further stirred misgivings. There were also persistent pockets of toryism among the laity. Boucher said that his parishioners all abstained from the Provincial Congress.[16] These Anglicans did not seem to be a majority, it is true, but their distress was real. It required delicate treatment by a Christian revolutionary government.[17]

Methodism was a movement within the Church of England, and the Revolution brought its adherents in America qualms of conscience which were similar to those experienced by other members of the once Established Church. But the Methodists underwent other difficulties peculiar to themselves.

In order to make the Methodist's problems clear, his relation to the Church of England should be understood. The inspiration of Methodism as expressed in its founder. John Wesley, called for reform and positive piety within the Church. The example and preaching of laymen were to be the instruments of this "awakening." Wesley had personally planted his religious movement in America. The preaching of Robert Strawbridge laid foundations in Maryland, which led to a phase of the Great Awakening. With such preachers as Strawbridge, Methodists developed the distinctive device of evangelizing known as the circuit rider. It came to be accepted as an office in the society.[18]

The Methodist experience during the trying revolutionary times centered around Francis Asbury. John Wesley had sent him to America in 1771. Two years later at Philadelphia he was given general supervision of the First Conference of "the society," as the Methodists referred to their organization, and he remained a leader after the War. Asbury personally experienced the worst disabilities of Methodists, having been arrested, fined, and compelled to live for a time in retirement in Delaware.[19] Throughout the Revolutionary War, Asbury adhered to the belief that Methodism should remain in the Church of England. He was thus identified with the anxieties of the Anglicans described above. At the end of the War he noted in his Journal: "I was shocked when first informed ... the design of organizing the Methodist into an Independent Episcopal Church."[20] This was also the sentiment of the native Maryland preacher. Thomas Haskins. He referred to Maryland Methodists as "generous & dutiful Sons of the Episcopal Church to Whom we have from time to time publicly professed ourselves to be associated ..."[21] The Conference of 1773 at Philadelphia had directed Methodists to receive ordinances, or sacraments, in the Church of England. "Guard against a separation from the Church, directly or indirectly," they were warned by a 1779 minute.[22] In 1780 Asbury and a native Maryland preacher sought to promote this view in Virginia.[23]

Even before the conclusion of the War, Asbury's pursuit of unity within the Church of England and the independent Protestant Episcopal Church in America, which was being formed from it, became full of frustrations, scruples, and misgivings. "After all my labour to unite the Protestant Episcopal ministry with us," he confided in 1779, "they say, 'we don't want your unconverted ministers; the people will not receive them.' "[24] During the War, the Methodist lay preachers met the spiritual need created by the mass resignation of ordained Anglican ministers who could not in conscience reconcile the revolutionary oath with that professed at their ordination rite, or with their political loyalty to the king and Parliament. This movement of preachers was precipitating a theological crisis regarding the very nature of the Anglican ministry. Many believed that the preachers might arrive at ministerial status without the traditional training-even, perhaps, without the ordination rite itself, currently such a source of scruple. A Methodist conference at Fluvanna, Virginia, in 1779 even repudiated the episcopal form of government and wanted authority vested in the preachers.[25] Thus the theological perplexities of the Methodist preacher exceeded in many ways those of the ordained Anglican.

The revolutionary government at times tended to suspect Methodists as a body. The extensive preaching and movement of the circuit riders, their pacifism, and occasional imprudence had much to do with this. A single dramatic episode during the War also provoked a trying condition of distrust. The Methodist Chauncey Clowe aroused three hundred Tories on the Eastern Shore, encouraging them to join forces with the British fleet in the Chesapeake Bay. Martin Rodda, a preacher, led this abortive insurrection, which ended in Clowe's execution.[26]

Methodists were clearly troubled by the obligations of their loyalty to the king and Parliament as head of their church and by doubts of the lawfulness of the revolt. "I must confess," said Asbury but six years after his departure from England, "Satan harassed me with violent and various temptations." He noted this on the occasion of hearing of the departure of a preacher for England. On a similar occasion three months later, he confessed, "I now felt some desire to return to England..."[27] Asbury seemed to be closer to Methodists in England than to the independent native preachers, even if he was not a loyalist. His great motive for staying on in America was the need souls had for his ministrations. He seemed to leave civil affairs in God's hands, and had no precise notions about the operations of the natural laws of society, which Bishop Sherlock indicated to White.[28]

The patriots among the preachers constituted a significant force of disturbance both to the individual and to Methodist unity. There is good evidence, indeed, that Asbury became sympathetic with the American cause. Yet he did not move any faster to its conclusion in independence than did any other conservative. He was also bound to John Wesley, who had ineptly come out against America. Asbury thus worried through the stages of advance toward independence under a cloud of misunderstanding on the part of many.[29] Both Thomas Haskins and Freeborn Garrettson gave greater evidence of belief in the justness of the American cause. Undoubtedly they reflected the general belief of the Maryland Methodists, if one allows for the progressive development of evidence for the American "case."[30] Haskins, for example, criticized the Tory writings of Wesley, who was not, as he put it, "infallible particularly with respect to the political, civil & religious affairs of America[.] [T]his may be discovered in some of his late writings on these heads."[31] Garrettson spoke of "an overgrown mother, who wanted to keep her children under subjection in matters wherein they thought they were capable of judging for themselves." [32] Wesley himself saw his cleavage with Methodists in Maryland. "I find a danger now of a new kind," he wrote to his brother in 1775, "of losing my love for the Americans: I mean their leaders; for the poor sheep are more sinned against than sinning." [33] However, Thomas Ware, who attended the Methodist Christmas Conference in 1784, found Wesley's agent, Thomas Coke, completely won over to the idea of American Independence, which Wesley only gradually accepted. [34]

On what principles did the Methodist conscience resolve the problem stirred by the American Revolution? The evangelical quality of the movements inclined many to remain aloof from the civil and political aspects. Circuit rider journals are extremely spare of comment on secular events. "Let us see how Providence opens itself," Wesley said, in support of aloofness. He committed all into the hands of Asbury, who in turn commended all to God. Asbury contrived no doctrinaire scheme of reconciliation between the civil and religious orders, between the old understandings and the new. [35] One would suspect that many of these Methodists were moving toward the realities of separation of church and state as they followed this policy of abstention from the political settlements. It was a matter of awaiting the decision of the civil process, as Thomas Sherlock (late Bishop of London) put it, and of Wesley's seeing "how Providence opens itself." This implied an autonomy of the secular order as something distinct from the spiritual and religious. Less than two months after Yorktown rather fully developed understandings on this topic had come into the mind of Thomas Haskins. In reading Burnet's *History of the Reformation in England* (1679-1714), he concluded that English policy initiated by Thomas Cranmer did not eliminate the type of power exercised by the Pope over Englishmen, but merely transferred it to the hands of the king. He noted that this accounted for the persecution of Baptists. The implication throughout this entry is that separation of such power from civil government was desirable. [36] The Christian revolutionary government was thus fostering such enlightenment.

Another source of Methodist distress under the impact of revolution was their pacifism. Unlike Anglican clergymen, some Methodist preachers held a religious belief which made recourse to war not only abhorrent but also unlawful. "But alas! We hear of bloodshed and slaughter," Asbury wrote, after hearing of the Battle of Long Island." "This is grief to my soul! Lord, scatter them that delight in war, and thirst for human blood!" [37] Shadford and Garrettson also gave witness to this belief. [38] Government records refer to Methodist laymen and preachers alike as opposed to warfare.[39] Out of these convictions arose difficulties and scruples calling for understanding by the Maryland government. Legislation, as will be shown, made exceptions for conscientious objectors to war. Yet Garrettson, for example, found difficulties with other laws. "I thought the test oath," he explained, "was worded in such a way as to bind me to take arms whenever called on, and I felt no disposition to use carnal weapons." This meant, as in Asbury's case, that he could not take the test oath of loyalty to the state, even though his sympathy was with the American cause. Thus it was that men often erred in estimating the loyalty of preachers.[40] Passages of the journals of these men bring out the real nature of the Methodist's moral and mental anguish. People understandably suspected treason in such refusals since, unlike Methodists, they thought the law said nothing contrary to pacifism. Nor did all of this leave the laymen beyond suspicion, as witnesses could later recall.[41] The laity were identified with the itinerant preachers who came into the community as strangers and suspects as far as non-Methodists were concerned.

Quakers, like Methodists, were identified with pacifism and under a similar cloud of doubt. In Maryland during the Revolution all could recall their dramatic abstention from the French and Indian War and withdrawal from the government of Pennsylvania on that account. In 1758 the Friends' official discipline made it clear that such a course was required of members. This and other past experiences, they continued to say in 1770, "teach us to avoid mixing with those in their human policy . . . who are not convinced of our religious principle of pacifism . . ." As late as 1794 there was still no mitigation, although a dissenting movement appeared during the Revolutionary Period.[42] Maryland Quakers were non-jurors. It was the practice of oaths as such, however, and not loyalty to the new state toward which oaths were directed, that was disavowed by them. So Marylanders would be inclined to understand them. Not so with the Methodists. Because they accepted the practice of oaths, they could not always explain satisfactorily to others that the test oath of loyalty to the state implied approval of war and that this and not loyalty was in question. This was not the problem of the Quakers.

What, then, were the peculiar trials in connection with their pacifism and oath opposition? Judged by monthly meeting records, tribulations did not seem to come from oaths. For about two years before 1778 no instances of censure for "Taking the Test to the Present Measured Government" are found in the Kent and Cecil County Minutes.[43] Exemption of the

Quakers from the oath became a governmental policy.[44] By 1780 a provision in law also excused religiously conscientious non-jurors from the treble tax Tory non-jurors paid. A law of 1781 explicitly excluded Quakers from the oath connected with the voting right.[45] The civil obligation of the bearing of arms, more than the oaths, caused the greatest problem for Quakers. The Kent Minutes as early as March 13, 1776, cited two of their members for "bearing of arms to Learn the art of War Contrary to the Rules of Friends. Disciplin[e]..."[46] Other instances are found throughout the records for the succeeding years until the surrender at Yorktown. Young men in these circumstances felt great anguish. Many were convinced of the justice of the American cause, but felt the means to its achievement was morally wrong or at least questionable. Quakers scrutinized their faith with a certain amount of agony at this focal point of revolution.

The procedure of the Monthly Meeting with members engaged in military exercise or service created further problems. Representatives were appointed to treat with the delinquent member. This often involved visiting the person in a manner not easily concealed from the public. Arguments were used to persuade him to give up military service. This put meeting representatives in an unfavorable light with the government. People might unjustly identify their work with that of Tory obstructionists. The alternative to service was a financial assessment by the revolutionary government. Payment caused a problem of conscience for many Quakers. Were not the financiers of war also participants in the immoral act itself? The resolution of this dilemma often forced the government to confiscate the Quaker's property, when he refused payment of the fee. This greatly tried the restraint and honesty of the revolutionary government.[47]

What about rendering obedience to the revolutionary government, established by unlawful war? There was less difficulty here than with specific policies and acts. Quaker other-wordly philosophy and evangelical Protestant spirit explains this. The kingdom of God was wholly within; its judgments were not about kingdoms of this world. Quakers must live peacably with what they found. When the politics of state, however, demanded actions which were immoral to the Quaker, he must abstain. He must not judge the government so much as its specific acts. The latter were either moral or immoral means to the legitimate purpose of a government, which in itself might not be so clearly immoral. While some religious groups had elaborated philosophical grounds for accepting or rejecting the revolutionary government, Quakers did not seem required by their beliefs to do either. In a Christian spirit, the Maryland regime did not intrude into this realm of conscience nor condemn the neutrality implied in the Quaker position.

Among Maryland evangelical Protestants was the sect known as Moravians. Like the Quakers, they espoused pacifism and came from the same background of German pietism which had influenced William Penn. Count Nicolaus L. Zinzendorf, beginning in 1772 in Pennsylvania, had led this reform sect, which considered itself related to German Lutheranism. Moravians, however, experienced less pressure from the Revolutionary War than did the Quakers. Their community, located in Frederick County, had developed from German Lutheran immigrants in the Monocacy River Valley. They were associated with the Bethlehem, Pennsylvania, jurisdiction, which sent preachers among them.[48]

John Ettwein, leader of the Moravians during this period, expounded the traditional pacifism in a way which differed from Quaker discipline. Some, according to him, receive a higher calling from the Spirit and are inclined to refuse bearing arms. "But if there be any to whom He has not given this spirit, we would not tie fruit on such a tree. Whoso[ever] was able hitherto to drill with calm heart, why should such a one be unable to sign the rule and regulations for the Association?"[49] It was also acceptable for the complete pacifist to pay the fee for military abstention without violating religious principle. "We are not warlike," as one of their spokesmen said, "nor are we Quakers."[50] All of this did not preclude debate with one's self and others, but it did mitigate the problem of adjusting to the country at war in a way not experienced by the Quaker.[51] The Maryland government was less severely tried in its dealings with Moravians.

The way thus remained open to both loyalists and patriots among the Moravians, as well as to those who would not identify themselves with either viewpoint. There were many who felt that they should remain loyal to the English king, prompted by a sense of gratitude. The House of Hanover had originally made it possible for the German Moravians to come to the colonies. European ties were, in the eyes of many, necessary to preserve brotherly union and to supply missionaries and settlers.[52] Evidently the American-born Moravian inclined toward the patriot's cause. Instances of this at an early stage of the Revolution were frequent among young communicants, who successfully resisted efforts to exclude them from membership.[53] John Ettwein pointed to what would seem to be a more representative alternative to active loyalist or patriot roles. "It is my duty," he explained in 1777, "to remain quiet and to evade the issue as long as I may." He did not believe that the government of Pennsylvania was legitimate. Yet his reasoning to this position was not along the Tory line. Rather, he complained that the state's assembly was not representative of the people. In order to avert public disorder, however, such a government had to be tolerated.[54] The same charge need not apply to Maryland. The Moravian conscience could thus more easily adjust to the revolutionary changes which had come so swiftly. Two days after the Declaration of Independence a generous settlement was made by the Maryland Constitutional Convention in favor of the Moravians.[55]

Lutherans, in contrast to Moravians, experienced little conscientious tension concerning war and revolution. Inclination to the loyalist side derived from sociological rather than theological sources. As German immigrants they had benefited from the Hanover policy which opened America to them. Although the crest of this movement had passed by 1750, a supply of clergymen still continued to be drawn from Europe. The American congregations were also tied to a jurisdiction there. Many Lutherans were therefore inclined to maintain a colonial union with Europe. The alternative of independence was too uncertain. There is no evidence that the revolutionary government disturbed Lutherans who peacefully refrained from the patriot cause.[56]

Presbyterians, Catholics, and Baptists in contrast to the Episcopalians, Methodists, Friends, Moravians and Lutherans, were actually militant in moving toward independence in Maryland. The revolutionary government acted in such a Christian fashion, that their consciences were not troubled. Its respect for law, exhibited in the debate over colonial grievances, established in their eyes the divine justification of a war of independence.

Even before the Revolution, Presbyterians were preparing theologically as well as politically for a separation from the mother country. The rise of the so-called covenanters hastened the drift away from the Established Church.[57] The First Presbyterian Church of Baltimore and its membership developed out of a reforming spirit which an Anglican pastor had occasioned.[58] To this pulpit came a militant pastor named Patrick Allison, who became the leader of Presbyterianism in the state during the Revolutionary period. Allison was indignant about the "problems grown under the unrighteous & irreligious Establishment..."[59] He had also played an important part in a concerted dissenter effort at preventing appointment of a bishop. A Philadelphia association, in which he was active in the 1760's, collaborated with New Englanders, seeking to undermine the growing political power of the established church in America.[60] The revolutionary government now promised to remove that threat to the spiritual well-being of Maryland.

In spite of grievances, Presbyterians in general and Allison in particular did not move headlong toward a break with the mother country, contrary to Galloway's unreliable report to Parliament on American Presbyterianism's view of union.[61] Allison himself gave an address which was sent in a conciliatory way to the king at the time of the Stamp Act crisis.[62] But on the eve of the Declaration of Independence, the conciliatory course of relations with England came to an end. Presbyterians were swift to realize this and from then on there was vigorous Presbyterian support for America. A synod, gathered early in the War, prayed that God "would graciously smile on our arms and those of our illustrious ally, by land and sea . . ." [63] There is evidence that Presbyterians worked against Tories in some parts of Maryland.[64] James F. Armstrong, a Maryland Presbyterian clergyman, was soon appointed a chaplain in the American Revolutionary Army. Before becoming chaplain of the Continental Congress, Allison served with Washington's troops. The radicalism of Samuel Purviance, a prominent Presbyterian layman and a Baltimore merchant, is found in the records of the first days of the Maryland revolutionary government. He had to be restrained from extreme measures in dealing with Governor Robert Eden.[66]

Like the Presbyterians, Baptists were generally regarded as enthusiasts for the cause of American independence throughout the colonies. What is known of them in Maryland during this period would not conflict with the generalization. While they were not numerous in Maryland, Jeremiah Moore as a Baptist had denounced the church-state understanding prevailing in Maryland before the Revolution. The revolutionary government gave promise of sponsoring Baptist religious policy and won their conscientious support. [67]

Maryland Catholics were no less enthusiastic for the cause of Independence than Presbyterians and Baptists. They plainly considered the religious discrimination of the mother country and the province increasingly intolerable. Charles Carroll of Carrollton's debate with Daniel Dulany in 1773 dramatized this feeling, which was also reflected throughout his letters during this period.[68] It has been said, however, that American Catholics feared greater discrimination at the hands of their fellow countrymen once independence had been won. Anti-Catholic statements following the Quebec Act principally made in New England have been cited to this effect. The law fully established Catholic Bishop Briand in the same power at Quebec which a bishop held under French dominion Samuel Adam's diatribe against Catholicism at this time made Massachusetts Catholics fear a transfer of power to such men. [69] It has been shown that such was not the case in Maryland, however, where the liberal utterances of Paca, Chase and others reassured Catholics. The dealings of Charles and John Carroll with John Adams and Benjamin Franklin on the occasion of the their joint mission to Canada early in 1776 also strengthened confidence in general tolerance. The narrowness of one state, furthermore, could not in the subsequent practice of state autonomy affect Maryland and Pennsylvania, where most Catholics lived. The Government of the Confederation also could not but reflect the liberal spirit in which the Revolution was being taken up and prosecuted. [70]

The military service of Catholics further indicates support of the War. Large enlistments came from heavily Catholic counties. An exception has been pointed out in Pennsylvania, where a Catholic loyalist force was recruited in Philadelphia. These, however, were largely recently arrived immigrants and neither their number nor role as loyalists was significant. The Catholic gentry, on the other hand, contributed outstanding leaders to the patriot cause in Stephen Moylen, Washington's aid-de-camp, and others. [71] In the English Catholic tradition, these men and their clergy were schooled in the legitimacy of rebellion against tyranny. The Maryland revolutionary government, they understood, rested on the legality of higher natural law.

The Catholic conscience of revolution was best reflected in John Carroll, the foremost representative of the Catholic clergy. He actively espoused the American Revolution and did not scruple to join a Congressionally appointed committee to enlist Canadian support against the mother country. He saw the overthrow of political tyranny from a religious viewpoint. "In these United States our religious system has undergone a revolution, if possible, more extraordinary than our political one." [73] "Since the object of war on your side is now confessedly... acknowledged to have been unjust" he explained to an English friend, "every measure to attain that object must likewise have been unjust." [74] There had been a centuries-long theological and philosophical discussion of the conditions under which a government or ruler might be overthrown by force. These conditions were now present in the American cause. The liberal elements in this tradition clearly exerted influence on this line of reasoning by Carroll. [75] With this background, Catholics had little reason in conscience to oppose the war and change of government. The Revolution easily won their support.

In adjusting to war and political revolution, then, the denominations showed great variety. Evidence of this process of thought and debate testifies to a degree of freedom from governmental coercion. Marylanders, as it were, had the liberty to hesitate, otherwise they would not have refined their ethics of revolution. Other evidence for this favorable climate of conscience must now be examined in the revolutionary government itself.

Those responsible for law and order had a most complex task in assuring the rights of conscientious dissenters. It was for them, as William Eddis said, "to stem the torrent excited by factious artifices." At the other extreme were those who would use religion's privileges for Tory purposes. Even those who innocently followed their own lights might through imprudence jeopardize the safety of the state at war with England. Yet the Tory Eddis put his hope in "many respectable characters," with whom this difficult business rested. "Considering the complexion of the times", he concluded optimistically, "their proceedings have been regular and moderate." [76]

Maryland government records make it clear that the state understood the difficulty of its position. Article 4 of the Proceedings of the Constitutional Convention had to make a forthright statement of the major assumption of any revolutionary government, even though this was offensive to the religious views of some. "The doctrine of nonresistance against arbitrary power and oppression, is absurd, slavish, and destructive of the good and happiness of mankind."[77] In the case of particular persons opposed to this assumption, however, the Maryland Council was to apply the liberal provisions in law for the protection of clergymen and religious objectors. [78]

The council and other officials did not find such interpretations easy. General William Smallwood illustrated the problem in the theatre of war. On the Eastern Shore many pleaded that their religion made them disaffected toward the Maryland government and then aided the British. "Tho[ugh] there are some exception," he explained, "wherein Ignorant men from their Religious Attachments have been deluded (those are readily distinguished & to be pittied) yet by far the greater number conceal their true motives, & make Religion a Cloak for their nefarious designs." [79] William Paca cited the example of two clergymen in support of this contention. He also graphically represented the feelings of one in Smallwood's position. "If in the Heat of Zeal," he wrote to Governor

Thomas Johnson. "I may advise any Extremity out of the straight Line of the Law for our Constitution I hope I shall be excused: as to Extremities from necessity they will need no Apology or Justification." [80] In these straightened circumstances, the constitutional convention and the assemblies which succeeded it strove to create the atmosphere of freedom, so that the conscience of revolt might operate. As early as 1775 the right of opposition to the war for religious reasons was established. After stating the citizen's obligation to defend his country and bear arms, this qualification was added: "Clergymen of all denominations and such persons who from their religious principles cannot bear arms in any case, excepted...." [81] In the records of the state government during these times of war are found frequent references of cases to higher authority because of their difficult nature. Restraining directives often come from higher to lower levels of jurisdiction. [82]

The Quaker Kent Monthly Meeting Minutes present evidence for the success of these laws in effecting conditions favorable to the free exercise of conscience. A reading of this record over the period following 1776 reveals few instances where Quakers were refused benefit of laws regarding pacifism. [83] The Quaker practice of encouraging others to pacifism in fairness could have been opposed by the government, but little difficulty is reported in carrying on such activity. Many refused to pay for substitutes in the militia. Nearly a year elapses before the first mention is made of any problem with the government. [84] The fund set aside to aid persons penalized by confiscations seems to have been free from any great demand. [85] Finally, it should be noted that use is made of minutes from the Eastern Shore, where the government would incline to be stricter in view of the danger found there. Treatment must have been even more lenient elsewhere. Methodists also received these benefits of protective laws. Reports by Coke and others might suggest the contrary, but a close examination of their words in context will show that they were not making a case of injustice with the government. [86] They did not always separate suffering due to clear sedition, such as Clowe's Rebellion on the Eastern Shore by militant tory Methodists, from much clearer cases of intolerance on the part of the revolutionary government. [87]

Asbury's own career during these times leaves a favorable view of the Maryland government in its efforts to give reasonable protection to dissenters and pacifists. His journal mentions minor annoyances and obstruction, but also tells of the local civil official ready to intervene and stop the instigators. [88] During the early years of the War he entered

Annapolis with misgivings, skeptical of Maryland assemblymen who assured him of a place to preach. "Contrary to my expectations," he later recalled, "I preached in the church..." [89] A few months before the surrender at Yorktown, he preached at the Frederick County Court House without incident. Attendance at his preaching during these difficult times was generally good. These considerations, together with the remarkable growth of Methodism, indicate that external mobility as well as internal freedom in the realm of conscience was created by the revolutionary government. [90]

Freeborn Garrettson, the native Methodist preacher, provides the best test case for the freedom of a dissenter in Maryland. He was unavoidably under suspicion by the state at the outset of his career. Martin Rodda, the rank Tory preacher, had once been his companion. Garrettson, of course, had to live down the common opposition to the pacifist. He did not make it easy for the public, however sympathetic and tolerant they might be. As Asbury explained. "Brother Garrettson will let no person escape a religious lecture that comes in his way." [91] On the basis of his Journal, it would be difficult to find an itinerant preacher who had seen more of Maryland in the 1770's and 1780's than Garrettson. [92] He therefore put Maryland to the test more than others did.

Even in cases where Garrettson was harassed, the revolutionary government and its officials came to his protection. He was dramatically rescued on one occasion by the intervention of a magistrate in Kent County. A bystander rescued him from soldiers and provided a horse which carried Garrettson to the magistrate. "I told him," Garrettson narrates of the magistrate, "I was determined to Preach if I went to the stake. God had Called me, and man should not stop me. I was determined to regard God rather than man. At that he [the magistrate] became very friendly." [93] A year later at Salisbury a military officer protected him against those who were demanding that he take the oath. [94] On another occasion when a Dorset County magistrate urged him to the oath, the sheriff and a gathering of people asked that Garrettson be allowed to go his way. "It is a pity to stop you," they said in respect for his zeal for preaching. [95] An Eastern Shore magistrate also intervened in favor of Garrettson's friend in Salisbury and an officer stood up to his military subordinates who were threatening Garrettson himself. [96] Many other instances of this kind are found in Garrettson's journal. Responsible civil officials clearly kept down the radical elements which would indiscriminately penalize religious-minded men.

When one considers a certain lack of prudence in Garrettson, there is further evidence of the indulgence of Marylanders. He was not content simply to refuse military service, for example, and pay the fee for a substitute. "I was determined," he himself stated. "I never would join the Multitude to serve the devil." [97] Yet, as at Salisbury, military officials kept him from harm at the hands of those who understandably were antagonized by such strong pacifist statements. [98] In addition, there were instances where the public at large showed sympathy for one in his position. A crowd of citizens disarmed a man who was trying to prevent Garrettson from riding on to another station of his circuit. At the height of the war a man who opposed his preaching came to him afterwards to apologize. [99] Beginning in the unsettled days preceding the outbreak of the war and into the war years themselves, he found treatment of himself improved rather than worsened. "God had . . . opened the eyes of one of the magistrates, so far (although before he was a persecutor) that he took my part . . ." [100] He noted that his "enemyes begin to be at peace." He especially found great improvement on the Eastern Shore and in Somerset County. [101]

Like Asbury, Garrettson made it appear that the law was not so much on his side in all of these situations as overlooked through the liberality of Marylanders. His own writings, however, disprove this contention. His comparisons of Maryland to other states often give rise to such misunderstanding. "I could claim a right in the Delaware state," he said in one place, "which state was more favorable to such *pestilent fellows* as himself." [102] Yet his treatment in that state was similar to what is found on occasion in Maryland, as far as abuse by crowds was concerned. [103] As explained previously, both Asbury and Garrettson seemed to have felt the Maryland oath obligated them to something they did not find in the Delaware oath. This still would not make things unfavorable in Maryland because there were generous laws exempting from the oath, particularly for religious reasons. Moreover, Maryland honored the Delaware oath as satisfying for its own requirement—a benefit of which Garrettson actually availed himself.

The Delaware sentiment aside, Garrettson directly stated in places that his mobility and his position as a preacher was clearly within the law of Maryland. One need only note how restricted he found himself in Virginia. His complaints of that state showed his implicit preference for Maryland's legal settlement. [104] He told of the effectiveness of the Maryland plan of paid exemption from military service. His Maryland birth and property was a basis of legal protection. Finally, in the eyes of military men and the people in general, he made it clear—as St. Paul had—that he was a citizen and entitled to the protection of the law. His presentation was so effective that on one occasion an officer spoke to a threatening crowd for him. "If they laid a hand on me," Garrettson told of this officer, "he would put the law in force against them. They withdrew to their homes, without making the sleightest [*sic*] attempts on me." [105]

The experiences of Episcopalians do not substantially change this picture of freedom of conscience in the face of military and political revolution. They put no strain on the liberality of the state by and pacifism, active or quiet, the way Methodists and Quakers did. Nor were Episcopal ministers itinerant preachers. Well known to those of their parishes, people would not be inclined to intemperate dealing with them as moderate dissenters. The gradualism of the Revolution and its political outcome was matched by a progressive theological adjustment by Episcopalians. They could sympathize with the Maryland government which encouraged formation of an autonomous church. Those clergymen who did not accept this broadening development, or who would not abandon their original tie by the ordination rite with Parliament, were not left to the coercion of an impossible alternative. A number of these, who returned to England, could look forward to a comfortable security provided by the crown to whom they were loyal. [106] If Jonathan Boucher is a good example, the revolutionary government manifested generous indulgence to the politically vociferous who happened to have such a religious connection.

It thus became clear that the Maryland revolutionary government was making its way under the guidance of a Christian conscience. It was, in a way, manifesting the aspirations to a Christian state which were found stirring in the debates of 1773. Proceeding as it did with respect for religious freedom, the aspiration of 1773 gave way to actual growth while confronting the realities of the rebellion. For Presbyterians, Baptists, and Catholics commitment to independence was a Christian involvement. Their attachment to the revolutionary government was seen in this light. The majority of the laity of the once established church espoused the new government in the abiding hope that their Anglican faith would find some new fulfillment. Methodists, Quakers, Moravians, and others whose situation was not so clearly defined could not but respect the new government for the conscientious manner in which it carried out its business. If it was not clear how the revolutionary authority stood with divine authority, there was at least hope that this condition would change. As for the emerging Christian state, it was salutary that the Marylander's freedom to develop his religious insights prevailed in the period of the revolutionary government.

REFERENCES

[1] For a detailed backround of this discussion see Nelson W. Rightmyer, *Maryland's Established Church* (Baltimore, Md., 1956); Arthur L. Cross, *The Anglican Episcopate and the American Colonies* (Cambridge, Mass., 1901); and Richard Hooker, "The Anglican Church and the American Revolution" (Ph. D. Diss., Univ. of Chicago, 1943).

[2] Walter H. Stowe, *The Life and Letters of Bishop William White.*

[3] (Philadelphia, 1937), p. 33.

[4] George B. Utley, *The Life and Times of Thomas John Claggett: First Bishop of Maryland and the First Bishop Consecrated in America* (Chicago, 1913), p. 30.

[5] White, p. 16.

[6] *Ibid.*

[7] *Letters from America, Historical and Descriptive: Comprising Occurrences from 1769-1777, Inclusive* (London, 1792), pp. 50-53.

[8] *Four Dissertations, on the Reciprocal Advantages of a Perpetual Union Between Great-Britain and Her American Colonies* (Philadelphia, 1766).

[9] William Smith, *Candidus, Plain Truth: Addressed to the Inhabitants of America,* Containing Remarks on a Late Pamphlet Entitled Common Sense.

[10] See Smith's address at the time he accepted Independence, in Protestant Episcopal Church, *Notices and Journals... 1783... 1789,* p. 26.

[11] *Observations on the Present State of Religion in Maryland: By a Clergyman* (Baltimore, 1795), pp. 47-48.

[12] Clare O. Loveland, *The Critical Years: The Reconstruction of the Anglican Church in the United States of America: 1780-1789* (Greenwich, Conn., 1956).

[13] White, p. 33.

[14] "My curate was but a weak brother," Jonathan Boucher recalled, "yet a strong Republican, i. e., as far as he knew how." See Boucher's *Reminiscences of an American Loyalist 1738-1789* (Boston, 1925), p. 119, *et passim,* where he reveals his own doctrinaire character as well as that of others with a different complexion.

[15] White, p. 6.

[16] Boucher, p. 120.

[17] White and Boucher are in disagreement regarding the number of loyalists. The purpose here is to show the fact of distress of conscience.

[18] For a general story of Methodism, see in addition to Cameron, Ruthella Bibbins, *How Methodism Came, the Beginnings of Methodism in England and America* (Baltimore, 1945); William W. Sweet, *Methodism in American History* (New York, 1933); and with reference to Maryland, Nathaniel C. Hughes, "The Methodist Christmas Conference: Dec. 24, 1784 - Jan. 2, 1785," *Maryland Historical Magazine,* LIV (Sep., 1959), 272-292.

[19] Matthew Simpson (ed.), *Cyclopaedia of Methodism...* (Philadelphia, 1881), pp. 58-61.

[20] Elmer T. Clark, *et al.* (eds.), *The Journal and Letters of Francis Asbury* (3 vols.; Nashville, Tenn., 1958), I, 471; Nov. 4, 1784 entry.

[21] Journal (Washington, D. C., Library of Congress), Dec. 22, 1784 entry. Haskins was born in Caroline County and began his circuit preaching in 1782. See William W. Sweet (ed.), *The Methodists, A Collection of Source Materials* (Chicago, 1946, pp. 113-14.

[22] *Minutes of the Annual Conferences of the Methodist Episcopal Church for the Years 1773-1828* (New York, 1840).

[23] Robert D. Simpson, "Freeborn Garrettson, American Methodist Pioneer" (Ph. D. Diss., Drew University, 1955), p. 72.

William Duke, also a native Methodist preacher during the War period, is a more striking example of an adherent to the Church. When Methodism decided to become autonomous after 1784, he became an Episcopal priest. See his Journal Md. Historical Society, Diocesan Archives of the Protestant Episcopal Church.

[24]Asbury, I, 322; Nov., 13.

[25]Hughes, 274-75, 277. Thomas Ware, a preacher of those times, is cited as witness to this division, and the declining strength of Asbury's opposition. It should be noted, however, that political events and the development of autonomous Episcopalianism logically led Asbury to modify his position as much as did the pressure from Virginia.

[26]Robert D. Simpson, p. 63.

[27]Asbury, I, 235 (Apr. 2, 1777); 243-44 (July 21, 1777). The persons involved were Shadford, Rankin, and on a third occasion, Rodda (228-29 [Jan. 21, 1777]).

[28]*Ibid.*, pp. 283-89; Apr. 12, 1777.

[29]Thomas Ware, "The Christmas Conference of 1784," *The Methodist Magazine and Quarterly Review*, XIV [New Series, III] (Jan., 1832), 102-104. Ware agrees with Asbury's writings about these events.

[30]The distinctive nature of Methodist pacifism must be understood if one would see that they were professing this, rather than Toryism.

[31]Journal, Dec. 22, 1784.

[32]*The experiences and Travels of the Rev. Freeborn Garretson Minister of the Methodist-Episcopal Church in North America* (Philadelphia, 1971), p. 170. See also his MS Journal (Drew Univ., Madison, N. J.) under Sep. 7, 1785. His free movements showed that he was on good terms with the patriots.

[33]Oct. 177, in Sweet, *Methodists*, pp. 83-84; Hughes, *Maryland Historical Magazine*, LIV, 273.

[34]Ware, *Methodist Magazine*, XIV, 102-104. Coke did not come to America until 1784. Wesley composed the *Sunday Service* as a discipline guide for Americans and it clearly indicated his acceptance of the American political settlement in Article XXIII. See Hughes, *Maryland Historical Magazine*, LIV, 287.

[35]Wesley to Dromgoole, Sep. 17, 1783 in *ibid.*, 274; Asbury, I, 243-44 (July 21, 1777) and 228-29 (Jan. 21, 1777).

[36]December 6 and 7, 1782.

[37]Asbury, I, 198-99 (Sep. 1, 1776).

[38]*Ibid.*, 229, editor's note; Robert Simpson, p. 60; Asbury, I, 266-67 (Apr. 11, 1778) and 346 (Apr. 24, 1780). Asbury calls the legislation "preposterous and rigid" in Maryland. The very taking of the oath threatened to scandalize others, according to him, apparently meaning that this would give approval to the war as a lawful policy of state.

[39]Instances will be discussed below in this chapter.

[40]R. Simpson, "Freeborn Garrettson," p. 60; Asbury, I, 266-67 (Apr. 11, 1778), 346 (Apr. 24, 1780). Asbury calls the legislation "preposterous and rigid" in Maryland. The very taking of the oath threatened to scandalize others, according to him, meaning apparently that this would give approval to war as a lawful policy of state.

[41]Hughes, *Maryland Historical Magazine*, LIV, 280.

[42]*The Revised Discipline...* (Baltimore, 1794).

[43]Photoduplicates (Md. Historical Society). No instances are found until June 6, 1778.

[44]*Proceedings of the Convention of the Province of Maryland, Held at Annapolis in 1774, 1775 and 1776* (Baltimore, 1836), p. 134 (May 15, 1776).

[45]*Laws of Maryland...* (2 vols.; Annapolis, 1799), Oct. 1780 Session, ch. lvi; Nov. 1781, Session, ch. xviii. See anti-Tory legislation under Feb. 1777, ch. xx. The large number of amendments to the oath indicates the sensitivity of the assembly to the consciences of citizens.

[46]Mar. 3, 1776.

[47]Kent Monthly Minutes, Feb. 11, 1778. Concerning substitutes for military service, see entry for Oct. 8, 1777.

[48]A. L. Oerter, "Graceham, Frederick County, Md. An Historical Sketch," *Transactions of the Moravian Historical Society*, IX, Parts I and II (1913), 119-305. The church diary of this community is used extensively in this presentation.

[49]Journal (Moravian Archives, Bethlehem, Pa.). See Kenneth G. Hamilton, *John*

Ettwein and the Moravian Church During the Revolutionary Period (Bethlehem, Pa., 1940), p. 136.

⁵⁰*Ibid.* This was the Moravian patriot Augustus Spangenberg.

⁵¹John T. Hamilton, *A History of the Church Known as the Moravian Church, or the Unitas Fratrum, or the Unity of the Brethren, During the Eighteenth and Nineteenth Centuries* (Bethlehem, Pa., 1900), pp. 253-54, *et passim*, describes this process.

⁵²Kenneth Hamilton, p. 137.

⁵³John Hamilton, pp, 252-54.

⁵⁴Kenneth Hamilton, p. 140.

⁵⁵*Proceedings of the Convention of the Province of Maryland, Held at Annapolis*, p. 199.

⁵⁶Abdel R. Wentz, *A Basic History of Lutheranism in America* (Philadelphia, 1955), pp. 43-45, 48. This study proved more useful than the more specialized books on Germans in Maryland.

⁵⁷William W. Sweet (ed.), *The Presbyterians: 1783-1840: A Collection of Source Materials* (New York, 1936), pp. 3-11.

⁵⁸John H. Gardner, "Presbyterians in Old Baltimore 1729-1859," *Maryland Historical Magazine*, XXXV (Sep. 1940), 224-55, makes extensive use of the manuscript records at First Presbyterian Church, Baltimore.

⁵⁹"The Rise and Progress of the Presbyterian Church in Baltimore Town 1761-1793; The Rise and Progress of a Small Presbyterian Society in Soldiers Delight 1766-1793" (Presbyterian Historical Society, Philadelphia). This is a contemporary account.

⁶⁰Carl Bridenbaught, *Mitre and Sceptre* (New York, 1962).

⁶¹Edward F. Humphrey, *Nationalism and Religion in America* (Boston, 1924), pp. 66-104.

⁶²*Ibid.*

⁶³*Records of the Presbyterian Church in the United States* (Philadelphia, 1841), pp. 481-82.

⁶⁴Minutes of the Lewistown [Lewes, Del.] Presbytery, 1758-1788 (Presbyterian Historical Society, Philadelphia), June 2, 1778 entry. This presbytery had jurisdiction over the Eastern Shore of Maryland.

⁶⁵William P. Breed, *Presbyterians and the Revolution* (Philadephia, 1876), p. 91.

⁶⁶*Proceedings of the Convention*, pp. 143 ff. (May 22, 1776).

⁶⁷Normay H. Maring, "A Denominational History of the Maryland Baptists" (Ph. D. Diss., Univ. of Maryland, 1948), pp. 8 ff, uses minutes and other papers of the Philadelphia and Baltimore Associations. On Moore, see his *An Inquiry into the Nature and Propriety of Ecclesiastical Establishments, in a letter to Howard Griffith*, Esq. (Baltimore, 1808); and William C. Moore, *Jeremiah Moore, 1746-1815* (Richmond, Va., 1933).

⁶⁸Hanley, *Charles Carroll*, pp. 233-40, ch. 14.

⁶⁹Charles H. Metzger, *Catholics and the American Revolution: A Study in Religious Climate* (Chicago, 1962), pp. 24-47.

⁷⁰*Ibid.*, pp. 262-63; Annabelle M. Melville, *John Carroll of Baltimore: Founder of the American Catholic Hierarchy* (New York, 1955), pp. 49-53.

⁷¹Metzger, chs. 9-10.

⁷²Hanley, ch. 12. See also John Carroll's 1776 memorandum on the mission to Canada (Baltimore, Catholic Archdiocesan Archives, John Carroll Papers, Special Case C-f).

⁷³John Carroll to Thorpe [?], [1784-87] (*ibid.*). See Peter Guilday, *The Life and Times of John Carroll* (New York, 1922), pp. 172-73.

⁷⁴John Carroll to Plowden, Apr. 10, 1784. (Photoduplicates of the John Carroll Papers, Catholic University of America Library, Washington, D. C.). See also Mar. 21, 1791, and Nov. 13, 1795, letters to Plowden (*ibid.*) for related ideas.

⁷⁵On the Canadian mission in support of the American Revolution, see Annabelle M. Melville, pp. 49-53. On the justice of the Revolution see Carroll to Plowden, Apr. 10, 1784 (John Carroll Papers). See a description of the English Catholic's philosophical education in Hanley, *Charles Carroll*, pp. 46-48.

⁷⁶Eddis, *Letters*, pp. 210-12.

[77]*Proceedings of Convention*, p. 297.

[78]*Ibid.*, p. 375; Nov. 11, 1776. One Nathan Perigo, for example, was said to be pretending to be a clergyman to avoid a tax for a substitute.

[79]Mar. 14, 1777, Snow Hill; *Archives of Maryland*, XVI, 176.

[80]Aug. 25, 1777, Cecil Court House; *Archives of Maryland*, XVI, 345. Paca described one Methodist preacher, John Patterson, as the "most provoking exasperating mortal that ever existed" (*ibid.*, 364-65).

[81]*Proceedings of Convention*, pp. 19-20, and 74, where a year later this provision was reiterated, widened, and special place given to Eden and his household.

[82]See, for example, the Proceedings of the Council of Safety, Mar. 1, 1777, and Mar. 13, 1778 (*Archives of Maryland*); XVI, 156 and 535.

[83]Dec. 10, 1777.

[84]Oct. 6, 1777.

[85]Aug. 10, 1785.

[86]*Extracts from the Journals of the Rev. Dr. Coke's Five Visits to America* (London, 1793), Dec. 5, 1784 entry.

[87]*Archives of Maryland*, XVI, 535 ff.

[88]Asbury, I, 154 (Apr. 20, 1775) and 473 (Dec. 12, 1784).

[89]*Ibid.*, p. 241 (June 27, 1777).

[90]*Ibid.*, p. 430 (July 21, 1782) and 155 (Apr. 29, 1775). Previous mention has been made of Asbury's sympathy with the American cause and how knowledge of this was withheld from state officials and the public in general. The active hostility of Wesley toward the Revolution could not but be identified with Asbury, which accounted for the ill regard in which he was held until the interception of his letter containing patriotic sentiments.

[91]*Ibid.*, p. 348 (May 5, 1780) .

[92]Garrettson, Journal, Book I, pp. 10-11 and 16 (1775). On Rodda relationship see Robert D. Simpson, p. 55.

[93]Garrettson, Journal (June 30, 1778).

[94]*Ibid.*, Feb. 28, 1779.

[95]Garrettson, *Experiences and Travels,* pp. 233-236 (July 20, 1779). This is a polished and, in places, an abridged version of the above-mentioned Journal of Garrettson, which the printed version follows very closely.

[96]*Ibid.*, p. 147 (Feb. 25, 1780), and 144 (Feb. 14, 1780).

[97]Garrettson, Journal, Book I, p. 22.

[98]*Ibid.*, pp. 21-22.

[99]*Ibid.*, Apr. 22 and June 6, 1779.

[100]*Ibid.*, June 14, 1779.

[101]*Ibid.*, Mar. 28 and Apr. 10, and May 5, 1779.

[102]*Experiences and Travels*, p. 155. Underlining is in original.

[103]*Ibid.*, pp. 128-20; Journal, Sep. 12, 1778.

[104]Garrettson, Journal, July 6, 1777; see Robert D. Simpson, p. 57.

[105]*Experiences and Travels*, pp. 122-125; see Robert D. Simpson, p. 57, on militia fee.

[106]Jonathan Boucher substantiates this generalization as outlined here. He himself was a highly intermperate Tory. Given the conditions of the times, the abuses he experienced were less delinquency on the part of the state and a tolerant public, than his own antagonistic personality.

III

CREATING THE CHRISTIAN STATE

Anxiety about the questions of legitimate government and the moral means of changing it deeply stirred the conscience of Marylanders. Individuals framed their reconciliation according to various patterns found in the religious thought of the time. The decision was made, the Revolution was won, and far-reaching consequences inevitably followed. Aspiration to a Christian state helped bring the revolutionaries to their courageous decisions and accounted for the Christian conscience of the revolutionary government. Very soon after July 4, 1776, Maryland patriots, under their guiding inspiration, turned to fashioning the legal foundations of the Christian state to which they aspired. The whole law under which Maryland had lived underwent revolutionary change as the new constitution came about in November, 1776. The religious provisions of the new order of law reflected the dramatic shift of authority away from the king and Parliament and the confessional state.

The most fundamental and striking feature of the new constitution, as far as religious provisions were concerned, was the end it made of the once established Church of England. Religious ties to the king and Parliament, once broken by any loyalty given to the new state, were not renewed by the Maryland government (as New Hampshire had done when it established the Protestant Episcopal Church). For the first time since the beginning of the century all Christian denominations were now equal before the law in Maryland. [1] The once established church, soon to be known as the Protestant Episcopal Church, continued to enjoy —together with other denominations—positive benefits from the government, but on an equal footing. This meant that Christians as individuals and as diverse groups were the object of special constitutional concern. Government itself, therefore, retained not only a religious character, but a precisely Christian one. The fact and significance of this condition must indicate how inadequate it is to describe the new church-state situation as a case of "disestablishment," or "separation of church and state."

The evolutionary and transitional spirit of the constitution was clearly heralded by the Christian revolutionary government. Treatment of dissent has been noted. There were other manifestations of a religious spirit. Progressive disengagement from unjust ministers, then from an arrogant Parliament, and finally with great reluctance from the king, who had forced the colonists down the road of independence, was accomplished as a process of justice. These dramatic departures were always upon the foundations of the British Constitution and the Maryland Colonial Charter. [2] The token of this spirit was found in the long retention of and deference for British Governor Robert Eden.

In another religious vein, Marylanders appointed a day of public humiliation and prayer in April, 1775, aware of the dangerous increase of strain on ties with the mother country. "Deeply considering the distress and perplexed situation of British America," the Convention confessed that, "the weakness of all human councils, and that the hearts of all men are at the disposal of the Supreme B[eing]..." [3] A year later, facing the solemn decision of a war for independence, the same moral and religious tone continued. "Whereas his Britannic King George had prosecuted a cruel and unjust war against British colonies in America . . . the good people of this province... cannot... pray for the success of his Majesties . . ." [4] As the war went on, the council was pleased to be addressed "May God send Victory to the Arm lifted in Support of righteousness, Virtue & Freedom..." [5] So in a religious spirit the new government set its course. We appeal to that Almighty Being," said the Declaration of Delegates in justification of independence, "who is emphatically styled the searcher of hearts, and from whose omniscience nothing is concealed." They professed to rely "on his divine protection." In this spirit a chaplain was requested to render a daily prayer during the sessions of the new government. [6]

In such a religious atmosphere the constitutional convention sought a legal understanding of religion in the new state. Some retained attachment to the notion of an established church as an appropriate provision. They saw the successor to the old establishment, the Protestant Episcopal Church, as a suitable official church. This, however, was impossible at the time of the drafting of the constitution, as many pointed out. The tie of Episcopalianism to the English government was unresolved by political independence. Even afterwards, when the adjustment and independence of the American church had come about, William White did not think the temper of the southern states would allow such an arrangement of re-establishment of his church. [7] Nevertheless, the attempt was made once the Maryland Episcopal clergy saw the possibility of their autonomy. William Paca took steps to attain an official legal position for his Episcopal Church, with what he considered fair assurances to other denominations. In the thinking of the times, there were forms of government which gave a particular denomination an official position not enjoyed by others. The state merely recognized the fact of preponderance by a particular body. Such an establishment intended no discrimination, as shown in the case of Massachusetts, where all religious groups benefited from state financial grants. It seems that Maryland Episcopalians had something like this in mind. They did not feel that it savored of the confessional state which had prevailed under the period of British domination. Yet echoes of the old confessional state philosophy could indeed be heard among leaders of the Episcopal Church. "The greater the unity of Americans in religion," Samuel Seabury said long after the state constitutions were written, "the greater, probably, will be their unity in political sentiments and conduct." [8]

The assembly act which Paca promoted in 1783 did not unfold a complete establishment plan as Massachusetts created. There was reason to believe, however, that it was to open the door to an ultimate place of preference for the Protestant Episcopal Church. For the present, Paca merely sought protection of the law for all property deriving from the period of colonial establishment. In addition to approbation of a charter with these benefits, the bill sought government approval of liturgical reform, clergy recruitment and ministerial education. Patrick Allison and his fellow Presbyterians immediately attacked the measure. Like their coreligionists in Virginia, they would not readily grant all land of the former establishment to the newly incorporated Episcopal Church. In a pamphlet, Allison also denied the propriety of a church seeking government approbation of its internal affairs. Such authority in the hands of the government constituted a carry-over from the colonial state philosophy. This was "illicit commerce with civil powers." [9]

It was indeed reasonable to suspect that Episcopalians entertained ulterior plans for preferment. William Duke, himself an Episcopalian, leaves their intentions under a cloud. "They were suspected of aiming at a good deal more," he candidly stated, "and it must be owned, that if this [a charter] was all they wanted, several things suggested in the petition whereby they obtained leave as above said, were quite impertinent." The Presbyterian attack was warranted by these circumstances. [10] It also called all parties back to their true aspiration to a Christian state.

While Duke was a somewhat conservative Episcopalian, he sensed the evolutionary nature of thinking about the constitutional arrangement. He clearly saw the inequities in the old system of establishment. "With what indignation must a sensible dissenter have surrendered a proportion of his property to maintain a minister, with not one evidence of his qualification but letters of ordination and letters of introduction." Religion in consort with "the arm of power" frightened him. "It soon grows sick of its successes," he believed, "and sinks under the load of its rotten acquisitions." Yet religion's link with government could produce an "engine of virtue." "The conclusion is, that as unanimity and uniformity give stability to everything that is virtuous or good, so it is to be wished that religion had been promoted by one common exertion..." It was a common idea that government be a party to this single "exertion."

Duke saw this role of the state fulfilled among other ways by the official confessions of Christian faith. "A confession of this sort goes a great way towards a public character of religion, and paves the way to such instruction as secures the most precious and durable benefits of christianity." [11]

How did this thoughtful commentator come to accept the equal footing of all denominations before the law? He felt that it was necessary, even at the inevitable cost of eliminating a more detailed profession of Christianity in evangelical terms. Both church and state had failed in their religious goals for Maryland before the Revolution: "As the spirit of religion, as it existed amongst us, was not adequate to such an exertion, and in order to produce its effect, was obliged to avail itself of the indirect motives of strife and emulation, we ought to regret its imperfection, and make the best of it." While Duke was not dogmatic about his recommendation of a creed, which was ultimately rejected, he did not close the door against the new understanding when he noted the disadvantages of pluralism. He surely found areas of great agreement about the new religious laws and their inspiration. Among these, he shared belief that the state benefited from a virtuous citizenry; that religion, particularly Christianity, best molds such citizens; that the state must, as before, promote religion with these understandings; and that a general profession of belief in Christianity was valuable.[12]

More than twenty years after drafting the Constitution of Maryland St. Anne's Parish in Annapolis revealed a last dying glimmer of the old order. Pews were specifically inscribed for the governor, president of the senate, speaker of the house, assemblymen, judges of the general court, and members of the council.[13]

Against this background it is not surprising to find the Constitutional article of disestablishment dealing gently with the once established church, its property, and its clergy. It was the only denomination specifically mentioned by name. Its extensive property had been assured to it by law. Episcopal ministers were to be left as their church had appointed them. Long accustomed to dependence upon the government for their salaries, they were encouraged to hope for a continuation of this arrangement, but as adjusted to an equality with other denominations.[14] In all of this one finds no severance with the old order so great as that found in political independence. Instead, in religious matters there was a more gradual evolution, a modification.

The new religious form of the state emerged unmistakably Christian, as the confessional state was cast aside. It was positively religious and specifically Christian. Everyone had a duty to worship God, Article 33 stated, and must be free to fulfill it. By way of special consideration, "All persons professing the Christian religion are equally entitled to protection in their religious liberty." Only Christian denominations were singled out for such positive favor. Commenting on one of these proposed benefits, Francis L. Hawks, an early historian of Episcopalianism, said: "This scheme, it will be observed, pre-supposed the recognition of Christianity, a recognition that but few of the States, as States, are supposed to have made; Maryland, however, made it." [15] Observers of the period itself confirmed this view Maryland as a Christian state. "It treats Christian ministers with respect." William Duke noted, "and favours the general advancement of Christianity." [16] Catholic John Carroll agreed with what Duke conceived to be the government's purpose regarding Christianity: "The less its purposes toward religion are affected by the peculiarities of any one party, the more essentially it will promote the common cause... by encouraging every measure that would make the people more virtuous." Throughout his book Duke contended Christianity best serves this objective. Carroll elaborated the principle by reference to government Indian policy. The national government believed that Christianity proved a most effective means of virtue and peace among the Indians.

The constitution promised that the new state would benefit every religious-minded citizen and Christian denomination. While English legislation against Protestant dissenters had progressively been mitigated in the eighteenth century, this had not been so in the case of provisions against Catholics. Now, however, "no person ought by any law to be molested in his person or estate on account of his religious persuasion..." The formerly less acceptable persuasions of Christianity embarked on a new era before the law. At middle age, and for the first time in his life, John Carroll could say, "I have never had any cause to fear speaking my sentiments with the utmost freedom." "In our new Constitution," he explained, "it is fixed as a matter of natural justice, that every person has a right to worship Alm: [ighty] God in that religious mode or form, which his conscience dictates..." [18] The protection of the state extended to those less conventional practices so long frowned on by other governments. The Moravian settlement of Graceham, for example, became something of a religious state within the secular state, "founded solely for such persons who, through grace are members of the Brethren's Church..." [19]

Must these preferences for Christianity be interpreted to mean exclusion of non-Christians from those rights "fixed as a matter of natural justice," to use Carroll's phrase? If one excludes the right to hold office, the answer would be, no. Certainly, coercion of belief was against the letter and the spirit of Article 33, and there would never be an obligation to contribute to the support of a religion other than one's own. Person and estate of the non - Christian was likewise protected by law.[20] Declaration of belief in Christianity was not required for voting; to hold office, it was. The constitutional convention seemed aware that the non-Christian exclusion from office conflicted with the general provision against religious discrimination. This is clear from the fact that the former law appended a provision that non-Christians could through the assembly be enabled in particular cases to hold public office without a declaration of belief in Christianity.

The broader religious context of the constitution throws further light on the reasons for the declaration provision. In the final analysis, Jews were not regarded as a threat to the Christian state and thus as the source prompting the declaration requirement. Ironically, nominal Christians accounted for this. Some of these, Duke pointed out, "according to the usual artifice of Deists, sap the foundation of religious belief under pretext of great good will, meaning only to clear away the rubbish of superstition." Methodist journals called them "professors of infidelity." Extreme forms of this tendency, in followers of Paine, Condorcet, and Priestly, became positively hostile to Christianity, which they hoped to negate as a social force in society. They espoused a doctrinaire politics which would refashion the moral and religious tone of government without Christianity as traditionally understood. If such an element became an ingredient of Maryland government, "vital religion" would suffer. The Maryland Christians must provide antidote by a strong assertion contrary to this by those who held office.[21]

The rise of evangelical Christianity created a sense of crisis regarding infidelity in the revolutionary era. Thomas Claggett and William Duke revealed the importance of government in the face of "infidelity's" challenge as well as the climate of opinion it created. Claggett wanted Duke to revise his manuscript of *The State of Religion* with an eye to attacking these enemies of Christianity. He further advised that the highest governmental officials be listed at the beginning of the book as subscribers. Claggett himself solicited these subscriptions. "It would afford additional evidence," he explained to these patrons, "that ye ruling powers in ye State of Maryland are most firmly attached to ye Cause of Religion..." [22] This was but an example of the way in which Duke said Christians were "forward to maintain their profession, both against the arts and sophistry and the petulance of impiety..." With such influence the name of Christ would be honored. "At least," he concluded, "this will be the case with a sufficient number to characterize the whole, and infidelity will think fit to acquiesce." [23]

If these commentaries continued generally through the period following the adoption of the Maryland Constitution, as obviously they did, the understanding behind them evidently existed at the convention which formulated the strong provisions in favor of Christianity. That profession of Christianity was not rejected by the convention testifies to the accuracy of the commentary exemplified above and developed below in a further discussion of infidelity. One must conclude, then, that the Christianity provisions were to a considerable .degree inspired by the challenge of infidelity. Historians, it is true, have shown the charlatanry practiced in public discussions which reduced adversaries to the category of infidels, or of unwittingly bringing others to infidelity.[24] Delegates to the convention were sensitive to this problem. They would have the assembly judge in particular cases if the person refusing declaration was intent upon overturning the Christian state. The mire to which such a device would lead was a lesson learned in subsequent decades. On the other hand, the original motivation and the viewpoint of those who drafted the constituion, was later overlooked. The whole approach was understandably rejected in the long reach of the American heritage, which understood that the non-Christian was not striving to overturn religion in society.

Professions of oaths and declarations were, therefore, a logical outgrowth of the general religious and Christian aspect of the state. These practices should be related to the state's general religious purpose of fostering virtue which, it was believed, guarded against excesses in civic life. [25] "There is a sense of divine authority," Duke commented on this premise, "and an excitement of conscience produced by religion, even in the most mismanaged state, that mends the moral disposition, and in some degree prepares the human soul for its engagements, whether temporal or eternal." Christianity preeminently had the capacity to produce this effect.[26] The state was not necessarily judging the truth of Christianity, though it reflected its common acceptance by Marylanders. "Whatever difference there may be," Duke explained, "between the influence of religion as it effects the salvation of an individual, and as it maintains the vigour of the body politic, it is equally necessary to both."[27] Ultimately, then, Christianity was judged good for the state in general and, in particular, was logically required of those who exercised civil authority.

To understand fully the insistence on oaths and declaration of belief in Christianity by office holders, the aristocratic structure of government in Maryland must also be recognized. The constitution, following a principle of aristocracy, made those with greatest authority the most remote from control by the people. Senators of the upper house were chosen from the state at large and by electors rather than directly by the people. It was significant that electors were never to be excused from the oath.[28] The governor was chosen by the assembly. Removed as they were from popular censure, these officials had to give evidence of being men of conscience, profoundly under the influence of religion and Christianity. Only then would they "maintain the vigour of the body politic." The people had to be assured that their welfare was in good hands, since they now had no direct control over it. Article 11 of the Constitution and Form of Government typified this aristocratic and religious spirit when it strove to provide, "That the Senate may be at full and perfect liberty to exercise their judgement in passing laws, and that they may not be compelled by the house of delegates either to assent to some other act of legislation, in their conscience and judgement injurious to the public welfare..."[29]

The motivation for, as well as the relationship of religion and the state was indeed very subtle. The clergyman saw the state as "an engine of virtue" because it fostered and was itself nurtured by Christianity. From the secular point of view, religion was an engine which produced a virtous and responsible citizenry. All of this was understood at the time, even by those who criticized the arrangement. William Vans Murray, the noted Maryland diplomat, was an example. He criticized exclusion of non-Christians from office and believed that religion was an improper instrument of state policy. By using religion in this way, he said, the state unwisely and unlawfully tempered with matters which stood only between the individual and God.[30] Vans Murray, however, did not properly appreciate the way in which his adversaries viewed him and his school of thought. In their view, he was himself a sectarian, one considered by Marylanders as an infidel. As an extremely unrepresentative group, they reasoned, it was unjust that his religious commitments should shape the state of a dominantly evangelical Christian people.[31] The case of the Jews was similar and their number even smaller except that they had no design to change religion by a secularized state. Apparently if there were no militantcy in persons with such non-Christian commitments, the assembly was empowered to grant them public office without oaths and declarations. Accordingly, the constitution's provisions for religious freedom was thus fulfilled.[32]

Fear derived from an awareness of an aggressive infidelity prompted some to call for even stricter provision for a Christian government than the constitution provided. The Talbot County Vestry, for example, petitioned the lawmakers to insist that qualifications for office rest upon the fact of actual registration with a Christian congregation.[33] This was a practical application of Duke's general principle which was so widely understood. "If the revealed knowledge of God," he wrote of Christianity's influence, "devoutly received affects individuals, most beneficially and delightfully, and if it conduces to useful society, and confers an air of dignity upon government, who that loves himself, that loves his neighbour, or his country could neglect it." [34] In a sense, the reasoning previously used against Catholics was applied to infidels to keep them from office. The royal government of the colony had considered Catholics a menace to the safety of the state. Now the constitution sought to prevent a force believed to be inimical to evangelical Christanity from using government against the influence of Christianity on social morality.

In the face of this somewhat conservative approach to constructing a Christian state, striking liberal features are easily overlooked. The constitution significantly broadened voting rights and civil liberties. Catholics, disfranchised for nearly eighty years, were now allowed to vote. Marylanders had long felt that Catholics constituted no danger, but a benefit to the state. There was no hesitancy about bringing their many gifted aristocrats into the highest public offices. A deepening sense of freedom had clearly taken root and repelled that unreasoning fear which had always used a plea of public security to suppress civil liberties.

The constitution sought to promote a Christian and religious aspect to government by requiring the oath of those who held offices of profit and trust. There was frequent litigation, constitutional amendment, and legislation on this matter as Maryland government and law stubbornly strove to retain the oath, particularly at the highest levels of authority. Exceptions in favor of conscientious objectors were made carefully and reservedly, assuring that the person in question was religious-minded and sympathetic to the Christian state. William Duke provides the best commentary on this care and reserve. He noted that a "sense of the divine presence" should attend domestic and civil business of a Christian people. "The ministers of civil justice," he wrote, "will make use of the occupation that their office suggests, of inculcating that idea of the divine government upon which our political as well as spiritual safety depends." A solemn oath reasonably accompanied the taking of office by such persons. "How can an honest magistrate," he asked, "administer oaths to thoughtless or profane people, without enforcing the obligation by the omnipresence and inviolable honour of the Deity? If he either loves God or his country, he will show it on such occasion." [35]

The constitutions's insistence on the operation of conscience in the office holder has been noted. The oath is the symbolic inauguration of conscience's function in the government. It is true that the state did not expect an act of God to strike down the man who violated his oath. The law, however, saw to punishment in this life. By Article 39 of the Constitution and Form of Government, the dishonest office holder must suffer more than the penalty of any theft he may have perpetrated as a private citizen. "He shall suffer the punishment for willful and corrupt perjury" in such cases.[36] All of this was but a way of affirming the motivation which consideration of further punishment in the next life provided. When later amendments to the constitution in the nineteenth century removed the requirement of declaring belief in Christianity, the state significantly required declaration of belief in reward and punishment in the hereafter.

In the case of the highest offices of the state, the state significantly rejected affirmation as a substitute for the oath. The first draft of constitutional legislation, for example, required that senators and delegates take the oath without exception. [37] The following day Samuel Chase moved to add "or affirmation" to the oath clause, but was defeated by the convention vote. [38] In the final version the oath clause stood as originally stated without exception for affirmation.[39] A similar attempt was again made in the case of the oath for electors of the senators and it likewise failed.[40] In 1788, however, a bill was proposed which would make it possible "to alter such parts of the constitution and form of government as prevent a citizen from taking a seat in the legislature or being an elector of the senate, without taking the oath to support the government." William Kilty, Maryland's first constitutionalist, asserted that this was an actual law which had no effect. He did not explain his view.[41] In any event, a law with a similar purpose was before the 1794 session of the assembly, which indicates that a concession had not yet been made.[42] This persistent demand for an unqualified oath gave evidence of the importance attached to it. When one considers the indulgence shown in other causes toward persons conscientiously at odds with the practice, the special view of the highest offices is apparent. Proposed amendments allowing affirmation instead of the oath dealt only with the lower levels of the civil structure. As for the governor, councilmen, and judges, there was no discussion of the possibility of affirmation in the article providing for their oath.

The oath played an important role in the court and in legal transactions. Here one finds the state "enforcing obligation of the omnipresence of the Deity," to use Duke's characterizations of the spirit of the oath in court.[44] "In all criminal prosecutions," the Declaration of Rights stated, "every man hath a right... to examine the witnesses for and against him on oath." When a man was to be removed from office there must be the same requirement. "His seat on conviction in a court of law, by the oath of two creditable witnesses, shall be void ..." In assuring the safety of person and property, the constitution again appealed to the sacred sanction of oath: "All warrants without oath... to search suspected places... ought not to be granted." [45] Although the once established church vestry no longer exercised authority jointly with the state civil law in matters of public morality, the oath was still retained in civil proceedings as a religious force for justice in these delicate matters affecting personal reputation.[46]

Oaths for court and legal procedures were insisted upon almost without exception, even though one might expect that the state would have allowed for affirmation by conscientious objectors. The original provisions for witnesses in criminal prosecutions and removals from office show the strictness of the oath requirement. Affirmations, however, were allowed in the case of warrants. Yet, legislation considered in 1797 showed that the law had a great reluctance to modify the oath practice. It took considerable time and proven cases of serious hardship to bring about extension of affirmation to court and legal practices in that year. "Persons conscientiously scrupulous of taking an oath," read one constitutional amendment, "labor under many and great inconveniences, owing to their not being admitted to make their solemn affirmation as witnesses in all cases instead of an oath." Only under such circumstances was there mitigation of the oath requirement.[47] It is noteworthy that only members of specific Christian denominations were mentioned in connection with the law. This gave foundation for believing that Jews were excluded from its benefits in court. One historian adds to this reasoning consideration of Article 33 of the 1851 Declaration of Rights where Jews are specifically mentioned.[48] However, were not the vast majority of eighteenth-century American Jews able to take the oath without any qualification? All that was required was belief in God, and Jews would not then seem to be troubled by the Quaker's objection to calling on God as a witness.

Education illustrates another area where the oath was applied by the state according to the pattern found in previous considerations. More exact requirements were made of county school trustees than of those in colleges. In Anne Arundel County, for example, the oath was used to assure belief in the Christian religion, loyalty to the state, and active opposition to toryism. Something similar was found in Kent County. While requiring the oath at Washington College, Chestertown, nothing specific was indicated for its content beyond support and fidelity to the state. Even less was demanded by St. John's at Annapolis; oaths and other requirements, in this case, were by law not to enforce "any religious or civil tests." County schools, it must be remembered, approximated the status of public schools more than did the colleges, so that the state could require more of them.[49] This inexactness regarding oath requirements in education contrasts with the strictness maintained at the highest levels of civil authority.

This strong conviction regarding the necessity of oaths inevitably led to difficulties for certain orthodox Christians. These men of faith believed it against the divine law to swear, or call upon God to witness the truth of one's word. How did the government and constitution reconcile their obligation to these dissenters with what they owed the majority of Christians who insisted on the oath? It has already been explained in a general way how the Christian revolutionary government maintained a delicate conscience in this respect. It remains to be seen how the committed Christian state provided some legal exceptions, while holding strong attachment to oaths as an important means to survival.

Article 36 of the Declaration of Rights made it clear: "That the manner of administering an oath to any person ought to be such as those of the religious persuasion... generally esteem the most effectual confirmation by the attestation of the Divine Being." Before proceeding to any exceptions, it was understood that every case under consideration must accept the idea of attestation to a Divine Being. The Article noted that Quakers had long accepted this basic understanding and that under colonial law they were allowed to affirm rather than swear by oath. This privilige was renewed as far as it applied to warrants and witnessing in courts—two basic civil needs.

It was significant that Dunkers and Mennonists (Menonites) were also included as beneficiaries of Article 36.[50] This meant that exceptions to the oath must be specifically named in law, thus assuring that only denominational believers would benefit. A petition by the Nicolites, or New Quakers, showed that they were excluded from the benefits of the article until they were mentioned by a specific law in their favor in 1783. This act assured that it was "for relief of the christian society of people," and that their "solemn affirmation" was founded on belief. This precaution of the law dragged out the process of winning exceptions, not only for specific denominations unnamed in the original article, but for those who had won it in some respects but not in others. It was not until 1794, for example, that Quakers succeeded in modifying the oath required for public office. [51]

Apparent in all of this was a struggle with two principles of Maryland constitutionalism. There was the will to free the individual's religious belief; and there was the will to preserve the state and society by force of the Christian religion. It was not until 1828 that the non-Christian believer in God won the right to hold public office. A decline of the aristocratic concept of government undoubtedly accounted for this development. It should be recalled how the prevailing aristocratic concept had originally called for a religious requirement of office holders. The Jeffersonian and Jacksonian influences in this process of political change, of course, was responsible to a great extent for the modification that took place.

What did the state do for the denominations specifically, besides granting special recognition of Christianity and its influence? The direct action of the old regime was exclusively toward the established church. The provincial government gave property to the parishes, both in land and buildings. Glebe-land, as a benefice to a clergyman, and taxes yielded a constant income to the parish, its rector and curates. Only clergy of the Establishment claimed salaries and aid from the province. What impact did the Revolution have on these arrangements? Examination of the constitution and other legal provisions will reveal striking changes, which were unavoidably involved in politics, touching other religious groups as well as the succession of the formerly Established Church. The constituional convention acted to safeguard the legal status of property held by all denominations. This was essential to them. "As they were all treated equitably," Duke observed, "and every party left in possession of what was properly its own, there were no complaints made." [52] This was surely an accurate commentary on Article 34 of the Declaration of Rights.

This article gave assurance not only of title to property, but to its use and transmission, so essential to any growing religious congregation. The state undertook to make good by legal force any of these matters submitted to it for sanction. The "gift, sale, or devise of land," which were intended as benefits to ministers or similar persons, denominations or religious orders, were honored. These benefits were, under such legal conditions, valid, "in succession, or... after... death... and also... for the support, use or benefit of any minister, public teacher or preacher of the gospel, as such, or any religious sect, order or denomination..." [53] This legislation gave the government some control in return for such legal benefits. Proposals for incorporation and other arrangements possible by Article 34 had to be approved by the assembly. St. Paul's Parish, for example, was strictly held to a stipulated formula for distributing its annual rents. [54] The assumption was, however, that revision of the conditions of incorporation was possible by a new petition of the assembly. The rights of church petitioners were so exact and detailed that it would seem the assembly could not but concur in any provisions for incorporation.

Because of its unique position, the Protestant Episcopal Church, as the formerly established Church of England in the Maryland Province, claimed special provision in the constitution. "Churches, chapels, glebes, and all other property," read Article 33 in part, "now belonging to the church of England, ought to remain to the church of England for ever." Shortly before the drafting of the constitution, the assembly of the province had enabled tax collections for church building and maintenance. The new government chose for the present year not to intervene in the execution of this law. However, the practice of assessment of tobacco at the county level was to be discontinued. The force of the provincial act for the support of the clergy was to continue its benefit to the support of the once established church's clergy until the end of the current annual period. [55] Routine business of the parishes were rendered legal under the new government, even though the ecclesiastical status of the Church was unclear. In the May Session of 1781, a vestry's negotiation for tobacco was validated. [56] The following year Shrewsbury Parish, Kent County, was legally enabled to sell its glebe-land and acquire other land which was more productive and more favorably situated. [57] It 1784 a Cecil County parish made a similar arrangement [58] and about this time there was an act to appoint a selective vestry for St. John's Parish. [59] In these ways the extensive landholding of a denomination was safeguarded. Secular law even sought to stabilize ecclesiastical government; it secured the mutual rights of pastor and vestry where civil litigation could develop from their contractual relationship.[60]

The other denominations took advantage of the benefits of Article 34. The Catholic church of St. Marys, Bryan Town, acquired legal incorporation. Besides such routine legal provisions, others of broader significance were gained. John Carroll found protection against the Roman Congregation of the Propagation of the Faith. "If any of our friends," he wrote the year that Independence was won, "could be weak enough to deliver any real estate into their foreign hands or attempt to subject it to their authority, our civil government would be called upon to wrest it again out of their dominion." [61] Presbyterians and Catholics, among minority denominations, had greater need of legal incorporation and other safeguards of this kind than did Methodists, Baptists, and Quakers, although petitions by this latter group were made. [62] The assembly also acted for the benefit of individual clergymen. In some cases these acts were made as aids in relief of the clergyman as a private party. [63] As for non-Christians, nothing in the laws prevented them from obtaining incorporation of property and houses of public worship. The only denial of a petition of incorporation was in 1829 and then the grant was made the very next year. [64] The general spirit of the constitution regarding worship was to proceed in a manner entirely different from what it showed in requiring certain religious qualification for office. This meaning was clear in passages on the exercise of religious liberty at the beginning of Article 33.

Much legislation was mere routine, perhaps most of it. The resultant legal benefits to religion, however, were not always free from rather deep involvement in the politics of the assembly. Indeed, submitting these matters to a political body, rather than to a judicial of quasi-judicial commission as is done today, had the odor of the old days of Establishment about it. It was not enough to get agreement among the clergy with their bishop on proposal to the assembly. Lay vestrymen of the church also had to concur. Dissidents along the line could engage in obstruction. Others, more happily, could seek assistance for passage of what was agreed upon within the church. The good will of other denominations became a factor in making a success of a given church's business before an assembly in which many members were of another religious persuasion. The whole political balance of members and non members of that church came into play.

All of these possibilities of a happier sort were verified in the 1788 Episcopal Bill. William Smith, organizer of the first Episcopal Conventions in Maryland, was struggling to have an important clause inserted in the existing vestry laws. He wanted the rector to have the power of calling a vestry meeting in the face of obstruction by vestrymen who wanted to prevent election of a minister or some other important matter. Smith revealed the kind of politicking such business required. "I have done the best with Mr. Chase's usual offices," he wrote to Samuel West, the Baltimore minister, "and the bill will be taken care of on its Passage through [the House] of d[D]elegates by Jere Chase, W. Tilghman & other members of our Church..." Maryland's highest ranking Catholic and Presbyterian clergymen entered the political proceedings in the Senate. "Dr. Carroll and Dr. Allison went with me into the Senate," Smith recounted, "and delivered the Clause, declaring that on the Insertion thereof, we were all agreed to the Bill . . ." [65]

In 1797 the complicated position of Episcopalianism before the assembly and law fell prey to unfavorable forces. The contest over the Vestry Bill of that year recalled the dispute of Samuel Keane in the days before the war. After great effort, he had prevented the assembly from assuming power over clergy appointments. [66] The Revolution had not swept away all capacity for jealousy in the secular power, for the new status of other denominations had changed the church's situation. "When the abrogation of the former government annihilated all political advantage," Duke accurately explained, "and put the several denominations of Christians in Maryland upon equal footing, they presently began to calculate the interest and ability of each other, with respect to a competition, in which they were left entirely to themselves." [67] The one favored church was still the most prosperous. "A glebe, or the ground-rent of two or three houses, becomes a matter of envy," Duke observed, "if not of admiration, and the proprietor is suspected of taking unfair advantages, and tampering with the legislature, to the detriment of other societies." [68] It surely had to be conceded that tampering was necessary. Suspicion and fear of loss by other denominations was only on a few occasions justified. Episcopalians who set about their legislative business in 1797, however, had to reckon with this unpleasant atmosphere. [69]

Thomas Claggett, by now Bishop of the Episcopal Church, described the complications of the Vestry Act. There was internal dissention and the dissenters appealed to those outside the Church to obstruct the bill.

"It is violently opposed by the vestry of St. Paul's [.] Baltimore," Claggett wrote. "They have sent forward a most formidable counter petition, signed by themselves & a large body of the most respectable Gentlemen of our communion in that City. It places y.ᵉ Clergy in a very degraded situation indeed..." [70] William Bend, the rector of St. Paul's Parish, did not attend the Annapolis session because he was in disagreement with his own vestry regarding the legislation. Further increasing the internal conflict, he collaborated with Claggett and Samuel Chase in drafting and promoting this legislation. Dispatching the bill from Baltimore with Chase, he encouraged Claggett to stay on at Annapolis and use his influence until the bill was passed. [71] Chase found much opposition among the other denomination, as well as within the Church. It became important to prevent the internal strife from becoming public and one assemblyman strongly urged Chase to attend to this. [72] The bill was finally passed in the form Claggett, Bend, and Chase had desired. The revolt within and opposition from other denominations seems to have been offset by strong support from Presbyterians and Catholics, whose alignment in these matters remained much as it was ten years previously in the earlier vestry bill. [73]

Claggett noted another way, though less important, in which his Church as well as others was involved in politics. The assembly plagued one vestry bill with postponement, as it wrangled about trivialities of a purely political nature. The Church could get no action on its plan for raising urgently needed money within the parish. Consideration of pew rent arrested the attention of the assemblymen, whom Claggett chastised for being too intent on mundane matters. [74] These, then, were some of the disadvantages mixed with the legal benefits found in the constitution. It was largely a condition, however, created by the prior existence of an established colonial church. Procedures for protecting church incorporation seemed to be wanting more than a sincere benevolence in the Christian state.

It is not surprising to find that such a state sought to aid religion directly by public funds. "The legislature may in their discretion," Article 33 of the Declaration of Rights stated, "lay a general and equal tax for the support of the christian religion, leaving to each individual the power of appointing the payment over of the money collected from him, to the support of any particular place of worship or minister; or for the benefit of the poor of his own denomination, or the poor in general of any particular county." [75] This was a carefully worded piece of legislation for an extremely delicate situation. The old provincial tax for support of clergy had drawn bitter attacks in the days before the War, but the new legislation had an equality about it which appealed to religious-minded men. There was no doubt about its being acceptable to a majority of those at the convention.[76] Whatever the recollection of the past, the principle upon which that aid now rested was readily accepted in 1776. "Dissenters in general were pleased to be discharged of every involuntary expense about religion," Duke said of the new atmosphere, "and churchmen were too sensible of the justice of the measure to express disapprobation."[77] Given this change of feeling in the new Christian state, Article 33 was in obvious harmony with the whole tenor of the constitution. Whatever the outcome, the door could not but be left open to direct support of religion in this form.

It was only natural that the successor to the once established church and its clergy should take the lead in implementing the right provided by Article 33. Vestry records as early as 1780 gave evidence of this growing feeling among Episcopalians. Chester Parish wrote its petition for legislation with attention to the position of the minority denominations. Attention was even called to those with no denominational connections, or with no desire to express them on this particular topic of aid; their tax might be designated for a charitable fund of their choice. Above all these people reasoned later that same year, the practice of "pious Ancestors" must be respected; for without religion Maryland would "fall prey to some haughty Invader!"[78] In 1783 William Paca, when addressing the Episcopal Convention, hopefully called attention to Article 33 in the face of the Church's decimated clergy and dilapidated chapels.[79] Two years later further efforts were made. St. Stephen's Parish, Cecil County, appealed to the familiar justification for aid to religion but pointed out the "unequal burden upon a few" which continued for want of action by the assembly. Vice and immorality would result from continued neglect.[80] All of this reasoning and support was not enough to bring agreement on an acceptable clergy bill. Throughout *The State of Religion,* Duke alluded to the factors which explained the failure. A new alignment of the denominations had taken place following the War. Reserve had developed in the general attitude toward use of the tax device for the benefit of the denominations.

While the Episcopalians took the lead in promoting the clergy bill, Presbyterians and Catholics at first willingly discussed its possibilities. It was evident that any significant sentiment which was categorically opposed in principle to such measures would earlier have prevented passage of Article 33. Presbyterians and Catholics could have done this, possibly alone, but certainly with an appeal to Baptist and other elements. At least one Catholic, Charles Carroll of Carrollton, as a member of the constitutional committee was in a position to prevent the article. Episcopalians, on the other hand, as the largest denomination, commanded the respect of these minorities. Yet, considering their past attacks on their own colonial clergy tax bills, it seems that some still questioned the advisability of renewing aid in the new constitutional form of equal allotment to all denominations. If one ascribes influence to the evolutionary tendency of religious lawmaking in these times, it will be apparent that this too was a factor in at least leaving the door open to some form of this past practice. All of these circumstances considered, the formulation of Article 33 was capable of uniting most of the viewpoints, since no one group had made up its mind, certainly not about details. The long period before action was finally taken on the matter confirmed this fact.

Against this background, Duke's description of the sequel to passage of Article 33 was what might have been expected. "They thought that an Act of Assembly might be of service to them," he wrote, largely in reference to Presbyterians and Catholics. "Hence they conferred, they disputed, they agreed and disagreed, and finally, since they did not very cordially co-operate, they left the business pretty nearly as they found it." [81] Article 33, then, assured only the possibility of this discussion; something else explained why "they did not very cordially co-operate." Since John Carroll also spoke of "animosities" in connection with the legislative effort, their fact and influence cannot be overlooked. [82]

According to Duke and Carroll, the Presbyterian-Episcopalian relationship was the source of greatest strain on the Clergy Bill. Duke believed Presbyterians had no real interest in such aid to religion, possibly due to their envy of Episcopal glebe-land. Their long experience in getting along without state support of clergy and church also inclined them to be slow to respond. In noting how Methodism diminished the number of Episcopalians, Duke indicated that Presbyterians as well as other denominations saw that this afforded "an evident gratification." The general treatment of Presbyterians by Duke, however, would lead one to take his observations on such a matter with some reservations. [83] John Carroll believed that the clergy bill tended to revive past animosities between the two denominations. [84] Methodists tended to view the measure in terms of denominational competition.

While there was less strain in Catholic-Episcopalian relations, there was little evidence that Catholics were inclined to concur with the clergy bill. They were able to support their clergy by corporate property holding, now more secure than ever by the new constitution. An impressive lay-aristocracy was equally assuring. As with Presbyterians, the custom of doing without such aid inclined Catholics to a different view from that of Episcopalians. Judging from John Carroll's writings, direct aid was viewed with caution and even suspicion. The only approximation of the proposed arrangement which he had ever carefully observed as accomplished fact was in English and French history. From study and experience he characterized the arrangement as a "surrender made by the Church to the State of the independence, it derives from God, and the nature of its destination." [85] Freedom from financial care, all the same, must have been attractive to both Presbyterian and Catholic clergymen. The demands of the liturgy, church government, and the care of souls bore down on them as they did the Episcopal clergy, in a degree not experienced by some evangelical denominations without a priesthood or episcopacy. All this explained how the door was left open for some time; but past experience and Presbyterianism's relationship to Episcopalianism ultimately prompted the other parties to withdraw support of the Episcopal effort for a clergy bill.

The view of the other parties is not hard to grasp. "Methodists, Baptists and Quakers," Duke explained, "were satisfied with an exemption from the *thirty per poll*" which had taxed these sects before the Revolution. [86] There is no evidence that they wanted a clergy bill. In addition to points noted in Catholic and Presbyterian experience which contrasted with the Episcopalians, these sects had the common tendency to compete against the Episcopal Church. The large number of Methodists and Baptists recruited from Episcopalianism gave evidence of their success. As consideration of the clergy bill continued inconclusively for nearly ten years after passage of Article 33, all the minorities came to feel that Episcopalianism inevitably—and unintentionally—stood to gain the most, everything considered.

In addition to these interdenominational elements of tension there was yet another weakness in the Episcopal policy. It was not Episcopal enough. There were too many members who were not convinced. In a passage describing the lay animosity for the clergy, Duke himself leads one to believe that there was a hard core of opposition, or certainly of skepticism. "Churchmen [Episcopal laymen] not only exclaim against the impositions of the late establishment," he stated, "whereby persons were erected into little popes, about the country, but they still see nothing sacred in the clerical character, and pass sentence upon the religious and moral principles of their own pastors, with as much petulance as they would upon those of an infidel." [87] In the face of this frank estimate, one can conclude that this recognizable element of the Church was reform-minded in the style of dissenters. The clergy bill was a logical point at which to join the dissenter opposition. Rather than disloyalty, there was found in this critical element of Episcopalianism the aspiration to a Christian state and society, which was stirring on the eve of the Revolution. Old understandings on church and state were too much to be found in the clergy bill. Significant elements of the Church, therefore, had by now joined the minority sects in drawing back from this particular tie to the state, "lest a surrender [be] made by the Church to the State of the independence, it derives from God..." [88] The confessional state was buried at last. That the Christian state was very much alive is seen in the great sensitiveness both to the generous aid to religion and to dangers hidden in only apparent goods for that purpose.

The Christian state manifested itself in still other ways. The matrimonial contract and ceremony adhered to the religious character it had always held in provincial law. By an Act of 1777 religious requirements were added to the usual secular provisions for annulment, alimony, and cases of consanguinity. To be valid in the eyes of state law, marriages had to be performed in the presence of a religious minister and in a house of worship. This requirement was so much insisted upon, that a marriage without it could be nullified by the state. [89] The Church of England had formerly exercised authority over many aspects of matrimony; the state now assumed jurisdiction in the conditions without a state religion. "The chancellor," the law stated in one case, "shall and may hear and determine all causes for alimony, in as full and as ample manner as such causes could be heard and determined by the laws of England in the ecclesiastical courts there." [90] Similarly provision was made in the cases of legitimacy, fornication, and other matters of sexual and matrimonial morality. The vestrymen and ministers under provincial law had been empowered to initiate investigations of these cases. Now only constables held jurisdiction. [91]

People understood that the Christian state must keep up such concern with matrimonial law. The Lewes Presbytery, for example, censured one of its members for disregarding one of these provisions, which were thought proper for a "government, where Christians live." [92] The new condition of that law, however, must be insisted upon in the spirit of Article 33, so that there be impartiality in the exercise of such power among the Christian denominations, where formerly the state religion held an exclusive role. John Carroll once made an issue of this on the occasion of an orphan's estate in which Catholic guardianship of Protestant children was denied, while at the same time Protestants were given guardianship of Catholic children. "This clause is inconsistent with that perfect equality of rights," Carroll noted, "which by our constitution is secured to all religions..." [93]

Sunday observance and censorship of blasphemy had been provided for in a law of 1723 and these enactments were renewed after 1776. The convention reminded electors of this before the constitution was drafted. About the same time it took occasion to warn officers and soldiers of these two matters while encouraging them to reverent attendance at divine worship. [94] Place was made for control of public morality, even in ways which probably infringed upon private morals. What are sometimes called "blue laws," were not considered out of spirit with these constitutional times. A law against gambling, for example, was passed in the belief that such games of chance led to the "corruption of morals." [95] Faro was specifically named. "The most innocent use of them," wrote Duke of card-playing, "was countenancing what is really criminal in others." [96] He felt himself singular at the time he wrote this, but within a few years the government was on the side of the reforming minister. A lottery, however, for church improvement, or the erection of a town wharf, were allowed because of the wholesome motivation and circumstances in which such a practice took place. [97]

The theater was an instance of governmental supervision by the law. [98] In 1780 the assembly also did not hesitate to revive laws prohibiting liquor and horseracing in one vicinity out of regard for a Quaker meeting house. [99] But when Benjamin Rush, Pennsylvania signer of the Declaration of Independence, sought support in Maryland for a general law against spiritous liquor, he had little success. [100] As far as Sunday observance was concerned, it was found that good results rewarded the state's vigilance. "Thousands who, a few years ago, spent the sabbath in a worse manner than any other day of the week," Duke commented at the close of the Revolutionary Period, "now devote it to the more immediate service of God." [101] Whether religious fervor produced the effect and then the law, or the other way around, is never easily settled. The common understanding after the Revolution was that the Christian state should provide more stimulus throughout the social process.

When this whole scope of constitution making, subsequent passage of laws, and application to society comes into view, the inspiration and character of the Christian state is unmistakable. It is clear that the old confessional state was thrown off under an authentic religious inspiration. The forthright implementation of that inspiration created the reality of a Christian state.

REFERENCES

[1]The Declaration of Rights was agreed to by the Convention on November 3, 1776, the Constitution and Form of Government, on November 8; together they formed the Constitution of the State of Maryland. For provision on religious equality, see Article 33 of the Declaration, *Proceedings of Convention*, pp. 314-15.

[2]See John A. Silver, *The Provisional Government of Maryland (1774-1777)* (Baltimore, 1895) for a general study of the governmental transition.

[3]*Proceedings of Convention*, p. 13.

[4]*Ibid.*, p. 156.

[5]Stone to Council, July 12, 1776; *Archives of Maryland*, XII, 36.

[6]*Proceedings of Convention*, pp. 203 and 217.

[7]White, pp. 1 *et passim.*

[8]*An Address to the Ministers and Congregation of the Presbyterian and Independent Persuasions in the United States of America* (Boston, 1797), p. 35.

[9]Patrick Allison, *Candid Animadversions Respecting a Petition to the Late General Assembly of Maryland in Behalf of Christian Ministers of the Same* (Baltimore, 1783), pp. 1-5. Gardner, *Maryland Historical Magazine*, XXXV, 248. This was "Illicit commerce with civil powers."

[10]*State of Religion*, p. 36.

[11]*Ibid.*, pp. 27, 37, 38, 48, and 8.

[12]*Ibid.*, pp. 37-38. The above is drawn from and over-all consideration of Duke's thoughtful analysis of religion and law in Maryland.

[13]Entry, Parish Vestry Records, July 13, 1797 (Maryland Historical Society).

[14]*Proceedings of the Assembly*, pp. 314-15.

[15]*Contributions to the Ecclesiastical History of the United States: Maryland* (New York, 1839), p. 324.

[16]Duke, *State of Religion*, p. 47.

[17]Pastoral Letter of May 28, 1792; to Baxter, Sep. 15, 1800, and to Washington, Mar. 20, 1792 (John Carroll Papers).

[18]Carroll to Plowden, Sep. 26, 1783, and Feb. 27, 1785 (*ibid.*).

[19]See Town Ordinances or Statutes Referring to the Civil Government of the Church Settlement of Graceham, in Carter, *Transactions of the Moravian*, IX, 289.

[20]Article 35 required declaration of Christian belief by office holders, but even this must be required by specific laws in each case (*Proceedings of Convention*, p. 315). These implications were all found in the Etting case, where a Jew unsuccessfully petitioned the right to hold office. Because the Assembly voted on petitions of incorporation of all religious congregations, Jews could—as any other gorup—be discriminated against.
    This topic requires a special study that is only partially satisfied by that of Benjamin H. Hortogensis, "Unequal Rights in Maryland Since 1776," *Publications of American Jewish Historical Society*, No. 25: (1917), pp. 93-107.

[21]Duke, *State of Religion*, pp. 12-13.
    For a discussion of Methodist journals as well as other sources for evidence in Rationalism and Deism see: Chester Parish Vestry Record, Mar. 14, 1780; Minutes of the Lawes Presbytery, Oct. 15, 1782; Claggett to Duke, Sep. 26, 1796 (Maryland Historical Society, Maryland Diocesan Archives).

[22]Claggett to Duke. Sep. 26, 1796 (*ibid*).

[23]Duke, *State of Religion*, pp. 12-13.

[24]Martin Marty, *The Infidel: Freethought and American Religion* (New York, 1961), pp. 11-32; 43-58.

[25]*Proceedings of Convention*, p. 36, August 4, 1775; *Archives of Maryland*, XI, 11.

[26]*State of Religion*, p. 5.

[27]*Ibid.*

[28]*Laws of Maryland Made and Passed at a Session of the Assembly* (Annapolis, 1788). ch. XII.

[29]*Proceedings of the Convention*, p. 351. See also the stress on conscience in reference to other offices: electors, p. 320; and governor, p. 326.

[30]William Vans Murray, *Political Sketches, Inscribed to His Excellency John Adams, Minister Plenepotentiary from the United States to the Court of Great Britain, by a Citizen of the United States* (London, 1787); "William Vans Murray on Freedom of Religion in the United States, 1787," edited by Alexander DeConde, *Maryland Historical Magazine*, L (Dec., 1955), 289.

[31]William James brilliantly revealed the religious commitment in the agnostic's stance and assumption. See *The Will to Believe and Other Essays in Popular Philosophy* (New York, 1927), p. 11.

The Supreme Court of the United States in its decision, *Torcaso v Watkins* (1960) took note of Secular and Agnostic Humanism as America's Fourth Religion.

[32]The Maryland Constitution pointed the way to a twentieth century resolution to the problem of freedom implied in this assembly procedure. Assignment of state grants to churches or humanitarian objects were to be determined by the individual citizen. Tax exemption, in a sense, meets the problem and honors the still prevailing understanding that the state is a collaborator with religion.

[33]St. Peter's Parish, Report to Claggett, 1797 (Maryland Diocesan Archives).

[34]*State of Religion*, p. 53. For a similar view see Keith to Kemp, Sep. 30, 1793 (Maryland Diocesan Archives).

[35]*State of Religion*, p. 12.

[36]*Proceedings of Convention*, p. 358.

[37]Article 28 of the Constitution and Form of Government, as of November 3d Session, *ibid.*, p. 382.

[38]November 4, 1776, *ibid.*, p. 333.

[39]*Ibid.*, pp. 355-56.

[40]See Baly's motion of Nov. 6, 1776, session, *ibid.*, p. 342. Final form was in Article 18 of the Constitution and Form of Government, p. 354. The preliminary draft retained the same Article number, *ibid.*, p. 320, but in the 1836 edition confusion arises from the inclusion of "or affirmation," which was an obvious error. At any rate, there was no doubt of the Convention's intention.

[41]State of Maryland, *Laws of Maryland*, 1788, ch. xlii; and William Kilty (ed.) *The Laws of Maryland...* (Annapolis, 1799), ch. xlii of 1788 Session and note to this Act.

[42]Article 50 of the Constitution and Form of Government, *Proceedings of Convention*, p. 360.

[43]Article 50 of the Constitution and Form of Government, *Proceedings of Convention*, p. 360.

[44]Duke, *State of Religion*, p. 12.

[45]*Proceedings of Convention*, pp. 358 and 313.

[46]On sexual morality cases see *Laws of Maryland*, ch xxxx of 1781 Session. In these court practices the same reluctance to concede affirmation in place of the oath is found which is seen in connection with office holding. Nearly all of the vestry records used in this study illustrate the way in which local church vestries functioned in these cases before the period of independence.

[47]*Laws of Maryland*, ch. 118 of 1797 Session. Only Quakers, Dunkers, and other specifically Christian sects are mentioned, which gives further evidence of the religious and Christian emphasis of law.

[48]Hortogensis, *Jewish Historical Society*, No. 25, pp. 101-103.

[49]*Laws of Maryland*, ch. ii, 1779 Session; ch. xix, 1781; ch. viii, 1782; ch. xxxvii, 1784.

This provision for St. John's College might in part account for Duke's impression that its educators and trustees, "throw aside all appearance of divine worship..." (See Duke, *State of Religion*, pp. 50-51).

[50]*Ibid.*, pp. 315 and 255.

[51]*Laws of Maryland,* ch. xviii, Nov. 1783; ch. xlix, Nov. 1794.

[52]Duke, *State of Religion,* p. 35.

[53]*Proceeding of Convention,* p. 315.

[54]*Laws of Maryland,* ch. xxii, Article 4, Nov. 1779.

[55]*Proceedings of Convention,* pp. 314-15.

[56]*Laws of Maryland,* ch. vii, May. 1781.

[57]*Ibid.,* ch. xiv, Apr. 1782.

[58]*Ibid.,* ch. ix, Nov. 1784.

[59]*Ibid.,* Nov. 1783.

[60]*Ibid.,* ch. xxxvii, Nov. 1795.

[61]Carroll to Plowden, September 26, 1783 (John Carroll Papers).

[62]See Duke, *State of Religion,* pp. 35-36, for the varying interest of the denominations in legislation affecting religious property.

[63]*Laws of Maryland,* ch. ix, Nov. 1779; ch. xxxvii, 1786.

[64]Hortogensis, *Jewish Historical Society,* no. 85, p. 99.

[65]Smith to West, Dec. [?], 1788 (Maryland Diocesan Archives).

[66]Utley, pp. 38-39.

[67]*State of Religion,* p. 35.

[68]*Ibid.,* p. 34.

[69]Previous mention has been made of Duke's candor in admitting grounds for suspicion of his Church. He was not inclined to claim too much for his own persuasion; in fact, Claggett found him too critical. Regarding other denominations, he was extremely temperate, considering the reasoned basis of his disagreements with them. What he describes in the present connection came from a good witness who had no reason to depart from that record.

[70]Annapolis, Dec. 7, 1797 (Maryland Diocesan Archives).

[71]Bend to Claggett, Nov. 13, 1797 (*ibid.*).

[72]Bend to Claggett, Jan. 21, 1797 (*ibid.*).

[73]Claggett to Kemp, Dec. 7, 1797 (*ibid.*). This letter gives grounds for the present writer's explanation of the outcome.

[74]Claggett to Gentlemen in Washington [1797/8] (*ibid.*). A manuscript editor dated this letter as in the spring of either of these years. The present writer is inclined to relate it to the first date and to the Bill of that year which was discussed in the previous paragraph. The letter would tend in this case to show how delay, willful or otherwise, could harm church government and serve those disaffected toward it, which was what Claggett suspected.

[75]*Proceedings of Convention,* p. 314.

[76]See Albert W. Werline, *Problems of Church and State in Maryland During the Seventeenth and Eighteenth Centuries (1632-1789)* (South Lancaster, Mass., 1948), p. 196.

[77]*State of Religion,* p. 35.

[78]Chester Parish Vestry Records [Talbot County], entries for Feb. 4 and Nov. 29, 1780 (Maryland Diocesan Archives).

[79]*Journals of the Episcopal Church of Maryland,* Address to the General Assembly, p 6.

[80]Vestry Records, Feb. 7, 1785 (Maryland Diocesan Archives).

[81]*State of Religion,* pp. 35-36.

[82]Carroll to Plowden, Feb. 27, 1785 (John Carroll Papers).

[83]*State of Religion,* pp. 19, 28 and 35-37.

[84]Carroll to Plowden, Feb. 27, 1785 (John Carroll Papers).

[85]Carroll to Plowden, Dec. 15 and Sep. 3, 1800 (*ibid*).

[86]*State of Religion,* p. 19.

[87]*Ibid.* Usually "churchman" refers to an ecclesiastical personage, but obviously not as used by Duke in this passage.

[88]Carroll to Plowden, Dec. 15 and Sep. 3, 1800 (John Carroll Papers).

[89]Laws of Maryland, ch. iii, Nov. 1794. For Act Concerning Marriages see *ibid.,* ch. xii, February Session.

[90]*Ibid.,* ch. xii, February 1777.

[91]*Ibid.,* ch. xlvii, November 1785.

[92]Minutes, June 2, 1778.

[93]To Charles Carroll of Carrollton, Nov. 11, 1783 (John Carroll Papers).
[94]*Proceedings of Convention,* pp. 98 and 186; Hortogensis, *Jewish Historical Society,* No. 25, pp. 99, 100, 103, 104.
[95]*Laws of Maryland,* ch. cx, Nov. 1796.
[96]Journal, January 10, 1787.
[97]*Laws of Maryland,* Nov. 1795, ch. xiv and lxxiii.
[98]*Ibid.,* Nov. 1783, ch. xxiv; see Duke, Journal, Jan. 21, 1794.
[99]*Laws of Maryland,* Oct. 1780, ch. xii.
[100]John Carroll to Rush, July 18, 1789 (John Carroll Papers).
[101]*State of Religion,* p. 49.

IV

REVITALIZING AN ANGLICAN FAITH

Men of different faiths and denominational affiliations drafted the Maryland Constitution in 1776. Their primary objective was to end the confessional state and lay the foundations for a Christian state which equally granted constitutional benefits to every denomination. They envisioned a total society of religious people as the object of their law making. In this broad view each of the constitutional members saw fulfillment of the general religious aspiration which Maryland had held on the eve of the Declaration of Independence. At the same time, each of these founders cherished the good of his own faith. They saw that the general provision for the Christian state served very well the more particular aspiration each man had for the improvement of his own church. Time was to prove that both their general and their specific hopes were realized.

Of all denominations, those of the Anglican faith had the least grounds of assurance that this would come about. Historians have not proven that it did. It is important, then, to examine the experience of the Church which succeeded the once established Church of England. The Revolution destroyed the confessional state on which the colonial church was reared and the new constitution was yet untried ground. As it turned out, the courageous and creative leaders of the Anglican community in Maryland proved that the new life-conditions after 1776 revitalized their faith. It must be seen what events and experiences brought this about. Something has already been noted in these matters regarding the revolutionary government and the new constitutional provisions as they affected all religious groups. A delicate regard for the freedom of the Anglican was shown. The inner life of the Anglican Church, however, must be another starting point to estimate the process of revitalization. The forces within, which were released by the outer circumstances of revolutionary change in Maryland, must be understood. This will further indicate the good effect of "conscientious rebellion" and the benefits of the new "Christian state" as the successor to the once established church experienced them.

Recalling the loss of many loyalist clergymen on the war issue, one would expect the old Church to be near the breaking point under the new order. Yet its condition was critical rather than chaotic, and became revitalized rather than moribund. In general, there was a vital movement from liberal to conservative leadership which terminated in a native episcopacy. The loss of membership was overshadowed by the integrating element in the post-Revolutionary process of the Protestant Episcopal Church, which was the new name of the old Church of Colonial times. A remarkable adjustment of Maryland's penchant for parish and vestry authority was made, while bringing strength to the church with the episcopal office as long viewed with fear by the Anglican laity and Marylanders in general.

William Smith, associate of Thomas Jefferson in the American Philosophical Society and former teacher of Maryland's wartime Governor William Paca, critic of the confessional state and established church, led the way into the future. Even before the smoke of the battle for independence had cleared, he had taken significant preliminary steps. In a sense, they were prompted by the Maryland Constitution. While it had assured possession of Church property, it did so under the title of the Church of England, no other foundation yet existing in 1776. By 1776, however, Smith and others, particularly in the Eastern Shore, sought to establish an independent church on the basis of existing parishes and the affiliation among them. They would thus avert any property control from London. With fellow clergymen Samuel Keane and James Wilmer, and twenty-four laymen, Smith succeeded in bringing together the first convention of the once established church. In the meeting at Chestertown, where Smith resided as rector of an Anglican parish, the long-felt Maryland aspiration to strong vestry and parish government took form. As sessions progressed the name *Protestant Episcopal Church* came into use and a plan of developed growth was outlined. This nucleus once formed, it was undoubtably understood that other parishes throughout Maryland would join with the Chestertown convention. A state-wide affiliation thus formed, Maryland Anglicans would finally be in a position to seek consecration of a bishop. The important legal standing of the Church, however, would be thus thoroughly established before this second step. Formal legislation in the assembly would in this way provide security that the Church lacked in the uncertain terms of the Maryland Constitution. [1]

The situation of the Chestertown convention, however, was precarious from several standpoints. As a preliminary to the meeting, a Vestry Act was authorized in 1779, which enabled parishes to conduct vestry elections and establish vestry corporate ownership of property. While the Church of England title was thus removed, it was clear that the relationship among parishes was uncertain and the ecclesiastical structure entirely inadequate. It was the purpose of the convention ultimately to establish a developed constitution, which was partially accomplished by 1780. This, however, was done more with an eye to preparing for, and influencing, a subsequent convention drawn from the rest of the state. Outside of the Church, suspicion and hostility were awakened, even though convention efforts at secrecy were made. There was also resentment in parishes not represented and many churchmen saw the role of Smith calculated to bring him the episcopal office in Maryland. The sympathetic and active assistance of Governor Paca gave greater impetus to opposition in 1783, when a subsequent convention with wider representation came together. Mention has already been made of Patrick Allison's attack as *Vindex,* which came at this time, accusing the Episcopal Church of seeking a preferred position with the government. [2]

The shrewdness, vigor, and tenacity of Smith, however, won out and kept the Anglican drive toward an integrated church structure in progress. On May 6, 1783, his friend Governor Paca recommended that the assembly accept the 1780 Chestertown proposals as the legal foundations for the Protestant Episcopal Church. In view of the fact that it was generally understood that a new convention would be necessary for any final formulation, the Paca-Smith efforts seemed rash. Equally offensive was Smith's trip to England at this time in quest of consecration as the first bishop of Maryland. He ultimately ran into two hornet nests. In London, no preparation had been made with the Bishop of London and his fellow prelates regarding all of the theological and ecclesiastical complexities in such a consecration. Smith failed in his efforts there. Samuel Seabury of Connecticut was successful in receiving consecration from non-juring Scottish bishops, but Jonathan Boucher and other opponents prevented Smith from obtaining a similar consecration. In view of subsequent events in the general American quest for an Anglican episcopacy, Smith's defeat was a benefit as a stimulus to later efforts.

By 1783 the Maryland Church was ready for its state-wide convention and it followed the direction Smith had established. [3]

The convention of 1784 appealed to a latent spirit which the Revolution had now released. In the minds of its ministers the Church of England had long felt it did not have the authority to succeed with its mission Writing of this problem in 1769, Addison pointed to the need of a bishop in America. Far removed from the Bishop of London, he wrote, that he found Maryland "deprived of discipline which every other denomination of christians can really exercise..." [4] Claggett agreed with this and attributed the condition of religion, which he found "at a very low ebb," to the need for a bishop. He confided to Weeden Butler that he would like to see Dodd in this role with Butler as his chaplain. [5] Politics was the great obstacle. An American bishop would loosen the hold the Maryland Assembly had on the Church. Both Addison and Claggett found the assembly a deterrent to Church life, although Claggett accepted at this time the need of some lay and state supervision of the Church. [6]

Under the colonial arrangement there seemed no way out of such a dilemma when one considers the layman's and the assembly's viewpoint. Dissenters had long kept alive anti-episcopal feeling by capitalizing on the Anglican dilemma. Assemblymen feared an appointed bishop as one more string tightly binding them to the mother country. At the height of agitation against clergy tax benefits, opposition to a bishop as a greatly needed office in the Maryland Church mounted. A native bishop might bring more political power to the Church. Claggett's optimism was questioned. [7]

The revolution dissolved this dilemma. Laymen and the assemblymen now saw deliverance from the Bishop of London. The state no longer had the legal burden which financing and supervision of the church had imposed. In all of this the laity were relieved of an old rancor and could no longer resent clergy initiative, even when it centralized authority in a native bishop; for he would no longer require a tie to a mother country.

The convention could now put down the foundations for an independent Protestant Episcopal Church of Maryland. "We consider it as the undoubted Right of the said Protestant Episcopal Church," read the convention Declaration, "in common with other Christian Churches under the American Revolution, to compleat and preserve herself as an entire Church..." This assurance, a response to Addison's complaint, rested upon another consideration even more fundamental. The same article asserted with fresh insight the spiritual nature of the Church. This required "the full Enjoyment and free Exercise of those purely *Spiritual Powers,* which are essential to the Being of every *Church* or Congregation of the *faithful,* . . . being derived only from CHRIST and his APOSTLES. . ." Even before settling the question of American ecclesiastical authority with the Bishop of London and Parliament, the convention severed these colonial ties. The Maryland State Constitution had already cut the church's other temporal connection by force of the Vestry Act of 1779, which viewed incorporated vestries as the legal basis of the Church's existence. The Church now professed to be *"independent* of every *foreign* or other jurisdiction, so long as may be consistent with the civil Rights of *Society.*" [8]

The convention proceeded with daring steps toward his concept of church and state. All those with orders—bishops, priests, or deacons— must not "subscribe any obligation of obediance, *civil* or *canonical* to any foreign power or authority whatsoever. . . ." If they have done so they must make a disavowal. [9] These provisions, however, caused a great obstacle to the creation of a bishop, an essential feature of the Maryland Church as the convention conceived it. Episcopal orders must come from those who possessed them in England, but dependence upon the crown and Parliament was a condition for reception. Nevertheless, on their own contrary conditions as stated in the Declaration of Rights, the Maryland Convention in 1783 addressed the Bishop of London, requesting a Maryland bishop. "For without such a remedy," they candidly and cogently reasoned, "the Church in this country, is in imminent Danger of becoming extinct." [10]

The liberal atmosphere of the times was evident in other provisions. "The duty and office of a Bishop," it was stated in one instance, differs in nothing from that of other priests except in the power of ordination and confirmation, and in the right of precedency in ecclesiastical meeting. . ." [11] Both clergy and laity were to have a voice in his selection. The laity also had a supervisory role over the clergy. [12] This was a strong statement of the co-ordinate authority of clergy and laity, although it was later agreed to leave choice of a bishop to the clergy. [13] Even the liturgy was touched by this spirit, as a memorial called attention to the need of revising it and the Service, "in order to adapt the same to the Revolution." [14] It was significant that Maryland was moving rapidly ahead of such states as Virginia and South Carolina in developing an autonomous Church. [15] Maryland Anglicans were already delving into details of securing the office of bishop and of seeking out its first occupant. Allison and Claggett stated that William Smith sought the office both in his retired life at Chestertown and on the occasion of his voyage to England in 1783. [16] There was no doubt, at least, that his convention role, liberal views, and qualities of leadership confirmed the likelihood that many conventioners wished the office for him.

As Episcopalians pursued their separate courses in each state —particularly in Maryland, Pennsylvania and Connecticut—three plans emerged for consideration at Philadelphia. Maryland had proceeded to win assembly acceptance of Church independence on a state level, intending to apply alone for an episcopal consecration in England. Smith's failure in England opened the way for general agreement to act with other states. This was the direction of federation toward which William White led the Pennsylvania Church. A national structure established, the Church of England could be approached more surely with a petition of consecration there. In New England, on the other hand, forces behind Samuel Seabury of Connecticut called for action based on the authority of the office of bishop itself rather than an association of state vestries or a federation of such church communities. Understandably the first two solutions had so much in common that the Maryland Church naturally came to Philadelphia in 1784 for a general convention. It should be noted in passing that a preliminary meeting had been held the previous year at Wilmington, Delaware. [17]

William West, who was Secretary of the Maryland Convention, has left his impressions of the framework of its proceedings. In his letter to William White in 1784 he made inferences from, and references to, revolutionary political understandings which influenced the convention's approach to its own independent form. The following passage carried discussion even down to the notion of political confederation:

> I think the Protestant Episcopal Ch. in each particular State, fully entitled to all the Rights & Authority that are essentially necessary to form & compleat an entire Ch. and as the several States in Confederation have essential Rights & powers independent on each other, so the ch. in each State has essential Rights & powers independent upon those of other States but still as each State harmonies with its Sister States for the Common Good of the Confederation, so, in like manner each particular Chh should harmonize wth. its Sister Chhs. in the different States for the Common Good of its ... society at large. [18]

The vigorous initiative shown in Maryland Conventions inevitably led to confederated action with other state conventions, as West clearly foresaw. Smith and others found that their efforts required the prestige and force of a national body. His own independent effort in England to obtain the episcopacy failed. Autonomous though the state convention was, it faltered short of an acquired episcopacy, which was essential to completing that autonomy. So it was that Smith led Marylanders to a "Meeting of Clergymen and Lay Delegates from sundry Congregations of the Episcopal Church in the State of Pennsylvania, May 25, 1784."

Here William White assumed the leadership. A native of Philadelphia, he became Rector of Christ's Church there in 1776 and remained in this office until his death in 1836. At the Philadelphia Convention of 1784, he introduced the principle of coordinate lay participation in the government of Church and was largely responsible for the draft of the new constitution on this occasion. This was similar to action taken by the Maryland Convention. White collaborated with Smith in drawing up an American revision of the Book of Common Prayer.[19]

The Convention attendants knew and appreciated White's views on an independent Church. He had to make the decisive point that control by the English church through the agency of English government was not essential to the Church. He called attention to traditional dissenters, who complained that the Church depended too much on human law enforced by a civil government. Others felt bound to the church only because civil laws so obligated them under the established religion. "It is to be hoped," White said, speaking of the latter, "they are comparatively few, and that the great majority of episcopalians, believing that their faith is rational and scriptural, have no doubt of their [view] being supported, independent of state establishment..."[20] This was a complex historical refinement of the Maryland Declaration of "those purely *Spiritual Powers*" of the Church, which required independence of the English church and state.

White carried his reasoning deeper into the new political reality of America. He foresaw an inclination in southern states to retain certain practices toward the Church from the period of establishment. "It would ill become those bodies," White said of such legislative action touching external church government, "composed of men of various denominations (however respectable collectively and as individuals) to enact laws for the Episcopal churches..."[21] Accommodation to political views was inevitably involved in such legislation. "This may be avoided in the present instance," he noted, "where all denominations of christians are on a level, and no church is farther known to the public, than as a voluntary association of individuals, for a lawful and useful purpose." This situation extricates the Church from politics with its blight of subservience and secularization. [22] But to attain these results, the Church must, "in common with others, claim and exercise the privilege of governing themselves." [23] Independence was the only form of life in the new nation. The Philadelphia Convention drew the logical conclusions from White's reasoning. The first of the Fundamental Rules stated: "The Episcopal Church in these States is and ought to be independent of all foreign Authority, ecclesiastical or civil." [24] This implied a disentanglement of the Church from the English and American states and suggested a movement of emphasis upon the spiritual nature of the Church.

In these matters the Philadelphia Convention had a compatible, organic relationship to the Maryland Convention. Both made those provisions with the same spirit and intent. Allowing for some exaggeration, Jonathan Boucher, the Tory, found the same revolutionary context of Maryland proceedings at the Philadelphia Convention. "How generally they went into the views of Congress," he exclaimed. Boucher, an opponent of all this, singled out Smith's conduct for particular vituperation. [25] Well he might, for, judging from Smith's writings and the Maryland Convention's decisions, it was not clear who influenced the other more, White or Smith. The liberal views of both were clearly dominant, however, as Boucher keenly observed. [26]

In coming to Philadelphia the Marylanders were seeking more than the foregoing features of church structure. They had, in fact, already succeeded reasonably well in these respects. The keystone, however—the episcopal office in succession from an English see was not acquired by Smith in England. The hope was that the more widely concerted effort from Philadelphia would yet succeed in this. Once received at English hands, the American could communicate episcopal powers to dioceses such as Maryland, which were now taking shape. The prevailing ritual would call for two or three bishops thus consecrated in England to be present at a consecration in America.

The Convention and White had to deal with both the risks of and the opposition to episcopacy. Arthur L. Cross has shown how widely this opposition prevailed throughout the colonies. He noted, however, the very political nature beneath it. [27] Sir William Johnson saw further into this situation, while expressing the desire for the spiritual benefits of episcopacy. "We cannot have a clergy here," he wrote. "without an Episcopate and this want has occasioned many to embrace other persuasions, and will oblige greater numbers to follow their example, of which the dissenters are very sensible; and by pretended fears of an episcopal power, as well as by magnifying their own numbers and lessening ours, give it all possible opposition." [28]

White appealed to those with Johnson's feelings but also brilliantly portrayed the opportunity which the Revolution provided for establishing a new status for episcopacy. Independence had made it impossible to equate the newly projected American episcopacy with that English version so long railed against by dissenters. In America, bishops would not be quasi-political agents of the state, which in times past had enforced theological concepts of the Church on dissenters. If, in addition to civil ties, ecclesiastical ones were severed from the Bishop of London, the validity of past attacks would fail. "A dependence on his Lordship [Bishop of London] and his successors in that See," White explained, "would be liable to the reproach of foreign influence, and render episcopalians less qualified than those of other communions, to be entrusted by their government..." [29] Independence would give a non-English status to episcopacy. In so acting the American Church was severing itself from any commitment to a philosophy of civil monarchical government, for "this supposed relation between episcopacy and monarchy arises from confounding English episcopacy, with the subject at large." [30] If some suggested this severance was not republican enough, that episcopacy itself must go, they stood condemned by their own principles. "It is submitted, how far such ideas encourages the suspicion of want of attachment to any particular church... except so far as subservient to some civil system." [31] The Church must not give up such freedom to have a bishop, who was desperately needed to place the keystone in the autonomous church it was now completing. White concluded his appeal to the feeling for "democratic religion" by advocacy of a regional and local control, but with bishops as non-executive officers and the laity in the new rule of overseeing, which Parliament formerly exercised in a civil-religious capacity. [32]

It is well to point out that even at this time the complete removal of the churches from assembly authority was only gradually appearing. Paca, for example, thought it proper for the Maryland Assembly to recommend a bishop in the case of Smith. Other assemblies considered recommending "ordainers" as a proper piece of legislation. Prelates and other authorities in England, moreover, while interested in an independent American church, looked for some kind of assembly approbation of any Americans they would consecrate. Non-juring bishops in Scotland, however, were critical of these and similar practices of the state in such matters. It was thus that Samuel Seabury, who had avoided them, won consecration in Scotland. [33]

At this point in progression of thought about an independent church, the liberal leadership of White lost its ascendancy. When the convention was about to take steps to acquire an American bishop, it disregarded one of White's main arguments that the proven need for a bishop in the American church itself gave divine power within that Church to create its own bishops. In this way White would surmount any obstacles Parliament, the crown, or bishops in England might put in the way of an American quest for episcopal consecrations. The convention also turned aside from the course followed by Samuel Seabury in 1784. This was a conservative trait which was clearly present in the Maryland Convention. Had not Smith gone to England to make some third kind of arrangement which was different from what White and Seabury sought? Some similar procedure was now taken by the Philadelphia Convention, but on a federated basis of several states which Smith's effort had lacked.

On October 5, 1785, the Convention made a moderate petition to the Bishops of London for the consecration of an American bishop. Reference was made to the spiritual tie between the two churches. Clear recognition was given to English bishops as the true ecclesiastical source of the consecration they sought. In restrained terms the petition called attention to the civil duties which the new nation legitimately claimed from them and asked that these be respected in the manner of consecration. [34] "We desired you to be persuaded," came the cordial response the following year, "that we on our parts will use our best endeavors, which we have good reason to hope will be successful, to acquire a legal capacity of complying with the prayer of your address." [35]

There were, however, amidst this cordiality, reservations which made it clear that the English bishops would not be indifferent to the American church form. "Those alterations (learned from rumor) are not mentioned in your address," they said in their reply, "and as our knowledge of them is no more than what has reached us through private and less certain channels, we hope you will think it just, both to you and to ourselves, if we wait for an explanation." [36] This was spoken from interest in orthodoxy and awareness of the liberal views of White, which, after all, were originally even in disagreement with the theological assumptions of the Philadelphia petition. The convention itself had also taken certain theological views at variance with the London correspondents. The Athanasian and Nicene Creeds were omitted from its formulations and the Apostles Creed modified. [37] The conservative element in America thus had a point of leverage in the influence that came with the rite administered in England.

As the bishops in England had hoped, an act came from Parliament empowering consecration as requested but with a lingering atmosphere of reservation previously expressed by the bishops:

> Whereas, by the laws of this realm, no person can be consecrated to the Office of Bishop, without the King's license for his election to the office.... it shall and may be lawful ... for the time being ... to consecrate persons ... of countries out of his Majesty's dominion ... Provided always ... that a certificate of such consecration shall be given ... and the farther description of his not having taken the said oath, being exempted from the obligation of so doing by virtue of this Act. [38]

In thus agreeing to give episcopal consecration the English bishops were in a position to exercise some initial supervision. It was no more than this. Once there were three American bishops, the Protestant Episcopal Church had what was required by the rite for consecration in America. Restrictions could no longer be made by English bishops. Each party appreciated this situation from its own standpoint. In August, 1789, the Philadelphia General Convention of the Protestant Episcopal Church expressed a filial gratitude for the compliance of the English bishops in ultimately making a consecration possible in America. [39] Thereafter the American church's autonomy was completed. Significant of this fact was the choice of White, now a slightly mitigated liberal, to become the first American to receive episcopal consecration at the hands of English bishops in full union with the Episcopal Church, who had expressed a position of orthodoxy at variance with White's views.

The Maryland conventions during this period of negotiation with England were undergoing a change away from the earlier liberal preponderance. As the national convention modified White's liberal views, so in Maryland an oblique turn was given the trend of thought previously formed by Smith's leadership. The conservative element in Maryland undoubtedly won strength from the cautionary attitude of the English bishops. But it also drew on the indigenous nature of the state. Politically, Maryland had its flaming liberal patriots in the hour of challenge from England and in the War for Independence; but a striking moderation was found in the same Marylanders when they proceeded with the details of peacetime government. They were conservative and Federalist throughout the Revolutionary period, both in constitution making and in subsequent legislative practices. It is not surprising to find this same temper in that Episcopal Church, which these conservatives dominantly professed. Once the thrust for an independent church was made, the conservative force revealed itself in the constructive period that in 1785 followed the previous phase of the Smith-led conventions.

Thomas John Claggett came forward as representative of this new element. His concern for a Maryland bishop was well known, even before the Revolution. Though a graduate of Princeton, he was at an early date wary of presbyterianizing tendencies and other liberal elements in the Church. [40] Though he did not go to England following the Peace of Paris, as Smith had, he sought information on Maryland Church settlements through Robert Eden, the former Governor of the colony, and other important persons there. [41] He may not have sought the Maryland bishopric for himself but he surely had zealous hopes regarding the office which he wanted realized. By 1786 Claggett began to controvert the liberal views of Smith. At Philadelphia, Smith and White were engaged in a revision of the Book of Common Prayer and matters which affected Church of England Articles of Belief and Creeds. A third party to the revision was Charles Wharton, whose position in this connection was suggested by the fact that he had earlier removed orthodox provisions from the Delaware discipline. [42] Similar settlements were imminent in Maryland as the National Convention's provisions were being proposed for approval.

Claggett made his complaint of these prospects to his deserving confidant, William Duke. "I'm tired, my dear Sir, of Being hurried about, merely to give a little sanction to measures which generally have received ye *Royal assent* before I hear of them." The doctrines he would oppose were already in print at Convention expense. "Ye Resistance to be overcome will be far greater," he complained, "than any Efforts of mine will be able to surmount." [43] Claggett, however, put hope in his own and other parishes. "The new reformers," he said in description of his own congregation's view, "have altered too much, & have Presbyterianized in many Instances, particularly they have virtually denied ye Doctrine of Regeneration in Baptism taught by ye Church of England." The authority of Sacred Scripture itself had been weakened. [44]

Claggett appealed to parochial support in order to stir Duke's opposition to the Smith faction. He analyzed the baptism question in relation to the Nicene Creed, in order to expose the undermining of doctrine. He found similar doctrinal significance in the liturgical provisions, the selections and omissions of Old and New Testament in its passage. In this and other ways Claggett attacked not only the Philadelphia Convention but the Maryland Committee which was sympathetically publishing these proposals for distribution in the state.[45] Having thus awakened his own ire and confidence by this communication to Duke, he proceeded to address nearly the same remarks to a committee member the following day. This was William West, an associate of Smith, since the first Maryland Convention.[46] The major outcome of all of this was to secure a clear inclusion of the Nicene Creed and other important conservative views in the official constitutions for Maryland, which were lacking in the Philadelphia provisions.[47]

Later that year, by force of unusual circumstances, Claggett moved closer to attaining the office of bishop, from which he would assure a predominantly conservative influence on the church of Maryland. As Claggett's letter to West suggested, Smith and the liberal sentiments of the committee on discipline were at the moment in ascendancy. It seemed reasonable to expect this to culminate in the election of Smith as bishop of the Maryland Church. There is evidence that these may have long been Smith's intentions and action seemed now under way to accomplish them.

The suitability of Smith's character for the office, however, became the object of suspicion. He was said to have been under the influence of alcohol on the occasion of the New York convention of 1786. Whatever the extent of the influence, it affected the October discussions of candidates for Maryland episcopal consecration. William West had put his name to a recommendation of Smith. Upon hearing of the New York incident from a Colonel Rogers of Baltimore, he withdrew his recommendation. Opposition also came in writing from John Andrews and was called to the attention of the group. It was left to Claggett to introduce as tactfully as possible this whole discussion, using Wharton as his source of information on the New York incident. Smith, however, did not want his name withdrawn, which would have been a likely step after loss of West's support. It was then ordered by the deliberating convention to leave the charges open to question, as Smith had requested.[48] The Convention could then make its choice of candidates. There was evidence of strong support for

Smith, but not sufficient to prevent his displacement by Claggett from the position of leadership which Smith had held since the first Maryland Convention. [49]

The conservative Claggett inevitably, if not logically or more meritoriously, came to be the acceptable candidate. Those who shifted their allegiance to him may not entirely have accepted those doctrinal emphases about which he spoke so strongly. On the other hand, those who had gone along with the Smith formulations had not necessarily underwritten his views. It is not possible to fix liberal and conservative trends exactly in these respects. Nevertheless, in 1789 Claggett clearly emerged from the scene as a conservative figure. This new ascendancy was seen in a letter of Smith to West regarding the Maryland-revised Book of Common Prayer, so much criticized by Claggett in its first version. Smith sought West's "whole & unreserved Sentiments & Advice respecting Our Church Affairs, & every alteration Amendment of Reservation respecting our Prayer Book w[ch]. you judge will then [tend] most towards Peace & Uniformity, & a general Acquiescence, may a cordial and pious Acceptance & use of the Book- [.]" [50] It should be noted that West, who had withdrawn his recommendation of Smith for consecration, was now harmoniously collaborating with Claggett. Thus Smith in effect was deferring to the new conservative leadership.

Whatever restrictions the Maryland Conventions may have put on the office of bishop, Thomas Claggett nevertheless viewed it as a decisive agent in the progress of the Church. He was anxious to see Maryland proceedings move as rapidly as possible toward culmination in the consecration of a bishop. He turned to Pennsylvania for encouragement, since in William White, returned from consecration in England, the Church there had made such progress. While the two ways were not as congenial doctrinally as Claggett would desire, White's presence at the Maryland deliberations would be helpful. Claggett did not hesitate to encourage him to come. "A Gentleman of your Character," Claggett wrote, "a Bishop of our Excellent Church presiding in our Church Assembly would give Weight & Dignity to all our Proceedings, it would have a direct Tendency to promote ye Church, to unite us all firmly together, & to fix us in a more desirable Situation than we have been in since ye Revolution." [51] Only the very ignorant outside the Church had difficulty in tolerating the episcopal office. Those within knew White's optimistic prediction for an autnonomous American church had come true, and that progress and stability were coming out of the Revolution through the medium of a bishop. "If the bishop should be attentive to his pastoral duties," Duke complained, "and the inferior orders properly concur with him in promoting a spirit of Christian holiness, I should have no doubt of success, in a greater degree internal happiness, and a more durable reputation then ever was derived from the civil power." [52]

A general view of Claggett's episcopate reveals the capital he made of his exchange of civil power for the right to be an American Maryland bishop. He undertook personal visitations, the first experienced in Maryland's history. In conjunction with this he initiated the bold plan of regional visitors who would advise him on conditions; each parish vestry and rector were in contact with him through questionnaires in these matters. Claggett's "Notitia" or summary on conditions, after trial of these procedures, showed the vitalizing effect of the first Maryland bishop. [53] The physical hardships of visitation, however, presented a serious obstacle. [54] The ever-present parsimonious member would suspect the soliciting of funds for this office. [55] More often, however, there was that appreciation which gave rise to talk of creating another diocese and bishop in Maryland, a reflection of the esteem of that structure.

Maryland now had a conservative bishop as a counterweight to liberal origins and structure. A look into the more important episodes of his administration will reveal that the Church yielded to this conservative influence and that the yielding provided the needed element of stability to a liberally conceived structure.

White and others called for an increase in the layman's role and the Maryland constitutions took a similar view. There were, however, inherent weaknesses in this policy, for which a bishop could compensate. William Duke, for example, called attention to the problem of lay delegates to the state conventions. The various vestry representatives usually travelled eighty miles or more and incurred additional expense by absence from employment. The most qualified often were not available for these reasons. Too many were in attendance, according to Duke, who were interested in religion only in a "rational way." [57] The phrase suggests an undue preoccupation with the secular and temporal factors of church life. The bishop would tend in this situation to be a third party in which some clergy might exist among lay representatives. Appeals to the bishop from both elements of the Church on these and other occasions, which will be considered, were logical and now available avenues of settlement.

At the parish level of lay power there was even more evidence of the stabilizing effect of Claggett. Duke's Journal frequently noted poor lay attendance at parish vestry meetings. This in turn became a drag on the initiative of the rector. [58] One questions whether the laity had any deep sentiment for extensive democratic practices in the Church. It would seem that they chiefly desired a supervisory role. Claggett appealed to this disposition in lay government when he implemented the 1794 Convention's provision for lay committees of overseers. In each period, committeemen were to report on the rector's administration of church affairs. Considering the psychological factors inherent in such a situation, it is not surprising that little cooperation was given. [59] However, where rector-vestry relationships were greatly strained, the vestrymen would appeal to the bishop for removal of the incumbent pastor. This further enhanced the authority of the bishop beyond its legal and written definition of the office.

From his position Claggett did not hesitate occasionally to move directly against a clergyman, whom the vestry from pious complicity or other reasons would not censure. In 1795, acting at a higher level of authority, he handed down a legal provision which removed Townsend Dade from the ranks of the clergy. [60] According to Utley, Claggett was consciously compensating for the weakness of the lay element in church government. [61] The conservative Claggett stood out among his fellows of episcopal rank by such action. There were apparently great degrees of latitude to be found in episcopal power, depending upon the man who held it.

A parish near Salisbury illustrated in 1795 how both parties to a dispute strengthened the bishop's authority and how the Church was stabilized by appeals to him. The rector Samuel Tingley was confronted with an overgrown parish and corresponding increase of subsidiary chapels. When he distributed his care among the various chapels, criticism arose in nearby Saratoga, one of the parish units. This congregation, under the leadership of a parishioner named Dashiell, sought the more frequent ministrations of another rector. Tingley objected to this on legal grounds. Saratoga was in fact constituting its congregation into a parish without any legal incorporation by the Maryland Assembly. [62] To complicate matters, Dashiell and his associates did not want parish status but rather what appeared to be a highly unorthodox congregational structure. [63] Claggett's role in settling his difficulty, then, was crucial from several standpoints. He successfully vindicated Tingley and the inherent parish structure of the Church.

About this time Claggett answered a challenge made to his

diocesan authority by some of its clergymen. Led by Ralph, a resident of Baltimore, they opposed the ordination of a man whom Claggett had recommended. Bend, Claggett's Baltimore correspondent on the matter, warned that the "Well-assorted trio," as he called the objectors, aimed at a goal beyond the immediate case. If this group became the source of standards by which candidates and ministers were to be recommended, the diocese would soon be divided. Also Bend implied there were fundamental differences in the views of both parties. Ralph believed, Bend wrote to Claggett, that "he can produce a schism in Church, seperate the two shores, & get himself dubbed Bishop..." [64] He seems to have continued in disagreement, but without success, following the incident of which Bend spoke in 1794. [65] The details of this story are not clear, much less all of Ralph's intentions; yet it is certain that there was no schism and Claggett's authority continued to unite the diocese against dissidents.

Besides "ecclesiastical politics," Claggett's conservative leadership extended into the field of doctrine. Here, too, he provided stability. This was accomplished through the power to recommend creation of new ministers and the admission of others to the diocese from other states. Also of importance was the part he played in assigning Maryland clergy to parishes.

Duke provides us a good example of this last-mentioned role of Claggett. Here was a man, doctrinally of the same mind as Claggett, who had a deep conviction of the divine character of episcopacy. He accepted Claggetts' interpretation of that office in Maryland. But Duke emphasized that administrative functions must serve primarily the inculcation of sound doctrine. "I have long been of the opinion", he wrote in 1789, "that the government of the church in great measure is left to the prudence and direction of its members [;] provided the doctrines of Christ are rightly taught and applied the names or arrangement of offices cannot be very material." [66] The right minister became the crucial factor in parish life, since his preaching was the medium of doctrine—a bishop's major concern. It was significant that this entry in Duke's Journal was made at a time when he had encouraged a Methodist friend to accept his own concept of episcopacy. To Claggett's satisfaction, Duke illustrated a bishop's influence for sound doctrine. In the course of his visitation, he found an Anne Arundel County parish in need of a rector. As commonly happened, Claggett was asked for a recommendation. He directed that the vestry write to Duke, requesting his acceptance of the office. Thus it is again evident that the vestry power did not preclude strong episcopal authority and, in this case, authority in fostering doctrines. [67]

The bishop could also influence doctrinal climate at another level, when ministers applied to Maryland from other states. Recommendations accompanying such transfers or previous inquiries first came to Claggett. In addition to character and other considerations, importance was given to the doctrinal assumptions of the applicant. [68] The case of a William Green from New England provides an illustration of this. Samuel Seabury wrote to Claggett concerning him, and indicated what teaching might be expected from Green's sermons. Seabury noticed that the applicant had been "rigidly educated" in the principles of Presbyterianism. Nevertheless, Green was presently so attached to the church that he found himself uneasy among his former associations in the area. [69] He would not find this circumstance in Maryland, where orthodoxy attracted him.

The conservative Claggett was also able vigorously to take the lead in unusual circumstances involving doctrine. This was shown in the case of James Wilmer at Annapolis. The new translation of the Bible, which Wilmer used gave rise to criticism. Parishioners found disturbing departures from the customary interpretations. [70] Claggett soon learned the views of the vestry and was sympathetic to them. William Bend and Mason Weems had evidently advised the vestry to complain to Claggett. [71] Inevitably Wilmer had to deal with the bishop. Some have said, Wilmer sarcastically wrote of his accusers, that "I had changed my religion. I was investigating the Truth solely for the Truths sake," he insisted. The new translation clarified the meaning of the older version of the Bible. He also answered charges of disbelief in the Trinity. Because Weems was said to be a candidate for Wilmer's parish, he would not be inclined to a favorable interpretation of Wilmer's doctrine. But as it turned out, Weems later came to a more favorable view after his meeting with Wilmer. [72] Bend was less gentle and bluntly asked Wilmer if he was really a clergyman of the Church, which provoked only scorn from Wilmer. Bend recommended doctrinal disavowal by Wilmer, but not the full penalty of removal from the ministry (degradation). Knowing Claggett's own conservatism, Wilmer proceeded with an understandable docility at this higher level, and seemed to have reasonably responded to the bishop's doctrinal inclinations, at least as far as public conduct was concerned. [73] This was further evidence of the influence of the bishop's office.

Related to the doctrinal problem were the inroads of Methodism into membership of the Episcopal Church. Here, too, Claggett proved a stabilizing force. He adjusted to the challenge of reform without yielding to the more radical course which was leading many out of the Church and into the ranks of Methodism. His modification of the Church liturgy provided an example of this.

Mason Weems first awakened anxiety regarding modification of hymn books and related liturgical practices. Claggett acquainted the influential William West with the situation. "Our friend Mr. Mason Weems," he wrote in 1788, "since ye breaking up of the Convention had adopted a Line of Conduct that I fear will be greatly prejudicial to ye Church: he has I understand introduced ye Methodist Hymns & Tunes in ye public Service." This had merely provided occasion of going much farther, when Weems was prevailed upon to preach in a Methodist chapel service. The whole intention of the Methodists, according to Claggett, was to win respectability so that it would be easier for disaffected Anglicans to go over to Methodism. [74] "His conduct," Claggett said of Weems, "has materially affected ye interest of our Church in this Quarter & I do suppose that should this example be followed by one or two more of our Ministers, that very speedily two or three Parishes will be entirely lopped off from our Church." [75]

Wesleyanism within the Church before the Revolution was respected by many as a reform spirit. It now retained some of that respect after severance from the Church in post-Revolutionary America; and Claggett understood the popular appeal in Methodist liturgy. He admired the zeal of Weems, but objected to the fact that "this Zeal & Diligence are applied to the Methodist interests," rather than to its spirit. [76] Four years later Claggett still recognized what was good in Weem's liturgy, admitted the fact of its popularity, and retained his friendship for the man, although he disagreed with much of what he did. [77] Claggett also found a similar situation on the Eastern Shore, where Episcopalians were considering adapting Baptist hymnology. Both approaches, Methodist and Baptist, conceivably could be used to win back Methodists and dispose those in sympathy with Methodism to remain in the Church. [78]

William Duke, Claggett' close friend, was immediately concerned with this aspect of adjusting to Methodism. His own Methodist affiliation before the Revolution left him inclined to greater warmth in worship. Yet he seems to have thought more profoundly and proceeded more cautiously than had Weems in the matter of hymnology. However, he was sympathetic with Weems. "Was sorry to see Weem's pedling way of life," he wrote his Journal concerning Weem's publishing ventures, "but God knows best by what methods we can most directly answer the designations of his Province [Providence]." [79] He found Weem's published views largely read out of curiosity, and in Baltimore subjected to ridicule. [80] Some naturally feared the Church appeared in these writings as too "Methodist a form." [81]

Writing to Duke from Easton on the Eastern Shore, Jackson found the same sentiments for adaptation. He did not, however, look to Coke, Wesley and Asbury to solve the problem of a hymn book, but to Baptist sources. "I think," he wrote in criticism of Methodist works, "its Tendency is rather too warm or awakened than really to edify . . ." [82] But here, as with Weems, there was too much inclination to the "interests" of other denominations rather than to their spirit and good will alone. The Easton rector, in fact, frankly told Duke of his hopes for an inter-denominational hymn book. [83] All of this would not be entirely according to the mind of Claggett. In the course of these developments Claggett acted at the decisive moment. He was fully aware that Duke thought with greater theological competence on the whole problem of adaptations from other denominations. This was evident from Claggett's letter evaluating Duke's book, *The State of Religion in Maryland.* [84] Duke held moderate views, compared with those of Jackson and Weems on the matter, and generally agreed with Claggett. He had the further qualification of an artistic temperament joined to a cultivated mind, as his journal and Common Place Book clearly show. Claggett wisely assigned Duke the role of settling the hymn book problem in 1796 and thus successfully stabilized an important feature of church life, thanks to Duke's skill and prudence. [85]

This development of episcopacy shows that the Revolution brought stability and vitality to the Church. The natural transition from liberal to conservative emphasis, from Smith's to Claggett's leadership, was essential to the process. All of this certainly implied an internal improvement of religious conditions of the church. Indeed the foregoing considerations give direct witness to the favorable growth of the church. William Duke, among others, professedly set himself to this task of giving a similar judgment in the light of what he found. *The State of Religion* was the published version of his observations.

Duke was in a good position to know the facts. Before 1784 he had been a Methodist circuit rider. After that he continued itinerant pastoral work as an Episcopalian. We note in his Journal for July 21, 1789, for example, that temporary assignments took him to Georgetown, Frederick, and Harpers Ferry. He proceeded even beyond these outposts and into frontier country. His inquiring spirit and propensity for analysis place his Journal in an historically different category from otherwise similar ones among Methodists. His shrewdness was reflected in this apparently naive entry: "I asked her [the lady of the house where he lodged] something about the state of religion in the neighborhood." [86] He knew she added something to what her husband might say; gossip could also be usefully evaluated. He became well acquainted with the Annapolis and Baltimore areas and, through his friend Jackson, with the Eastern Shore. More important personages, such as Bishop Claggett and his visitor, Bend, provided other sources. "I actually made the observations contained in the following pages," Duke could say with justice in *The State of Religion in Maryland*, "and upon reflection, was satisfied of their truth." [87]

There was not much danger of his views being distorted by any deep, dishonest persuasion of thought or character. Bend pronounced him "irreproachable," and his writings give abundant justification of this. Scholar that he was, his analytical spirit made him aware of his own assumptions as he passed judgment upon a problem. "I know that to have my pamphlet briskly circulated amongst any one society," he wrote revealingly on this point, "I should have undertaken to prove that society [Episcopalian] to be eminently, if not exclusively the church of Christ, and dealt out abundante obloquy on all the rest." [89] He chose otherwise and guarded against the influence of such a mentality, inviting others to help in this, "to see it confuted . . ." [90] Claggett's main complaint was that the weight of Duke's criticism of the clergy rested more heavily on Episcopalians than on others. One would be inclined to agree with the complaint, although this is evidence of a healthy counterweight in Duke. This gave substance to his claim that misstatement or ommision of fact was due to lapse, not the tendentiousness of a biased mind. His Journal and took both support his profession that he did not "cherish an infriendly disposition towards individuals." [91]

Duke was thus in a position to know the facts and was sufficiently guarded to avoid a biased dealing with them. Yet he frankly confessed that he freely gave expression to interpretation of facts. "I thought I could not err much," he told Claggett, "in exhibiting the impression [,] supposing I did not mistake the facts . . ." [92] But Duke passed far beyond this. He carefully stated in *The State of Religion in Maryland* the generalizations which he accepted as a guide to his interpretations of the facts. He revealed what he thought constituted the good in religion and what he found was uncertain. One cannot easily be misled by such "open" interpretation, and his witness to the internal improvement of church conditions can be successfully weighed. There was, for example, the general assumption of a reformer approach to his estimate of what constituted improvement. Even here, however, his journal shows that Duke had a scholarly balance and rationality. "In those Revolutions," he wrote of an historical type of reformer, "which interested persons have endeavour[ed] to qualify with the Idea of a Reformation of Amendment, [he] has only exchanged the Load [of 'universal depravity'] or diversified its real Character by a Rotation of predominant Vices." [93] His reasonable interpretation is thus clearly open to evaluation so that his views cannot be in any instance gratuitously dismissed as mere opinion.

In his own judicious way, Duke found that religion improved among Episcopalians, thanks to the new structure which the Revolution brought about in the church. "The most numerous and wealthy church in Maryland," he said of pre-Revolutionary times, "was also the most supine and careless of its interests . . ." Dissoluteness in its members seemed inevitable. "Everybody who had worn out all impressions of religion, and considered nothing more than convenience in choosing a profession, was drifted into this church." [94] Some shock was needed. "I am afraid," Duke said, "the people of Maryland, twenty years ago, were too secure to be awakened without some violence of their former habits of thinking, and consequently a reiteration of acknowledged truths, and an enforcement of customary forms, would have made no moral or spiritual alteration." An established church under an affluent but distant see at London was not enough. Wealth and power became a twofold source of false security. Its uprooting by revolution could not be such a great tragedy. The new growth that was planted, a church and native episcopacy independent of the state, already in 1794 had fulfilled the hopes of fifteen years before. [95]

Amendment and improvement appeared only when viewed against this pre-Revolutionary background. "In the Protestant Episcopal Church, notwithstanding a general aversion to serious religion," Duke believed, "there are some evident marks of amendment." As a reformer his standard of "serious religion" was above average and this statement about such improvement must have been safely made. [96] Duke indicated how well he had analyzed the inherited conditions as they affected post-Revolutionary improvement. It would take time to build up responsibility in the laity and clergy for a church which had been so much in the hands of the state and the Bishop of London. They now had an estate, without much experience in its management. [97] It would be natural for the least religious-minded members, for example, to demonstrate their zeal by un-Christian carping at Methodist evangelists, treating them as enemies of the religion of their ancestors. [98] The weakness of the parish would allow only a gradual raising of vestry and communicant standards, "considering . . . the licentiousness that has been tolerated . . ." [99] Duke even frankly assessed the leakage of unregenerate leadership. The heartless, nominal member gave only the appearance of religion. His departure now under freer conditions could be no great loss to the church, even if pre-Revolutionary times viewed such things otherwise. [100] Disbelief of various kinds in such members who might remain should not alarm anyone.

Claggett did not take exception to Duke's general impression of improvement in the religious spirit of members. Considering disagreement Claggett freely expressed on other points, he would certainly have done so on this occasion had his experience been otherwise than Duke's Claggett made statements elsewhere complaining of a want of "serious religion," but they were clearly instances of a reformer's impatience with his flock that, "they eat, they drink, they fiddle, they dance, they play, & some of them lie and swear much as they use to do . . ." [101] In the content of his convention sermon in 1794, Claggett expressed a similar spirit, complaining that piety among the people did not seem to increase. Exhortation required such rethoric to motivate zeal. On the same occasion he noted that the pre-Revolutionary period held "the flattering prospect of brighter days, marked with rational zeal, [;] and ardent piety with hope enlivened this melancholy period..." [102] Again, however, he spoke rhetorically, looking at a threat on the horizon. In the wake of the French Revolution he rang the alarm in fear of infidelity and called for greater exertions. Duke has put this point in perfect perspective, which is not found in Claggett's sermon. Claggett would have spoken up against Duke's estimate in writing him about Duke's manuscript, had infidelity been an accomplished fact of something more than the vagary of the already spiritually dormant. [103]

Duke found that the rebuilding of churches and chapels had progressed and that worship itself had been enkindled in Maryland following the Revolution. He noted Baltimore as an example where the sanctuary and other externals were properly adorned. Such things were important signs. Where they were lacking, the less religious person found a further obstacle to Christian improvement. "Will they not conclude," he said, "either that such a form of religion was not worthy of the patronage of Providence, or that the people who professed it necessitated the abolition of it, as a punishment of their own unfaithfulness?" [104] Duke was not entirely satisfied with worship in such well-maintained edifices. Attendance should be better, singing more spirited, and knowledge of baptism greater. "But bad as it is," the conservative reformer noted, "it has been worse. I have observed something like a revival of the emotions of self-preservation in several congregations since they have been left, as it were, to shift for themselves." [105] This stabilized zealous adherents to the church and won others to join them. These were so many observations that "an evangelical form of public worship" was gaining wider acceptance The prayer book modification was further evidence of it. Surely this "form" was a sign of vitality. "I conclude," Duke said, it "will operate most efficiently toward the mortification of pride, the dissolution of vain confidence and intire submission to the will of God." [106] At the same time this did not preclude a corresponding intellectual formation in the congregations. "The doctrines of the gospel" were now better known. Claggett claimed this was even more clearly the case than the gad-fly Duke would allow. [107]

Writers on religious conditions correctly make much of the caliber of the clergy. Claggett had criticized Duke for his harsh judgment, especially with regard to the pre-Revolutionary clergy. Nevertheless, Duke still judged that there was an improved clergy. "The clergy of the Protestant Episcopal Church is still behind several others in zeal and assiduity," he frankly confessed, "but notwithstanding, I believe if they had never been more remiss than they are at present, there would never have been such alarming defalcations from almost every congregation in the state." [108] It is clear to Duke, therefore, that the emerging Christian state remedied a poor pre-Revolutionary condition which accounted for any loss in the last twenty-five years of the eighteenth century. The quality of the clergy was a decisive factor in the results, good and bad. What must be added from other evidence than Duke is the bad effect of the pre-Revolutionary confessional state on that quality and the improvement with the Revolution.

Quality and zeal evidently offset numerical limitation in the clergy in the new era. In 1775 there were fourty-four ministers of the Church in Maryland. [109] The losses sustained immediately following this time had not been made up by 1792, for the convention record for this year listed only thirty-four. [110] Seven years later there were forty-one. [111] In 1790's, however, the stability under the first bishop was becoming evident, two new parishes being formed in the western part of the state. [112] Consistent growth of the clergy took place following the time when only twenty-five ministers took the revolutionary oath. Claggett's letter in 1783 to the Duke of Marlboro at the height of his clergy crisis noted that lay-leaders partially compensated for the loss of ordained ministers. Instruction through this medium did much to offset the hardship of less frequent ministrations caused by a diminished clergy. [113] In addition, such readers were being encouraged to take up the ministry. All of this bespoke growth rather than decline, intensity rather indolence, in the clergy and the church generally.

Claggett's apparent incidental disagreement with Duke will show a misunderstanding about standards of judgment rather than about a favorable view of church conditions. Claggett primarily contested Duke's view of pre-Revolutionary clergy, and he failed to see that Duke had not denied "that in the worst of times there were *some good and pious men* amongst the clergy . . ." [114] This admission once made, Claggett would in general agree that the conditions of the clergy were stifled.

Boucher did not give evidence that the pre-Revolutionary clergy was as satisfactory as Claggett implied in his discussions with Duke in 1795. "I was always of a social temper," Boucher once candidly confessed, "and always had a numerous acquaintence, these too often led me to hard drinking, tho' never, I thank God, to intemperance." [115] He was also given to contracting debts; and left America owing three or four thousand pounds sterling. "This habit of running in debt has stuck by me through life," Boucher admitted. [116] He had taken the Maryland office, where Church preferment was so much better than it was in Virginia." [117] Claggett, indeed, had forgotten his own harsher estimate made in 1768: "I am very anxious to see an able & good ministry in his province, too many of my brethren at present being a shocking set (to say no worse of them) having neither abilities, a sense of the importance of their duty, nor (what is worse than all) an inclination to perform it." [118] Boucher and Claggett were giving evidence of the "supine" condition of the clergy, also noted by Duke. Add to this less edifying confessions, which some of Boucher's contemporaries were unwilling to make and which the delicate Claggett was not later inclined to describe, then Duke's views of the pre-Revolutionary clergy stands as very judicious. Claggett actually confirms them. This matter is important to both men in establishing their views that the Revolution brought improvement.

Claggett, in fact, had good reason to believe that the Church after the Revolution was improved more than Duke would admit. Careful recruitment of clergy was proceeding. [119] The instances of clerical vice were few and mild. He complained, for example, of one young man whose charm was not confined to the pulpit, but exercised itself too much at the race track and the card table. [120] Claggett's standard and viewpoint, then, would seem to rest on instances of scandalous conduct in the clergy. Duke was going beyond this to an estimate of superior zeal for religion in the great majority who were free from "scandal." "They seem in general," he said, "not to interest themselves & see." Coming to particular persons, however, he finds a spirit of "interest" and zeal which is a sign of clergy improvement.

The presence of this spirit gave scope to the "evangelical form," or that fixed desire for a more virtuous life, which Duke found stirring in the Church. The clergy must more and more have the capacity to bring this inner vitality to fruition. This had not been previously done. "When any of their [clergy's] hearers became seriously thoughtful about religion," he explained, "one would suppose it natural for them to consult their stated pastors; but when they [the hearers] remembered that these pastors in the course of so many years had not administered to them any sufficient instruction, they [the clergy] resented the imposition, and neglected them [such members] in their turn." For those fervent souls to continue in the Church promised them no satisfaction. "They found that the way they were in was not likely to issue in anything like the design of the gospel, and therefore did not hesitate to take the chance of a change." Conditions were now better, however, and these members were no longer left with this alternative. Some clergy had "the design of the gospel" in a high degree; more must realize it. [122] At the same time the Church must change the attitude of the laity toward the clergy and make them confident that they would find a pattern for the higher life in them. This was not easy in the light of the pre-Revolutionary experience with the clergy. Yet the acceleration of clergy improvement promised to arrest any leakage of memberships. Special clergy-appeal to this higher element in the Church would offend the less zealous members. A loss of the latter could not compare with departures among those seeking "the design of the gospel." Duke thus found within the Church the remedy for possible conversions to other denominations.

All that has here been said of the condition of the church in terms of quality clearly puts the single fact of some numerical decline of clergy in perspective, so too some church membership loss. William Eddis at the time of the Revolution found that the established church membership exceeded the aggregate number of dissenters of every denomination. [123] Duke believed that this condition continued until shortly before 1790. [124] He felt, however, that membership among other churches at that time grew more rapidly than was the case with Episcopalians, who nevertheless, still constituted the largest single denomination. Undoubtedly he concluded this from the fact that other denominations drew almost exclusively from Episcopalians, rather than from one another. The fact of Methodist growth, as will soon be seen, gave grounds for this view. [125] It would seem that the more fervent among those discarding Episcopalianism went over to Methodism, and hence concern for these departures was greater.

The uncertain fact of denominational proportion aside, evident growth of a new generation as well as the improvement in quality of the remaining one must not be overlooked; nor should some conversions to Episcopalianism. Duke himself had spoken of the tendency of those of other denominations, who were without a local minister or church to join Episcopalianism. It should also be said that Eddis, writing in the 1790's, did not find Maryland an exception to the general condition of numerical growth of Episcopalianism in the states. [127]

Claggett and Duke were less concerned with numbers than quality in their estimate of the conditions of the Church. The evidence makes it clear that the Revolution brought the stability of episcopal government which they had so long sought, and they were not disappointed in the improved religious conditions which it produced. It is therefore very clear that the emerging Christian state created an environment that was highly favorable. It satisfied the pre-Revolutionary aspiration and marked the event of Independence as a social blessing to this the largest segment of religious life in Maryland.

REFERENCES

[1]Loveland, chs. 2-3, *et passim*, gives a comprehensive presentation of these matters.
[2]*Ibid.*, pp. 25-27; and Robert W. Shoemaker, *The Origin and Meaning of the Name "Protestant Episcopal"* (New York, 1959), ch. 6.
[3]Loveland, pp. 107-08 and 212-13.
[4]To Bishop of London, Oct. 24, 1769 (Maryland Diocesan Archives).
[5]Sep. 19, 1769, Utley, p. 24.
[6]Addison to Bishop of London, Oct. 24, 1769, and Claggett to Bishop of London, Sep. 20, 1769 (Maryland Diocesan Archives).
[7]Barker, p. 359.
[8]Declaration of Certain Fundamental Rights and the Liberties, *Journals of Episcopal Church in Maryland*, p. 10.
[9]*Ibid.*, p. 16.
[10]Maryland Convention to Bishop of London, Aug. 16, 1783, Albert F. Gegenheimer, *William Smith, Educator and Churchman* (Philadelphia, 1943), p. 193.
[11]Fundamental Principles II, June 22, 1784: *Journals of Episcopal Church in Maryland*, p. 15.
[12]Hawks, 298.
[13]Loveland, pp. 74-75.

[14]Petition to the Assembly 1783; *Journals of the Episcopal Church in Maryland*, p. 8.

[15]Utley, p. 57.

[16]Claggett to Duke of Marlboro, Sep. 20, 1783 (Maryland Diocesan Archives); and Patrick Allison [*Vindex*].

[17]Loveland. p. 60.

[18]West to White [?], 1784 (Maryland Diocesan Archives).

[19]*Webster's Biographical Dictionary* (Springfield, Mass., 1943). Unless otherwise indicated basic biographical data hereafter is from this source.

[20]White, p. 34.

[21]*Ibid.,* pp. 7-8.

[22]*Ibid.,* pp. 8-9.

[23]*Ibid.,* pp. 7-8.

[24]May 25, 1784, *Journals of the Episcopal Church in Maryland,* p. 13. William Smith, in preparing the records of the first Maryland meetings, included the Philadelphia Rules. The Philadelphia gathering may not have been as much a general convention of the Church as those which followed.

[25]Boucher, p. 100.

[26]See, for example, *Plain Truth,* p. 14.

[27]Cross, pp. 263-72.

[28]*Ibid.,* p. 271, n. 1, quoting William S. Perry (ed.), *Historical Collections Relating to the American Colonial Church* (4 vols.; Hartford, Conn., 1870-1878), I, 418.

[29]White, p. 7.

[30]*Ibid.,* p. 18.

[31]*Ibid.,* p. 19.

[32]*Ibid.,* pp. iiff.

[33]Loveland, pp. 30-31, 83-85; Shoemaker, p. 107.

[34]Protestant Episcopal Church, *Journals of the General Conventions of the Protestant Episcopal Church in the United States of America...* (Philadelphia, 1817), pp. 12-15.

[35]*Ibid.,* p. 20.

[36]*Ibid.*

[37]Gegenheimer, p. 201.

[38]*Journals of General Conventions,* pp. 37-38.

[39]*Ibid.,* pp. 136-39.

[40]Utley, p. 9.

[41]Claggett to Duke of Marlboro, Sep. 26, 1783 (Maryland Diocesan Archives).

[42]Carroll to Plowden, Nov. 1786 (John Carroll Papers).

[43]Claggett to Duke, June 19, 1786 (Maryland Diocesan Archives); see also, Utley, pp. 49-50.

[44]*Ibid.*

[45]*Ibid.*

[46]Claggett to West, June 20, 1786 (Maryland Diocesan Archives).

[47]Hawks, pp. 306-07.

[48]Samuel Johnson to John Andrews, Oct. 31, 1786, in Gegenheimer, p. 197.

[49]David Griffith to Bishop White, Oct. 20, 1786, *ibid.,* p. 195. See his reasonable interpretation of the intemperance incident, *ibid.,* pp. 198-99.

[50]William Smith to West, June 10, 1789 (Maryland Archdiocesan Archives).

[51]Claggett to White, Apr. 21, 1787 in Utley, p. 53.

[52]Duke, *State of Religion,* pp. 39-40.

[53]Claggett, MS "Notitia," 1812-1813 (Maryland Diocesan Archives).

[54]Hawks, p. 323.

[55]Bend to Claggett, July 18, 1796 (Maryland Diocesan Archives).

[56]St. James Vestry Records (Anne Arundel County), entry for May 12, 1791 (Maryland Historical Society).

[57]*State of Religion,* p. 24.

[58]Duke, Journal, Apr. 9 [10 ?], 1787.

[59]Hawks, p. 318; Thomas C. Gambrall, *Church Life in Colonial Maryland* (Baltimore, 1885), p. 301.

[60]Hawks, pp. 316-17.
[61]Utley, pp. 71-72.
[62]Tingley to Claggett, Sep. 20, 1796 (Maryland Diocesan Archives).
[63]Dashiell to Claggett, May 16, 1796 (*ibid.*).
[64]Bend to Claggett, Nov. 4, 1794 (*ibid.*).
[65]Claggett to Bend, July 30, 1798 (*ibid.*).
[66]Duke, Journal, Aug. 8, 1789 (*ibid.*).
[67]Claggett to Duke, Sep. 26, 1796 (*ibid.*).
[68]Beach to Claggett, July 20, and May 6, 1794 (*ibid.*).
[69]Seabury to Claggett, No. 2, 1793 (*ibid.*).
[70]Wilmer to Claggett, Nov. 5, 1793 (*ibid.*).
[71]Wilmer to Claggett, Aprl. 27, 1794, and Bend to Claggett, July 18, 1796 (*ibid.*).
[72]Wilmer to Claggett (*ibid.*).
[73]Bend to Claggett, July 18, 1796 (*ibid.*).
[74]Claggett to West, Aug. 23, 1788 (*ibid.*); See also Utley, p. 51.
[75]Claggett to West, Aug. 23, 1788 (Maryland Diocesan Archives).
[76]*Ibid.*
[77]Claggett to Duke, Jan. 28, 1792 (*ibid.*).
[78]Jackson to Kemp (*ibid.*).
[79]Duke, Journal, Sep. 12, 1792.
[80]*Ibid.*, June 29 and 30.
[81]Ogden to Claggett, Dec. 11, 1799 (Maryland Diocesan Archives).
[82]Jackson to Duke, Nov. 18, 1796 (*ibid.*).
[83]*Ibid.*
[84]Duke to Claggett, June 29, 1795 (*ibid.*). This letter tells the contents of the one Duke had received from Claggett which is part of the evidence for the explanation followed here.
[85]Duke to Kemp, Dec. 3, 1796 (*ibid.*).
[86]Duke, Journal, July 21, 1789.
[87]Pp. iii-iv.
[88]Bend to Claggett, June 7, 1797; Utley, p. 98.
[89]*State of Religion*, p. iii.
[90]Duke to Claggett, June 29, 1795 (Maryland Diocesan Archives).
[91]*Ibid.*
[92]*Ibid.*
[93]Duke, Journal, Jan. 13, 1787.
[94]*State of Religion*, p. 14-15.
[95]P. 23.
[96]*Ibid.*
[97]*Ibid.*, pp. 10-11.
[98]*Ibid.*, pp. 42-43.
[99]*Ibid.*, p. 23.
[100]*Ibid.*, p. 11.
[101]Claggett to Duke, Jan. 28, 1792; Utley, pp. 54-55.
[102]*Ibid.*, p. 74.
[103]Claggett to Duke, Jan. 28, 1792; *ibid.*, p. 34. Claggett suggested that Duke refute Paine; but this does not indicate more than a danger of infidelity, nor put Claggett in disagreement with Duke's explanation.
[104]Duke, *State of Religion*, pp. 38-39.
[105]*Ibid.*, pp. 25-27.
[106]*Ibid.*, pp. 9-10.
[107]Duke to Claggett, June 29, 1795 (Maryland Diocesan Archives). See also, Claggett to Duke, Jan. 28, 1792, to Butler, Sep. 19, 1769, and Diocesan Address, 1794 in Utley, pp. 34, 73, 24.
[108]*State of Religion*, pp. 21-22.
[109]Perry, XV, 345-347.
[110]*Journals of General Conventions*, p. 133.
[111]*Ibid.*, 254-255.

[112]Ethan Allen, *The Clergy in Maryland of the Protestant Episcopal Church Since the Independence of 1783* (Baltimore, 1860), pp. 98-100.
[113]Claggett to Duke of Marlboro, Sep. 26, 1783 (Maryland Diocesan Archives).
[114]Duke to Claggett (*ibid.*).
[115]Boucher, p. 42.
[116]*Ibid.*, pp. 30-31.
[117]*Ibid.*, p. 53.
[118]Claggett to Butler, July 1, 1768; Utley, p. 20.
[119]Bissett to Claggett, Nov. 14, 1793, and Seabury to Claggett, Nov. 27, 1793 (Maryland Diocesan Archives).
[120]Claggett to Duke, Jan. 28, 1792 (*ibid.*). Duke, Journal, Apr. 25, 1791, noted one of the few instances of any serious delinquency in the clergy. The congregation urged that an intemperate minister be retained, perhaps due to the difficulty of getting a replacement. He would not seem to be an extreme case, and very likely in the minds of the congregation possessed redeeming qualities.
[121]Duke to Claggett, June 29, 1795 (Maryland Diocesan Archives).
[122]Duke, *State of Religion*, p. 19.
[123]Eddis, p. 46.
[124]*State of Religion*, p. 14.
[125]*Ibid.*, pp. 25, 44-45.
[126]*Ibid.*, p. 16.
[127]Eddis, p. 53, note.

V

THE EVANGELICAL IMPULSE OF METHODISM

The evangelical impulse of American culture in the 1740's has been well established by historians as the Great Awakening. After 1800 this movement once again came to the surface. Maryland, particularly under Methodist influence, experienced the impact of these awakenings. What is not generally clear is the fortune of evangelical Christianity between these two periods. A study of Maryland reveals continuity. After a decline in the 1750's and 1760's it developed in more vitalized form during the Revolutionary era. It is important to see that this was so, how it came about, and how the Revolution fostered it. Attention has already been called to the general aspiration in the colonial period to a vitalized religious life; Marylanders sought to achieve this by reshaping prevailing religious and secular structures of society. The Revolution gave the opportunity for this religious fulfillment. In Methodism especially, this whole story comes forward as evidence of a great evangelical, social movement. Its dynamics, particularly in Maryland, revealed all of the nuances of this social process.

The career of the Methodist preacher, Robert Strawbridge, throws light on the transitional survival of evangelical piety. By 1750, George Whitefield and his preachers, together with some Presbyterians led by

Gilbert Tennant, had brought about awakening in the region in which Maryland stood. Although considered a Methodist, Whitefield did not, however, organize local societies as John Wesley prescribed. Strawbridge, who arrived in America certainly by 1760 from Ireland, employed both the preaching style of Whitefield as well as local organization to assure enduring results of awakening. He built upon the lay preachers who survived Whitefield in the 1750's as well as the many families who had been schooled in his evangelical forms of piety. More local lay preachers were gathered into the revival as he zealously rode his Baltimore, Frederick, and Eastern Shore circuit. This success was due to the more orderly style of ministry which Strawbridge learned in the Wesleyan Methodist circuit in Ireland. [2]

In time, however, he came into controversy with Wesley's agents, who arrived in America in the latter 1760's. His free style in administering the sacraments or ordinances of the Church offended them. Since he was not an ordained minister of the Church of England, he was not, according to the Wesleyan and church discipline, free to administer the sacraments. He ignored their wishes, however, and in the 1770's came under censure. While Strawbridge had some order in local society, by 1770 Methodist piety needed the support which greater fidelity to the Wesleyan rules provided. Hence the organizing activities that ultimately culminated in the superintendency of Francis Asbury after the war met a very pressing need, if awakening were to have permanence in its religious effect. [3]

A school of preachers coming from Strawbridge and his period should not be overlooked in seeing the promise of expansion fulfilled in the war years and thereafter. Unlike him, they submitted to the Wesleyan rule and its agents. Philip Gatch, for example, was one of these. Nathan Perigau, a local preacher for Strawbridge, converted the Gatch family and Philip soon found his place in the ranks of preachers in the early 1770's. Freeborn Garrettson's case showed the persistent influence of the awakening. He had conversed with a man who had heard a Methodist preacher. Young Freeborn was moved to further inquiry and concern for his religious life, soon becoming a lay preacher himself. After 1770, he was, with Gatch, officially registered as a preacher by the conferences and respected the regulations on administering the sacraments. William Duke and others were among these and other young preachers who would be active during the Revolutionary Era. [4]

It is significant that the War did not destroy the beginnings of organizational integration reflected in the experience of these preachers.

It is also possible to say that the spirit of political independence created an atmosphere which fostered both enthusiastic preaching and awakening as well as integration. Some social theorizing makes the case that the unrest of revolutionary experience in society fosters this kind of decisive action. Discontented with past conditions and insecure with present trends, society, like the Methodists, felt the urgency to provide structure for the future. [5] The idealism of the war, itself, of course, instilled enthusiasm for a better order in human freedom. Methodism in America became a congenial pilgrim in the ranks of those forming the new republic, and sought a truly Christian state, and society. Methodists also hoped to enlarge their own ranks. The ultimate formation of the independent Methodist Episcopal Church and the remarkable growth of membership in the 1770's and 1780's provide evidence for the soundness of this generalization.

It can be said, therefore, in the light of Maryland's experience, that the First Great Awakening survived, but moved toward integration as well as expansion. With the beginning of the Revolution, such integration was adequate to support the growth from awakening preaching. This continued even more significantly in the 1780's and 1790's. So did the revivalistic style of Whitefield, Tennant, and Strawbridge, particularly in such native preachers as Garrettson, Gatch, and Duke. This means, then, that the Great Awakening as a national phenomenon after 1800 was not preceded in Maryland by some kind of a trough, as has been generally implied in the literature on this phenomenon of awakening. The Revolution, similarly, cannot be called a deterrent, as more writers seem to say, but rather an impetus. Jameson's notion of the Revolution as a social movement finds more detailed support in the scene described. The details of this story of the Methodist experience during the era must therefore be seen in this broader context.

With this kind of prelude and background, the significance of events in the 1770's are clearly seen. One of the highlights was a series of conferences which culminated in the meeting of 1776. The story in general centers in Francis Asbury and other Methodist preachers who came from England in the late 1760's. The work of these men reformed the tenuous structure of the Strawbridge phase. Sent by John Wesley, they were intent upon establishing local societies on the rules developed in England, calling for membership certification and regular attendance. While quarterly meetings or conferences were probably held by Strawbridge, these now became more correct and the number of regions for conferences increased. The conferences and the assistants who presided over them assigned circuit riders and authorized their lay preachers. Responsible and zealous persons were thus chosen for these important roles. Circuit riders, were, of course, the source of direction for the local societies and their preachers. [6]

The growth of Methodism in the late 1760's and early 1770's therefore was not surprising. While capitalizing on the latent interest in evangelical piety from Whitefield's day, the new development secured a lasting effect in permanent members who came forth from the large general congregations to which preachers spoke. The phenomenon of these years thus confirms the case for a religious aspiration in Maryland. The numbers recorded for membership must be understood as revealing persons who committed themselves to a strict adherence. But it should also be noted that far greater numbers were influenced, even if less profoundly, since preaching to congregations brought Methodism to persons of several different religious identification. The fact of such gatherings is a sign of revival that mounts through the war years and into the last decade of the eighteenth century.

Theological developments in Methodism prior to 1776 prepared the way for benifiting from the spirit of the Revolutionary era. Wesley's break with Whitefield was found in this area as much as in the matter of Methodist organization and practice. Wesley abhorred the notion of reprobation found in Calvin and emphasized in Great Awakening preaching by Whitefield, Presbyterians, Congregationalists, and Dutch Reformed revivalists. God did not, he believed, foreordain the damnation of those who had not been elected for salvation. Emphasizing freedom, the damned came to their lot by their own deeds. The grace of salvation was won by Christ for all men coming into the world. Grace was thus free. Yet with Whitefield and the awakening preachers, Wesley could say that justification came with conversion, which was the fruit of revivalism. But a second justification in the last day of judgement alone could bring salvation which depended upon the deeds of a true Christian life of virtue. One might succeed in the first case but fail in the second. [7]

Very clearly, reprobation theology, or at least emphasis on it, was not suited to the mood of the Revolutionary era and its message of man's dignity. Wesley's free grace and justification were. It is not surprising, then, that the story of Methodist growth through the fostering of such an evangelical piety came to mark this period in Maryland. It is necessary to detail the evidence for this phase which establishes the revolutionary emergence of the Christian state and what this implies for religious life in the period.

"One would have imagined," John Wesley wrote of the Revolution, "that ye 'fell [cruel] monster War' would have utterly destroyed the work of God. So it has done in all Ages and Countries: So it did in Scotland a few years ago. But that his work should increase at such a season was never heard of before! It is plain, God has wrought a new thing on Earth, shewing thereby, that nothing is too hard for him." [8] Many were not so optimistic during the War. A corn crib would hold all the Maryland Methodists, it was said. [9] To save the crib would be a miracle. The unexpected did come about, however, and Wesley proved correct. In viewing the events of Methodism during the Revolutionary period one comes to share Wesley's surprise.

In the decade and a half before 1790, a great expansion of Methodism took place and many men attested to what Wesley found. Thomas Haskins tells throughout his diary of the growing crowds that attended his preaching and worship. On one occasion in 1783 he was heard by fifteen hundred souls. [10] From Caleb Belt, ministering a southern Maryland circuit, he had reports that the revival started there did not abate. [11] There were full congregations at Baltimore. [12] Freeborn Garrettson's journal reads with crescendo as he describes the response to Methodist preaching. As early as 1778 he frequently blessed God for the day's harvest. Soldiers, magistrates, common folk came. [13] The following year found the Eastern Shore promising. "This neighborhood," he wrote of Somerset County and the town of Salisbury, "begins to flourish in religion. . . ." [14] Finally, in 1788, with enthusiasm, he said that in Talbot County: "The people in this part of the country seem as if . . . they would be all members." [15] The scholarly and sober Thomas Coke, recently sent by Wesley and writing a few years before the crest noted by Garrettson, agreed. "Perhaps I have in this little tour," he said, "baptized more children and adults than I should have in my whole life, if stationed in an English parish. [16]

The personal commitment to Methodism and the mathematical accuracy of membership lists perhaps are subject to some reservations apart from the context of this study. This is not so when one is estimating the general religious condition of Maryland. The fact of frequent preaching to large congregations, without evidence of personal results, also has significance as a sign of religious vitality. Methodist claims do not seem to be extravagant in this general view, particularly when non-Methodist sources are considered.

Methodist evangelizing was widely distributed throughout the whole state, which was further evidence of its process of growth. Robert

Strawbridge in the 1760's and 1770's rode circuit throughout the northern portion of the Western Shore. [17] In addition to Garrettson, Asbury himself toured this area, advancing even into the northwest extremity. [18] William Duke, when he was still a Methodist, also evangelized this portion, passing from Frederick beyond the mountains. [19] The Eastern Shore, of course rapidly became a Methodist stronghold. "If I cannot keep up old Methodism in any other place," Asbury stated confidently, "I can in the Peninsula. . . ." [20] By 1787, only Charles and St. Mary's Counties seemed to have been without this continued and intensive cultivation. [21] Methodists successfully evangelized neighboring Calvert County. Here, and to a lesser degree, elsewhere, the large number of Negro members testified to the extensiveness of Methodist growth. [22]

Conferences kept statistics which substantiate this picture. They do not provide all the accuracy one would desire, but with other evidence they constitute reliable confirmation. Circuit riders and others responsible for records may not or could not have reported all members. Qualifications for recorded membership were exacting. Large numbers attended congregations, hearing sermons, but mere attendance as recorded by observers are not necessarily reflected in membership records. Though not precise to the decimal point, then, this source furnishes proof of substantial growth along the lines described in journals and other material. It should be added that the large attendance in congregations gave evidence of religious vitality and influence apart from the fact of recorded membership in local Methodist societies.

Several areas grew rapidly before 1784 and then leveled off. Frederick, for example, noted 175 members at the start of the decade before this date, which marked the beginnings of independent church status for the Methodist society. In 1784, 516 were listed. Kent and Somerset Counties progressed according to a similar pattern. This was not the case, however, with Baltimore, Dorchester, Calvert, Talbot, and Caroline Counties. In these areas growth continued apace until 1790. [23] After 1784, account must be taken of new areas where Methodism took root and flourished before 1790, just as it had before 1784 in Somerset County. Montgomery and Harford Counties were examples of this. They began with no members on the 1784 register, but grew rapidly. The former had approximately 750, and the latter, 650 members in the 1790 listing. Counties with previous continuous growth, in this second period now had a very great increase in memberships. Calvert County went from 340 to over 1,800.

The journals of circuit riders provide descriptive evidence which parallels growth statistics. Asbury noted how important men were now concerned with religion in the midst of the troubled times. He mentioned Captain Ridgely, "who appeared to be under some small awakening." Others were stirring after long neglect. [24] The Eastern Shore, where statistics before 1784 showed gains in membership, was much travelled by Freeborn Garrettson. In this early period he found that many "did not know more of Jesus Christ than Indians." Elsewhere, in Somerset, a similar need was found. "I believe some attended," he said of one congregation to whom he preached, "that never heard a sermon in their lives." Revival began to appear shortly before 1780. In Kent County the poor especially began to show signs of spiritual vitality. [25] He found the "beginning and progress of the work of God" in Dorset County, where previously had been found men "universally enemies to the life and power of religion." While blaming the established Church for this condition, he nevertheless found some families of enduring faith fostered under earlier evangelical preaching. [26]

Asbury's experience of the Eastern Shore were no different. Speaking of congregations of 100 or more, he commented on "the revival of religion" in the period before 1784. [27] After an unfavorable view of Baltimore he was afterwards able to speak with greater optimism. "My heart was greatly enlarged," he wrote, "especially there is a very apparent alteration in this place." [28] Conditions in the environs of Baltimore contributed to this general impression. As he moved westward, however, and to the south, he was quite discouraged, with what he found in the 1770's and the early 1780's. But these regions would soon come under the impact of the great power of Methodism's evangelical piety. [29]

In the light of these statistics, Methodist witnesses to this growth do not seem to be overstated. Asbury himself took cognizance of these highly favorable statistics, noting the nearly 12,000 members of American Methodism in 1782, of whom the vast majority were Marylanders, [31] providing the spirit that carried it elsewhere. Descriptive evidence again confirms the impression of these statistics. Writing in 1787, Garrettson revisited an area in Talbot County where he had preached in the 1770's. He found the religious condition of the county greatly improved from what it had been. [32]

After 1790, however, there were indications that the pattern of growth changed from what has just been described. William Duke gave evidence that there was a reversal, noting in 1791 that Baltimore Methodism was "in a bad state." [33] It should be noted that he spoke as one who had stayed within the successor of the once established church, unlike most Methodist preachers in Maryland. He believed that a segment of conversions to Methodism were short-lived. "Many of their most violent professors," he wrote in 1794, "kindle at earthly objects, and after flaming to heaven itself, sinking into the residuum of fleshly lusts. I only take notice of what is obvious to every observer. . . ." [34] He believed this to be an inherent liabiltiy of the revivalistic piety to which Methodism extravagantly resorted during its period of greatest growth. He clearly saw that Methodism had lost some of its members.

Duke's testimony is trustworthy, certainly not given to excessive optimism for results of the enthusiastic style of Methodist preaching. In the face of some unfavorable conditions, he generously noted the genuine reform and stable membership of Methodism and respected the many good results. "When we observe drunkards to become sober," he wrote, "swearers to converse decently, idlers to mind their business, and mere worldlings to venerate the word of God, a Christian spirit would dispose us to congratulate them [Methodists], with unfeigned thankfulness to God for such an accession to the interest of vital religion." [35] What Asbury wrote in 1799 seemed to suggest agreement with Duke's estimate. He spoke of a recovery being sought at this time, evidently after finding a setback in the preceding ten years. The effort at recovery, however, seemed to be succeeding in only four of six districts from which he had heard. [36]

Not all of the potential loss was made up of capricious, worldly souls who originally were superficially attracted by revivalism. Many who had left Episcopalianism for the "evangelical form" they saw in Methodism might readily return when they saw it appearing in their former church. Of these, some undoubtedly felt as averse as Duke did to extremes in "experimental religion" and "enthusiasm" found in Methodism. In 1794, Jeremiah Cosdon resigned his Methodist ministry and became an Episcopalian. "He was always very generous," Asbury said of him, "and did not serve us for money." [37] Such defections of the clergy had been made to other denominations [38] and, in earlier times, were likely to be among the "disorderly preachers" [some imposters], [39] who plagued Methodism. But in the period of greatest growth there were acquisitions of clergymen such as James Barton, the Quaker preacher. [40] Now, however, greater stability was developing on all sides, particularly within Episcopalianism, as has been shown. In terms of the general condition of religion in the emerging Christian state, none of this behavior indicates a decline in vitality. Moreover, loss in membership growth arose in Virginia, rather than in Maryland. There, James O'Kelly, an opponent of episcopal government, brought about a schism which affected

Methodism after 1790. Total membership figures at annual conferences were affected more in the area of Virginia. In Maryland, it was a case of the dramatic growth prior to 1790 merely levelling off thereafter. It was crucial that the church withstood this storm, leaving the solid structure upon which the growth of Methodism had taken place. [41] Jesse Lee, who ministered in Virginia for the most part, called attention to the fusing that took place within Maryland by 1788, reflecting the growing impact of a better organized Methodism. Visiting the Eastern Shore, he was greatly impressed by the intensity of piety there, noting that assistance from Virginia preachers like himself had contributed to the evangelization of Maryland. [42]

In the light of the foregoing, the former movement toward Methodism was only modified after 1790. The statistics show a tendency to level off. Prince George's County was one of the few instances of notable growth as a field of fresh endeavor. [43] The Revolutionary period thus properly singles out Methodism among minority denominations on the basis of its remarkable growth and vitality. Implied in this is the progress made organizationally. So well were the circuits maintained and with such success, that the Church order provided a proven pattern for growth in the new areas of the west. Influence on the more settled areas were not left untouched by the Maryland impetus, where the center of Methodism was found.

What conditions in the Revolutionary period caused the remarkable growth of Methodism? Certainly, there was a favorable atmosphere, a spirit of reform abroad. Men were critical of the colonial government and its established church. Marylanders criticized clergy, resented taxes for the clergy's benefit and made much of any worldliness they found among them. In this situation, the Methodist society could not but win respect before the Revolution, for they sought to exemplify an unworldly spirit within the Church. After the Revolution they thus stood as a vindicated element in the religious structure of Maryland. The longcriticized clergy of the once Established Church themselves tended to conform to the reform spirit which Methodism dramatized. Duke and others believed them to be accepted as the image of this spirit. Whenever an itinerant clergyman or stranger possessed the outward bearing of a religious man, he was believed to be a Methodist. [44] The curious would offer such a person some whiskey. If he refused the drink, it indicated that their surmise was correct. [45] When one found himself reproved by another for swearing, it was common to ask if the admonisher was a Methodist. [46] Tavern operators could expect to be visited by Methodists distressed at the spread of swearing and drinking. [47] Some folk were violently antagonized by such zeal. Asbury attributed attacks on Methodist property to this reaction. [48] Garrettson was personally assaulted for the same reason, and so were others. [49] More often, however, such crusading put the Methodist in high respect, certainly among those most capable of reverence. Duke found that other reformers did not achieve as high a position. Presbyterians were not nearly as effective in shaping a town's attitude toward religion and morality. Quakers were even likely to be ridiculed. The Methodist preacher, on the other hand, received noteworthy remarks of reverence and even won the title of "reverend." [50]

The heroism of the circuit rider also appealed to the spirit of the times. More than anyone else, he won esteem for Methodism by the image he gave of the reform spirit. It has been shown how Garrettson, by his personal sacrifice and zeal for preaching, often led people to put aside their political suspicion of him. Haskins told how austere was the life of a circuit rider. "This running up & down I don't like," he once complained; "the Methodists are in some things an inconsiderate people." [51] For he had to call not only at chapels, but at private homes far removed from his circuit route. "Oh God give me more grace in this Circuit," he prayed in hunger. "There is no danger of a preacher eating too much." [52] The Conference did not allow him or other riders to receive any money by subscription. They were discouraged from marrying in order to have greater freedom to meet the demands of the circuit and the poverty accompanying such a life. [53] These were some of the things which were added to the standard chores of preaching a hard doctrine, even extending to abstention from liquor and superfluity of apparel. [54] Finally, there was the call to missionary work in the back country, which Methodists faithfully answered. [55] The obvious ingredient of heroism in this role of the circuit rider did not go unnoticed, nor, for the most part, unappreciated.

"There is evidently more concern, more inquiry." Duke wrote, "and more practice now than was twenty years ago, and it cannot be denied that it has been chiefly excited by the Methodists." [56] The word *excited* was appropiately chosen, for excitement or revivalism was particularly suited to the revolutionary times. With disestablishment of official religion, people had a peculiar need. Many were uneasy about eternal things. "However satisfactory a man's circumstance may be," it was observed, "without some comfortable respect to an hereafter, grounded upon religious experience, he becomes, not only disgusted, but positively miserable." [57] Both the extreme secularist and the epicurean had at least a passing experience of these thoughts. Such persons as well as others were disposed to listen to what promised them relief. There would have to be something new in the approach, for their experience of religion heretofore was not compelling. "Taking into account," Duke said of this situation, "those who were betrayed by their own curiosity, and those whom accident had thrown into the vortex, we cannot wonder that a sect, right or wrong, should succeed in such a state of affairs as we have now under consideration." [58] As things stood, fire and brimstone were needed to "excite" people to concern for religion, and this Methodist revivalism produced. "But whether there be more smoke or fire," Duke reflected without complaint, "I am persuaded Christ is glorified and I therein do rejoice and will rejoice. Religion with some irregularity is better than no religion at all." [59]

As the Revolutionary War progressed, Duke himself experienced the growing appeal to revivalistic preaching which grew on the ever-increasing response it was getting. As a Methodist preacher he was instructed by Thomas Rankin, a highly successful preacher, not to be too intent on the pursuit of things intellectual, much less introduce any of those subleties into preaching. "Pray much and converse much with the people." Rankin said, "and you will find that this is the way to gain spiritual knowledge. . . . This is a Methodist preacher's calling, and ought to be his alone business." [60] Daniel Ruff, another correspondent of Duke's days with Methodism, also encouraged him in revivalistic preaching. "If you never are a means of Saving a soul," he wrote in 1779, "your Preaching may rise up in Judgement against thousands who must be left without excuse in that day. . . ." [61] With such conviction one must preach the hard realities of Christ's message. While Duke later saw that such preaching was suited to the times, he did not then or later go along with its extremes. He and other Episcopalians did employ milder expressions of evangelical Christianity.

Outstanding Methodists, all the same, continued to capitalize on the dispositions of the times, which were so favorable to revivalistic preaching. Haskins, while moderating revivalism more than most preachers, continued with the Methodist movement. [62] He fully realized the calm English church meeting did not suit America. [63] When he preached he might find a man in the congregation speaking out, possessed by the power of God, [64] As the war was drawing to an end, he found a member of his congregation telling of the imminent second coming of Christ. Garrettson was a more aggressive advocate of revivalism. He showed that the "word began to decline" where his style lost influence among preachers and vigorously defended "what some called hollowing [shouting] meetings. . . ." [66]

Both Asbury and Coke agreed with Garrettson and noted that revivalism was widespread and in a unique form among Methodists in Maryland. Throughout the 1780's Asbury found striking results. "Some sinners fell and shook," he frequently noted in his journal. Next day at Rowe's [house meeting] there was a shaking." [67] This praying and praising aloud." Thomas Coke wrote in 1790, "is a common thing throughout... Maryland... The work is surely a genuine work, if there be a genuine work of God of honor. Whether there be wild-fire in it or not, I do most ardently wish that there was such a work at this present time in England " [68] Coke believed that these practices came with the Revolution. "This praying and praising aloud has been common in *Baltimore* for a considerable time; not withstanding our congregation in this town was for many years before, one of the calmest and more critical of the Continent." The elder preachers gave up the old ways, "and entered with all their hearts into this work." [69]

In an age of growing social democracy initiated by the Revolution, Methodism made an appeal to the lower economic and social levels of society, which were also the most numerous. Special note will later be taken of Negro slaves in this connection. Revivalism was most suited to these people, and the direct contact of the circuit rider paid them a respect which a person awaiting parishioners in polite church surroundings failed to render. More than one preacher had a preoccupation with the idea that his gospel was destined for the poor and was likely to be a scandal to the mighty of this world. [70] The lowly were thus freed in religion from a form of subservience to class. Having thrown off political subservience, they welcomed a removal of it from religion at the hands of simple preachers. The journals of circuit riders leave no doubt why Methodist growth took place at this broadest base of society. Asbury was zealous in keeping a spiritual orientation of the Methodist evangel to the poor, as the rules of English conferences stated. "Do not affect the gentlemen for God's," it was said. The Christmas Conference was as strong in its support of this view: "This is no time to give any encouragement to superfluity of apparel." [71] Haskins criticized the Anglican rector Samuel Keane as he preached to "a gay careless. . . section" in a style too much accommonodated to the worldly and well-born. [72]

All of this is not to say that Methodism lacked appeal to other classes, and indeed to all age levels of society. [73] There were, however, special difficulties in the way of acceptance by the wealthy, which might suggest an apparent lack of universal appeal in the Methodist Revolutionary growth. An anti-intellectualism in some preachers like Rankin and extreme revivalism may have offended the well-educated among the wealthy.[74] Methodists inveighed against demonstration of wealth in one's manner of life. When Methodism took a radical stand against slavery in 1784, it showed that the wealth and prestige of the plantation gentleman was not the powerful element in the Church. One Methodist witnesses that there was a gradual division of the society in the upper economic classes,[75] the earlier broader base remaining.

In spite of these obstacles, Coke gave evidence that the wealthy had a genuine interest in Methodism. Dorset Gough was the most prominent example. Although he did not give up the majestic surroundings of Perry Hall, one of Maryland's finest mansions, he did put it in the service of the preachers. Persons of all classes and races would attend religious services there. In his travels to the Eastern Shore, Coke found similar instances in Somerset and Dorset Counties.[76] Here and in Caroline County he mentioned several military men, doctors, and civil magistrates as connected with Methodism.[77] One wealthy gentleman of Kent Island gave up fox hunting out of devotion to his decision to become a Methodist.[78] The Western Shore provided other examples.[79] In Baltimore and Annapolis the wealthy answered the Methodist appeal, as Garrettson and Asbury noted.[80]

Evidently the Methodist ideal of poverty of spirit was a matter of individual judgment and sufficiently flexible, so that these persons of wealth and gentility felt equal to the religious challenge. In time, some adjustment also developed on the question of the manumission of slaves. Rigid requirements of members were mitigated but with a strong appeal to idealism still remaining from the immediate period of the war years. Methodism's great desire for the freedom of slaves made strong appeal to the idealism of liberty awakened by the Revolution. This in turn attracted many Negroes to the church. Preachers and conferences proclaimed the doctrine effectively and put it into practice. Black interest eventually brought about an African Methodist Church.

The present consideration is concerned entirely with Methodist growth as affected by black membership. On the broader topic of the Methodists and slavery carrying up to the Civil War years a different story is told, which has not the complimentary narration developed here. The vigorous movement for the manumission of slaves begun during the Revolutionary War years played out. Strong stands taken in the initial conferences of Methodism were progressively watered down by 1790, but it would seem that this force largely came from Virginia. Furthermore, the ideology of freedom which waxed strong in this period was maintained in spite of some regression in the application of it. It is also true that the formation of the African Methodist Episcopal Church was greatly prompted by resentment at segregation and discrimination in many congregations. [81] Nevertheless the period of disenchantment among blacks was preceded by enthusiastic attachment. The growth of religious life among them for this reason continued and owed its origin to the Revolutionary period.

The force of religion by its good works will be considered in a later chapter. But in this whole area of black religion it is necessary to see the problem within the period under consideration here. The specific phenonomen of the evangelical impulse of Methodism which resulted from the revolutionary movement helped bring about the emergence of a Christian state and a society that manifested a vitality not found earlier.

The growth of evangelical Christianity among blacks was very real and significant evidence comes from expansion in this segment of society. This black chapter was thus extremely important.

Asbury was typical of the tenacity of preachers on the slavery question. "I visited the old gentleman [John Wilson]," he wrote in 1783, "hoping he had done with disputation; the subject of slavery being introduced, he acknowledged the wrong done by taking them from their own country, but defended the right of holding them; our talk had well-nigh occasioned too much warmth." [82] On other occasions he would abruptly leave a home out of resentment at the manner in which his host dealt with slaves and the slave question. [83] Thomas Haskins had similar experiences when he "went fully into the matter about the freedom of slaves." [84] He also freely participated in legal action to bring about the manumission of individual slaves. [85] Thomas Coke became intransigent in the face of compromises which were urged by Devereux Jarratt and others in Virginia. He would not allow preachers to be sent to those circuits which openly advocated the need and justice of slavery, contrary to early conference rulings. [86]

As early as 1780 Methodism took an official stand against slavery. In Question 7 of the April 24 session representatives acknowledged:

> ... that slavery is contrary to the laws of God, man, and nature, and... this society; contrary to the dictates of conscience, religion, and doing that which we would not others should do to us and ours. ... [and] we pass our disapprobation on all our friends who keep slaves, and we advise their freedom. [87]

Assistants of the preachers were themselves to meet with blacks, who were to have place in common with others at church assemblies and meetings. [88] Three years later some preachers reported difficulty in releasing their slaves due to real or apparent obstacles in civil law. [89] In 1784, the conference suspended those preachers who still held slaves. Those who openly opposed such manumission were forbidden to continue as preachers, and increasing pressure was applied to the laity who held slaves. [90] But objections and obstacles began to gather in the way of the noble movement. In the fall of 1784 John Wesley intervened and urged postponing enforcement of the conference resolutions on slavery passed earlier that year. Yet Methodism, Wesley said, must continue to be bent upon the destruction of slavery by all wise and prudent means. [91]

In June of 1785 a conference in Baltimore reversed the 1784 decision calling for a manumission rule. Jesse Lee from Virginia had led the moderate group, who were now supported by Wesley. The new decision which they won removed as a membership requirement manumission of slaves. Thomas Coke far more than Asbury was an opponent of the gradualism led by Lee. To some extent it was a contest between Virginia and Maryland Methodism, the latter being more favorable to compulsory manumission. [92]

It was not the fault of Marylanders that the crusade fell short of the liberation upon which they had early fixed the eyes of American Methodism. Thomas Coke, not given to compromise of principle on this issue, explained the situation. "We thought it prudent to suspend the minute concerning slavery," he said in recognition of Wesley's directive, "on account of the great opposition that has been given it. . . ." The Church had not yet been safely established. "Our work being too infantile, it would be unwise to push to extremity." [93] Methodists hoped that a strong Church would one day decisively act to remove the blight of slavery. For the present, the leadership of Methodism must reinforce the idealism of racial equality, looking to voluntary manumission of slaves by owners. Preachers gave abundant evidence of that effort.

It was not strange in a day of heroic crusading for political liberty that Methodist preachers gave spiritual dimension to this ideal by their effort to liberate black Americans from slavery. Their pastoral labors were distributed on a basis of racial equality. Haskins often recorded with satisfaction that large numbers of Negroes heard his preaching of the Gospel. [94] Asbury had no misgivings when more than one race was in attendance at his preaching of universal salvation. [95] The popular Negro preacher, Harry Hosier, served as welcome associate of Asbury on long ministerial journeys. [96] Freeborn Garrettson had the pracuc. conducting Bible class on the same basis. [97] He was proud to record in his journal that his own recently "awakened" black brother "became a leader of a Black & a white Class." [98] Garrettson reflected the Revolutionary idealism of the day when he described this leader's charitable and zealous activities:

> He had 40 or 50 Souls to watch over. Tho' the greatest part of them was Black, God gave him a great love for them. He seemed as if he loved them as his own soul. When any of them would be careless he had a heart to weep over them. — I conversed with him several times, and I had reason to think he was struggling for all that was in the Blessed Jesus. [99]

This idealism was alive among the laity. In 1795 Francis Asbury told of a prominent physician of the Eastern Shore who manumitted his slaves. [100] "This society," declared a conference of 1787 in Calvert County in another instance, "will not hold their fellow-creatures in bondage." [101] This was after the earlier and more general conferences of Methodists in 1784 and 1785 had removed manumission as a condition of membership. "We were agreeably informed," Coke wrote of a similar case, "that several of our friends in *Maryland* had already emancipated their slaves." [102] This practice continued, and many hundreds of slaves were freed by their Methodist masters, even though not strictly required to do so.

As it stood, this situation was favorable to the growth of Methodism. Preachers could win adherents by appeal to social democracy, which at least began to level even racial barriers. At the same time, those who were not equal to the full demands in the idealism of emancipation were not driven from the Church. Most important of all, the zealous and charitable call to blacks did not go unanswered. The numbers that came into the church were remarkable. In some counties the Negro proportion ran close to half of the total membership. In Calvert County, where the strong stand against slavery noted above was taken, more than half of the Methodists were Negroes. [103] Except for Quakers, no other denomination stood so firmly upon these grounds of equality. Had Methodism not been made an independent church by force of the events of the Revolution, such an appeal could never have been made. [104]

Asbury and others in the government of the church responded generously to the desires of black members. A large number in Baltimore wanted a separate congregation, "forming a distinct African, yet Methodist Church." [105] "The Africans of this town," Asbury explained, "desire a church, which, in temporals, shall be altogether under their own direction, and ask greater privileges than the white stewards and trustees ever had a right to claim." [106] The movement continued to develop and merged with a similar one that had begun in Philadelphia. Out of this came the African Methodist Episcopal Church. Shortly after the turn of the century this Church convened at Philadelphia to select its own bishop. Stephen Hill represented Baltimore on this occasion and played a prominent role in the transactions. [107] Another part of this spirited growth of Methodism among Negroes was the "African Academy" of Baltimore, which Asbury encouraged. [108] This first harvest was a response to the idealism of freedom awakened by the Revolution which was probed with all of its implications by these religious men. From Asbury's journal account the separate black church arose from a desire to please black Methodists and give them wider responsibilities.

It is important to see, however, that significant numbers were restive under the gradualism philosophy of the 1785 conference. "For ages there [was] not a sufficient sense of religion nor of liberty to destroy it," Asbury sadly remarked of slavery in 1798. "Methodists, Baptists, Presbyterians, in the highest flights of rapturous piety still maintain and defend it." [109] Such men were responsible for at least ending the slave trade. Their published writings relentlessly attacked the whole degrading nature of the institution. Ezechial Cooper especially crusaded in Maryland. [110]

Apart from the story of black Methodism, other democratic ingredients accounted for its remarkable growth generally. St. Peter's Parish, Talbot County, revealed one of these in its report to Bishop Thomas Claggett. "Upon the whole," its vestry wrote of Methodists in 1797, "the Strong fort of the Sectaries seems to have lain in mischievously directing that Pride which everyone (in some degree or other) feels at being A free agent . . ." [111] There was a distinctive liberality, the vestry believed in ecclesiastical discipline of Methodism. More important to an age that was preoccupied with the rights of man and his universal aspirations was the truth that a religious realization of these desires for greater freedom was possible. Many sects had called this truth in question by their interpretation of predestination. Methodist doctrine was not saddled with this disability. Methodists elaborated and effectively preached their optimistic version of man's freedom to attain eternal happiness through free grace. Wesley and Asbury wrote professedly on this doctrine; circuit riders noted many conversations and sermons on the topic. More than once they recorded the fact, of long, and even heated, controversy with those who espoused an extreme Calvinistic explanation of predestination. Methodists believed that reprobation in this system destroyed free grace. The *means of salvation* in their system was open to all. The Calvinist view of election held a different meaning and the whole controversy affected man's freedom, a sensitive point in the eighteenth century age of Enlightenment.

Thomas Haskins' journal gives an example of the preachers preoccupation with this issue which was vital to his faith and to the peculiar attraction it held during the Revolutionary era. Like other circuit riders, and contrary to the impression historians often give of them, Haskins read considerably. Amidst the turmoil at the conclusion of the Revolutionary War, he spent the day "chiefly in retirement [and] read Mr. Sellon's Works." He found the author's arguments against those who would impugn free grace "masterly." [112] "His criticism on those Scriptures," he said, "Which the Calvinists urge to support their peculiar tenets are great. I could not have thought that the Scriptures were so grosely perversely translated, as he represents them to be in these passages which countenance Predestination Redemption . . ." [113] The reprobation theology of many non-Methodist evangelical preachers was rejected. Haskins was also acquainted with the writings of John W. Fletcher (1729-1785), long associated with John and Charles Wesley. He found satisfaction in Fletcher's views, "Particularly his plan of reconciliation of Bible Calvinism & Bible Arminianism." [114] There was a moderation in such an approach to the problem of freedom, which prevented offense to Protestant views of Calvinistic origin, for it attacked reprobation without denying God's special call in free grace. Rationalists such as Priestley and their disciples gave no place to such special action by God. From this doctrinal standpoint Methodists promised to bridge a doubt of the times without the loss of traditional Christian faith. It was not surprising that, for this and other reasons, they were accessible to other denominations, with whom they successfully sought contact. In this situation the growth of Methodism was even further enhanced.

Methodism demonstrated another democratic tendency, further showing that it appealed to the times. Its preachers cut across all denominations, even finding place in their pulpits. Mention has been made of the welcome the Episcopalian Mason Weems gave to Methodists. [115] There were also others, since Methodists did not easily lose a relationship that had been fostered within Episcopalianism before the Revolution. There was no memory of that acrimony fostered among dissenters outside the Church. After the Revolution Episcopalians found enough of the old church in Methodism to balance the reform spirit for which even they now had a taste in milder form. Duke candidly admitted the unique and timely attractiveness of Methodism. "They have become numerous, and obtained the consideration of a church. . . ." [116] He noted how Methodist liturgy reflected the forms of Anglicanism. The gradual evolution of the office of superintendent into that of bishop prevented any undue offense to a feeling for Anglicanism, so often attacked in the past by dissenters because of the Anglican esteem of episcopacy. So also the office of vestryman was respected. Modification of the Sunday Service Book had a similarly favorable effect. [117] All of this has significance when one sees Asbury record instances of Episcopalians becoming Methodists. This was particularly the case when he tells how Garrettson or others won over a "great churchman." [118] Yet these acquisitions of members occurred without exciting jealously or resentment in other denominations, as Duke explained; nor had it done so in the case of Duke himself. who had once been a Methodist preacher.

With such dissenters as Presbyterians, Baptists, and Quakers, on the other hand, the Methodist had another basis of kinship; and also with pietist sects. Evangelical simplicity appealed to all of these, and so Methodists were welcomed to their services. The journals of circuit riders and preachers tell of many occasions of this. Interdenominational amity, which will be discussed at length in a later chapter, was verified by these recorded instances, which shows how Methodism served as a natural bridge. This Methodist contact and aid to growth in other groups obtained in the case of the German and other pietist sects. [119] Asbury for a long time had contact with the Quakers. [120] He attended their services and they, in turn, came to his. His friendship with the German pietist, Phillip Otterbein, was a story in itself. Garrettson was able to speak in German at a Dutch Church at Reisterstown, and there were similar occasions farther west in the state. [121] Haskins had the same experience and on one occasion was sought out for advice and encouragement by a Mennonite. [122]

With all of those conditions favorable to Methodist growth, church independence itself was decisive. Without an autonomous church the unique qualifications of Methodism for the Revolutionary times would have remained unfruitful. Its evident initiative would have played out without the integrating force of a completed ecclesiastical structure. The collapse of established Anglicanism and the departure of half of its clergy from Maryland came with the War. In these circumstances Methodism, like the emerging nation, gravitated inevitably toward independence. In this sense, the Revolution produced the major instrument of that growth which has been described in Methodism during these times.

In the troubled circumstances of war, Methodists had felt themselves abandoned. They were convinced that only their own action could save them and their work for God. "In America there are none," Wesley wrote of the absence of bishops, "and but few parish ministers; so that for some hundred miles together there is none either to baptize or to administer the Lord's supper." [123] Methodists began cautiously to deal with the problems. In 1780, certain Virginians led a premature schism from the Church of England and Asbury was sent from Baltimore to deter them. The conservative Marylanders urged reception of ordinances only at the hands of ordained ministers. [124] Robert Strawbridge, it will be recalled, had precipitated this question a decade before when Asbury and other assistants were designated to exercise control over preachers. [125] In this way an effort was made at retaining a semblance of church structure which for the moment required continuance within the Church of England. But this determined action by the conferences was an omen of final independence, given the condition of that Church as yet without its final Protestant Episcopal structure. An accustomed manner of action began to intrench a feeling for independence as Methodism evolved toward the Christmas Conference in 1784. "Abandoned abroad and suspect at home," one writer accurately stated, "the American Methodists came to view their own independence jealously." [126]

Although they patiently awaited the providential outcome of the war as a lead to their own steps, Methodists were prepared by a spirit of independence for that day when it arrived. "Let us leave God to govern the world," Wesley advised Edward Dromgoole shortly before the Battle of Yorktown "And he will be sure to do all things well. And all will work together for the glory, and for the good of them that love Him." [127] Wesley had put aside his former hostile view of American independence and now understood Methodist Maryland preachers. "It is well," he wrote a year before Church independence, "that you 'agree to disagree' in your opinions concerning Public Affairs. There is no end of disputing about these matters. Let everyone enjoy his own persuasion." [128]

Marylanders followed their own persuasion in changing Wesley's plan for their church. Francis Asbury reflected their feeling when he insisted with Thomes Coke, who brought the plan from England, that

all of the preachers pass upon it before it became law. [129] With this
new ingredient of self-government the plan became more acceptable. "The
preachers and people seem to be much pleased with the projected plan,"
Asbury said; "I myself am led to think it is of the Lord." [130] He carried
the democratic principle into the settlement of his own place in the
church. "If the preachers unanimously chuse me," he wrote shortly
before becoming superintendent, "I shall not act in the capacity I have
hitherto done by Mr. Wesley's appointment." [131] In saying this he was
calling attention to the passing of authority from Wesley to the Conference, which followed upon the Revolution. [132] The Baltimore Christmas
Conference thus became a counterpart of Independence Hall.

Methodists clearly recognized the advantage of independence and
even its necessity, given the fact of political independence. "By a very
uncommon train of Providence," Wesley believed in September of
1784, "many of the Provinces of North America are totally disjoined
from the Mother Country and erected into independent states." [133] He
was aware that the ecclesiastical authority of the English government
over the American church was nearing its end. "No one either exercises,"
he wrote, "or claims any ecclesiastical authority at all." [134] This created
an impossible situation. Ministers of the gospel were desperately needed
but under the circumstances could not possibly be created by bishops
of the Church of England. "If they would ordain them *now*," Wesley
feared, "they would likewise expect the government [of them] . . . How
grieviously this would entangle us . . ." "Our American brethren," he
observed of the Episcopalians at this time, "are not totally disentangled
both with the state and English hierarchy." Wesley's advice to the
Methodists was compelling: "Be they not entangled again either with
the one or the other." [135] These were assumptions upon which he submitted to the Americans his Sunday Service and the Articles of Religion. In Article XXIII he stated the following realistic conclusion:

> The Congress, the general assemblies, the governors, and coun-
> cils of the states, *as the delegates of the people*, are the rulers of
> the United States of America, according to the division of power
> made to them by the general act of confederation, and by the
> constitutions of their respective states. And the said states ought
> not to be subject to any foreign jurisdiction. [136]

On the face of it, one would expect a period of intense involvement
by Methodists in the Anglican adjustment in an independent Protestant
Episcopal Church. Only a few, such as William Duke, saw this and

stayed in the new structure. A few others were aware of the issue. The pessimistic estimate of Wesley evidently represented the prevailing view and prompted the independent Methodist course.

Thomas Coke gave a doctrinaire basis for the independence of the Methodist Church. After landing in America as an emissary of Wesley he soon aroused suspicion that he would recommend that course. Many saw this significance in his abstention from Episcopal Church services before the Christmas Conference. [137] When he arose to give the major sermon to that deliberating body, December 26, 1784, at Baltimore, he proceeded to elaborate a theological justification for what Wesley and certain Americans otherwise explained by the force of providential and inevitable circumstances. He called into question the whole prior church-state status of Methodism and the Church of England. He categorically indicted the whole notion of a national church, a tradition to which the Church of England —and Methodism with it— had adhered. Constantine had originated this perverse relationship with the Church whereby "*his* religion became the established one of the empire. And *now*, the pernicious influence of that bane of truth and holiness, a *national church*, began to pervade the Christian world." [138]

Coke traced the consequences of this. "The overseers of the flock of the humble Jesus, were raised above the princes of the earth." Now ambitious, worldly men sought these offices, which formerly were cherished by religious and zealous souls. The church itself became a "mere tool and stalkinghorse of sinister and ambitious men. The natural consequences of this was *infidelity* in all its various shapes. The religion of *Jesus* must be turned and twisted . . ." Those who then arose to oppose this perversion stood as Athanasius against the world *(Athanasius contra mundum).* [139] Coke did not hesitate to say that he found the Church of England caught in this web of history and "filled with the parasites and bottle companions of the rich and great." The Revolution and church independence were hailed. "The antichristian union which has subsisted between church and state is broken asunder." [140] Coke left no doubt that he gave a liberal acceptance of American conditions, considerably beyond what the Episcopal Church had chosen to do. The severance from England was complete in an ecclesiastical as well as in a political sense for Methodists, who evidently did not foresee the possibility of this for the Episcopalians.

Coke's proclamation of church-state separation went even beyond what the Maryland Constitution required or seemed to want. American Methodism, of course, accepted all the implications of the political break from England. In the ecclesiastical realm the problem of English bishops was simpler than it was for the Episcopalian Conventions. Asbury told of the way in which the office of bishop came to Methodism from within the American Church itself. [141] In the consecration of Coke as a Methodist bishop, reference was made to the Church of England in which he was a presbyter and to his title of doctor of civil law which he had acquired in England. Yet, in neither case was there anything other than a spiritual kinship and an academic status implied; and certainly no subsequent exercise of authority by the English church was granted. The power of ministerial consecration now came in democratic fashion from the Conference itself and its superintendents. [142] Some Methodist reasoning on church authority found in America was based on considerations White had once used. In particular, the *need* of the church was a guide to its judgment as to what powers it had to create superintendents and bishops.

The Revolution had clearly released the liberal forces that now followed Coke's lead. The few voices of dissent at the Christmas Conference confirm this fact by contrast and bring out the dramatic shift of direction which took place within Methodism. Thomas Haskin's journal provides one of the best examples. As early as February, 1783, he took his stand against the advocates of Methodist independence. A dissenter's tract against the Church of England and union with her brought his condemnation. "How hard a thing it is for a prejudiced person to reason thoroughy & impartially." [143] Haskins' own reasoning about ministerial orders and the rite which communicated them led him in June of 1783 to arrange for his own reception of orders in England. [144] He watched the proceeding of the Episcopalians with great hope that they would secure a native bishop and other means of providing ordained ministers for the church in which he hoped Methodists would remain. It was remarkable that views changed so rapidly in Maryland Methodism and that there were so few who approached the Christmas Conference with Haskins' understandings.

His journal for the Christmas Conference period showed a keen awareness of the predominantly liberal innovations. He urged that Methodists await the outcome of the Episcopalian deliberations before they act. Coke's recommendations came down to nothing more than "presbyterianism," that divisive bent which long had marred the unity of the Church. He boldly noted that Wesley had been wrong before in his views of America, a reference to Wesley's earlier analysis of the right and need of American political independence. Native American preachers such as himself, Haskins seemed to reason, were uncertain of the local conditions. How could Coke, Wesley, and Asbury, recently arrived from England, recommend such radical measures when natives were as yet uncertain of current trends. "Have felt my mind exercised," he wrote in distress, "on what was done in Conference—I fear *haste will make waste* if we don't take care." [146] This conservative voice was out of tune with the Conference and his temperament out of sorts with the sanguine feelings of the first days of American independence. It was this feeling which prevailed and created an independent American church.

This liberal spirit left its stamp on the discipline adopted by Methodism in Maryland. Wesley had already made substantial modifications in the Articles of Religion of the Anglican Church. His Sunday Service Book did away with many articles touching excommunication, the role of civil magistrates, descent into Hell, works before justification, predestination and election, and the authority of the Church. The nature of the ministry within the congregation had likewise been changed by Wesley, and the Maryland Conference made a further revision. It made more liberal allowance in the qualifications of preachers and ministers. American Methodism had removed the rigorous requirements the Episcopalians had put down for a valid American superintendent and bishop. Unordained Methodists were now allowed to administer the Lord's supper, baptism, and other rites prescribed by the liturgy. [146] At the same time, a strict procedure was followed whereby ordination to the ministry was conferred only on those who were qualified, and candidates were examined at the Conference. A vote by democratic process decided their suitability. [147] By such a liberal means the Conference did not deter the gathering stability which underlay the extensive growth of Methodism during this period. [148] Instead, these disciplinary measures equipped Methodism to respond effectively to the unique opportunity it had, thus bringing about orderly but dramatic expansion.

The key disciplinary feature was the superintendent, which office soon became that of bishop. According to Thomas Ware, who attended important conferences during this formative period, superintendency was calculated to strengthen the circuit rider and his method of preaching The superintendent had power to appoint riders to the circuits. [149] Asbury and the conferences thought that this kind of centralization was essential to maintaining itinerancy as the greatest instrument of Methodist growth. They strenuously and successfully opposed the

Virginian, James O'Kelly, who demanded that preachers have the power
to appeal to the Conference against the ruling of a superintendent or
bishop in a given case. [150]

Ware may have had the office of bishop in mind when he said
that "ecclesiastical polity and discipline would not be formed on the
model of our civil institutions, or other churches . . ." [151] He failed
however to observe that the state government of Maryland had its
own conservative traits, that the Episcopalian bishop had also made
his office a conservative force, and that in other respects Methodism
possessed a more democratic spirit than most denominations, as has
been previously described. That same spirit, when needed, operated
in restraint of superintendent and episcopal power. The Conference
of 1787, for example, made Coke sign a certificate giving assurance
that he would not exercise the power of superintendency when absent
from the United States and it struck the name of the absentee Wesley
from the list of superintendents. Asbury, a superintendent and witness
to these proceeding, realized that his subordinates were capable of
"warm and close debates" on the exercise of powers such as he possessed. [152] Had he not agreed that the validity of these powers derived
from the consent of the preachers whom he would govern?

The native preacher, Nelson Reed, of Anne Arundel County,
Maryland, gave dramatic effect to this democratic spirit. One attendent
at the 1796 Conference had cried, "Popery, Popery!" at what he
thought high-handed procedure by Coke. "Do you think yourself equal
to me?" Coke responded. At this Reed arose and delivered a piece
of timely oratory:

> Dr Coke had asked whether we think ourselves equal to him
> —I answer, yes, we *do* think ourselves equal to him notwithstand-
> ing he was educated at Oxford and has been honored with the
> degree of Doctor of Law— and more than that we think ourselves
> equal to Dr. Coke's king. [153]

Reed merely reflected the point of the Conference. The previous year
it gave thanks "for the admirable revolution," which still simmered
within the religious conference hall. Natives might readily flare up
under provocations which were reminiscent of the old order. This was
but a part of the whole train of events related to the remarkable
growth of Methodism thus set in motion by the American Revolution.

The interaction of Methodism as evangelical Christianity with the
Christian state and society was indeed very real. It shows the fact

of growth as well as explains how this was helped by the Maryland revolutionary environment. The Methodist impulse had some areas of penetration and interaction that are more difficult to establish; but the effect of Methodism on the Protestant Episcopal Church is better seen. Some insight into this process of interpenetration is found in the writings of William Duke, who had wide experience of religious forces at work during the period.

At the crest of Methodist growth in 1787 he did not hesitate to say that one Episcopal congregation received him so well because he still maintained much of the Methodist style of preaching. Three years later his journal contains veiled praise for the warm Methodist preacher. "His zeal," he commented on a Methodist, "seems too ardent for the health of the body whatever may be its effect on the soul —poor me I have neither health nor zeal." In 1791 he could not but admire another preacher, although he felt the need for greater intellectual content in his evangelism.[155] About this time he had discussed this whole problem of the proper amount of warm preaching in his own work and that of other Episcopalians. "What good I might do myself and others," he exclaimed to William West, "were I to speak freely of the reality and importance of this subject!" He implied that some degree of this style of preaching in Episcopalianism would bring Methodists to his congregations. There was also a minor note of resentment at Methodist growth. [156] It would seem, however, that his discontent came from its ecclesiastical organization and separation from Episcopalianism. There was no hostility to evangelical piety in the tradition of the Great Awakening. "A secret enmity," he said of Methodists, "gradually embittered them." Insults were sometimes heard. [157]

In the 1790's Duke continued to explore the theological and other aspects of evangelical piety, thus reflecting the pervading influence of the Methodist impulse in the era. He believed that sound Christian spirituality and piety should normally progress away from the world of emotion to that of intelligence. "I queried myself again," he explained, "Are not grovelling vitious spirits who became religious suddenly liable to much inconsistency and absurdity in their conception of a future state and consequently so much irregularity both in their affections and practices?" Hasty conversions were not always lasting and at times were followed by the indulgence of passion. On the other hand, he was willing to admit: "God can work with and by whom he pleases and He glories in the meaness of the instrument . . ." All the same Duke continued to be wary of awakening preaching and its results. "We ought not to take anything for the work of God but what appears to be so with sufficient evidence." It is very significant that at the time that he wrote in this vein he was corresponding with Devereux Jarratt, the Virginia Episcopal priest who had long conducted his ministry in the spirit of the Great Awakening. Duke made notations on a manuscript of Jarratt, which he sent to a friend with an accompanying letter. This friend had been employing Jarratt's method. One sermon was a matter of lengthy discussion with a third party. [158] At this time Duke was copying Jarratt's sermons and entered into correspondence with him. [159]

It was significant that Duke also studied the sermons of William White, which stood in contrast to the awakening preaching of Methodists and Jarratt. In 1780 the Bampton Lectures in St. Mary's, Oxford, were initiated in honor of John Bampton, Canon of Salisbury (d. 1751). About 1790, the American Episcopal Bishop White gave one of these lectures and Duke commented on it. He found White's metaphysical flights ill suited to the fostering of Christian piety. "Upon the whole," Duke judged, "however ingenious he may be or friendly to Christianity his book it not calculated to edify the bulk of believers." Duke admitted that some of his own compositions had these defects in them. [160] Whatever the extent to which Episcopalians like Duke were going over to the evangelical style of Methodism, the fact remains that the highly rational and restrained sermon traditionally rendered in Anglican parishes was under more severe criticism. In all of this context, the matter of singing at the Episcopal service further revealed the penetration of the Methodist impulse to evangelical piety. In 1792 Duke had taken up the practice of singing after the sermon. [161] He continued his interest in Jarratt at this time and corresponded with him the following year. There is also evidence of Methodist influence scattered through other sources on Episcopalianism to confirm what Duke gives with greater detail and clarity.

The spirit of the Great Awakening, then, was being experienced in Maryland throughout the whole Revolutionary era. As a final note, it should be said that this process was out of the pattern described in some comprehensive literature on the subject, but David Mathew's essay has found support for his hypothesis which emphasizes the Methodist feature. There was not, then, any major role given to the Congregational, New England tradition of the Great Awakening in Maryland. It is also not likely that evangelical membership stood in contrast to Anglicans regarding support of the Revolution. The structure of party politics, however, particularly in the 1790's, might prove to have a different explanation. Some sociologists maintain that unsettled conditions account for evangelical preaching and its favorable reception. In the scene surveyed here, it might be said that the uncertain condition of the successor to the once established church contributed to the rise of Methodism. The religious, rather than the general social and political order accounted for the growth of evangelical piety; but there are reservations here. There was a general aspiration for evangelical piety which was already cultivated to some degree on the eve of the Revolution. As an evangelical impulse, it was found in a general religious condition, reflected in Duke. Methodism thus was an effective and well-organized mode for expressing it; and served as a stimulus among those with a different affiliation. [162]

Apart from Methodism as a source of growth and penetration with evangelical piety, a more difficult matter arises. Was such a thrust disturbing and lacking ecumenicity? This question undoubtedly affects an estimate of qualitative improvement in religion during the Revolutionary era. It has been said quite critically that American Methodism drifted from the directions on which Wesley had originally set its course. It became "an isolated revivalistic movement." It had an "indigenous and virtually autonomous character" which diverted its first American inspiration. [163] As already explained, the Christmas Conference of Methodism in 1785 decided on an autonomous status, encouraged by the uncertain condition of the Protestant Episcopal Church with which it had a natural kinship. There are other justifications to be noted here. To the mind of Methodists, receptivity was wanting among American Anglicans and there is evidence to support the contention. When Thomas Coke conferred with the Episcopalians John Andrews and William West in December, 1784, he found agreement in doctrine. But, as Asbury noted, there were significant differences in "experience and practice." In the past only four Methodist preachers were favorably received in parishes and in 1784 there was little hope that bishops in England would be willing to go as far as Andrews and West promised in accepting the sacramental powers of Methodist ministers and in the creation of ministers from the ranks of preachers. The unorganized condition of the Episcopalians destroyed any confidence in a fusion of the religious groups. When in the 1790's Bishop James Madison of Virginia moved that episcopal conferences take up the same overture which Andrews and West had made, he found little support. The conditions of union were similar at both times. [164]

The "experience and practice" of Methodists had indeed brought them extremely important values, which could not be assured apart from their organized status after 1785. Only a limited number of Episcopalians like Duke and Jarratt held these values. Historical retrospect has provided perhaps greater insight into the convictions that led to Methodist independence than what people at the time understood. The local society was deeply esteemed as a "foretaste of heavenly fellowship." The local preacher as well as the circuit rider preached to responsive congregations; but where the smaller circle of the society membership came together, something more profound was added to revivalism. Here the Reformation doctrine of the priesthood of all the faithful found full scope as society members actively received the preacher's words, enlarged them, and even corrected them. It was the itinerant preacher, as Frederick A. Norwood explains, who as an institution brought this doctrine into full play. The whole world was his parish and society members who heard him became part of that world in their priesthood. The O'Kelly schism, it is true, threatened to destroy the concomitant authority in superintendents and bishops, while carrying out what seemed an implication of the universality of priesthood. [166] But by 1800 Methodists felt that they had by a special providence attained a balance between extremes, a balance that explained the growth and influence of their evangelical pity.

From the viewpoint of Methodist aspirations, then, the Revolutionary era in Maryland had brought fulfillment. It will be noted later that this was also accompanied by a mitigation of the bitterness between Methodists and Episcopalians found before the war. Qualitatively as well as quantitatively religious life in the Christian state was thus enhanced.

REFERENCES

[1]Donald G. Matthews, "The Great Awakening as an Organizing Process," *American Quarterly.* XXI (Spring, 1969), 25-43.
[2]Emory S. Bucke, ed., *The History of American Methodism* (3 vol.; New York, 1964), I, 69-76.
[3]*Ibid.,* 123-25.
[4]*Ibid.,* 140-41, 295 and Nathan Bangs, *The Life of Freedom Garrettson* (New York, 1829), p. 22. Bangs largely draws on the subject's journal, p. 2.
[5]Matthews, p. 34.
[6]Bucke, I, part. I, chap. 3.
[7]*Ibid.,* chap. 4.
[8]To Dromgoole, Sep. 17, 1783, Sweet, *Methodists*, pp. 13-14.
[9]Hughes, p. 272.
[10]Haskins, Journal, May 18, 1783.
[11]*Ibid.,* Feb. 12, 1783.
[12]*Ibid.,* Nov. 25, 1782.
[13]Oct. 1.

[14]*Ibid.*, Mar. 14, 1779.
[15]Garrettson, *Experiences and Travels*, p. 228 (May 28, 1787).
[16]Thomas Coke, "The Journal of Thomas Coke," *Methodist Review*, XLIV (Sep.-Oct. 1896), 11, entry for Dec. 6, 1784; see Hughes, p. 280.
[17]Matthew Simpson, "Strawbridge."
[18]Asbury, I, 462 (June 29-30, 1784).
[19]Duke, Journal, Sep. 19, 1774.
[20]Asbury, I, 346 (April 23, 1780).
[21]*Ibid.*, p. 555 (Dec. 20, 1787).
[22]*Minutes of Methodist Conferences*, p. 69.
[23]*Ibid.*, pp. 5 ff.
[24]Asbury, I, 180, 154 (Apr. 22, 1775), 234 (Mar. 19, 1777).
[25]Garrettson, Journal, Apr. 10, 16-17, 1779; June 20, 1778.
[26]Garrettson, *Experiences and Travels*, pp. 140 (Jan. 1780) and 115 (May 1779).
[27]Asbury, I, 525 (Dec. 4, 1786).
[28]*Ibid.*, I, 151 (Mar. 9, 1775), 154 (Apr. 16, 1775), I, 154.
[29]*Ibid.*, 192 (July 15, 1776), 489 (May 14, 1785), 513 (June 13, 1786).
[30]*Minutes of Methodist Conferences*, pp. 5 ff.
[31]Asbury, I, 425 (May 24, 1782).
[32]Garrettson, *Experiences and Travels*, p. 222.
[33]*Duke, Journal*, Nov. 30, 1791.
[34]*State of Religion*, p. 30.
[35]*Ibid.*
[36]Asbury, II, 202 (Aug. 5, 1799).
[37]*Ibid.*, p. 51 (May 9, 1795).
[38]Minutes of the Presbytery of Baltimore, 1786-1853 (Presbyterian Historical Society Library, Philadelphia, Penna.), p. 3; Asbury, I, 188 (June 2, 1776).
[39]*Minutes of Methodist Conferences*, pp. 16-17 (May 21, 1782).
[40]Haskins, Journal, Sep. 9, 1783.
[41]Bucke, I, 444; 440-52 gives a general discussion of the schism.
[42]Jesse Lee, *A Short History of the Methodists in the United States of America* (Baltimore, 1811), pp. 97-99.
[43]*Minutes of Methodist Conferences*, pp. 16 ff.
[44]Duke, Journal, Aug. 5 and 6, 1774.
[45]*Ibid.*
[46]*Ibid.*, Nov. 4, 1774.
[47]*Ibid.*, Dec. 19, 1782. "We think it wrong in its nature and consequence," a Baltimore conference said of drink on May 6, 1783, "and desire all our preachers to teach the people by presenting an example to put away this evil (see *Minutes of Methodist Conferences*, p. 18).
[48]Asbury, I, 613.
[49]See Chapter II above.
[50]Duke, *State of Religion*, p. 42.
[51]Haskins, Journal, Aug. 4, 1783.
[52]*Ibid.*, Feb. 23, 1785.
[53]*Minutes of Methodist Conferences*, pp. 11 and 25.
[54]Hughes, p. 286.
[55]Matthew Simpson, p. 82.
[56]Duke, *State of Religion*, pp. 41-42.
[57]*Ibid.*, pp. 17-18.
[58]*Ibid.*
[59]Duke, Journal, Aug. 9, 1789.
[60]To Duke, Feb. 14, 1776 (Maryland Diocesan Archives).
[61]To Duke, Feb. 12, 1779, *ibid.*
[62]See his Journal, May 1, 1783, for an example of his intellectualism.
[63]*Ibid.*, Jan. 22, 1785. Haskins said of Wesley's Sunday Service Book: "I scarcely think it will be of much use among us as a people." This would indicate Haskins' allowance for the native type of revivalism.
[64]*Ibid.*, July 4, 1783.
[65]*Ibid.*, Jan. 24, 1783.

[66]*Experiences and Travels,* p. 223 (June 3, 1787).
[67]Asbury, I, 649 (Aug. 2, 1790).
[68]*Ibid.*
[69]*Extracts of Journals,* pp. 109-110.
[70]Garrettson, Journal, May 10, 1779.
[71]Cameron, pp. 104-106; Asbury, I, 497.
[72]Huskins, Journal, June 8, 1783.
[73]Garrettson, Journal, Aug. 5, 1778. Asbury, I, 425 (May 24, 1782) noted the appeal of Methodism to all age groups.
[74]See Rankin to Duke, Feb. 14, 1776 (Maryland Diocesan Archives).
[75]Cameron, pp. 87-88.
[76]Matthew Simpson, "Gough,"; and Coke, *Extracts of Journals,* p. 22 (Dec. 17, 1784).
[77]*Ibid.,* Dec. 6-8, 1784.
[78]*Ibid.,* pp. 21-22 (Dec. 10 and 13, 1784).
[79]*Ibid.,* pp. 45-46 (May 27, 1785), 26 (Mar. 7, 1785).
[80]Garrettson, Journal, July 8, 1779; Asbury, II, 128 (June 18, 1797). Note Haskins' assistance from the wealthy (Journal, Dec. 25, 1782).
[81]Bucke, pp. 104-116.
[82]Asbury, I, 442 (June 15, 1783).
[83]*Ibid.,* June 8.
[84]Haskins, Journal, Apr. 1, 1783.
[85]*Ibid.,* Feb. 23, 1783.
[86]*Extracts of Journals,* pp. 39-41 (May 6 ff., 1785).
[87]*Minutes of Methodist Conferences,* p. 12 (Apr. 24, 1780).
[88]*Ibid.,* p. 18 (May 6, 1783).
[89]*Ibid.,* pp. 20-21 (May 28, 1784).
[90]*Ibid.,* pp. 20-21 (May 28, 1784).
[91]Wesley to Colby *et al., ibid.,* p. 24 (Sep. 10, 1784).
[92]Matthews, pp. 12-13.
[93]Coke, *Extracts of Journals,* p. 46 (June 1, 1785).
[94]Haskins, Journal, Apr. 9, 1783.
[95]Asbury, I, 441 (June 2, 1783).
[96]Hughes, pp. 279-280.
[97]Garrettson, Journal, I, p. 21 (1775).
[98]*Ibid.,* Aug. 30, 1778.
[99]*Ibid.*
[100]Asbury, *Journal and Letters,* II, 52 (June 11, 1795).
[101]Garrettson, *Experiences and Travels,* p. 222 (May 31, 1787).
[102]*Extracts of Journals,* p. 46 (June 1, 1785).
[103]*Minutes of Methodist Conferences,* pp. 5 ff.
[104]This judgement is based on the influence of official Episcopalian positions on slavery and emancipation. These did not compare with Methodist crusading.
[105]Asbury, II, 51 (May 30, 1795).
[106]*Ibid.,* p. 65 (Oct. 25, 1795).
[107]Matthews Simpson, "African Methodist Episcopal Church."
[108]Asbury, II, 128-129 (June 25, 1797).
[109]Asbury, I, 151.
[110]Matthews, pp. 23-24, 14-17.
[111]No further date (Maryland Diocesan Archives).
[112]Haskins, Journal, Aug. 27, 1783.
[113]*Ibid.,* Sep. 12, 1783.
[114]*Ibid.,* Nov. 7, 1784.
[115]See above, Chapter IV.
[116]Duke, *State of Religion,* p. 33.
[117]*Ibid.,* p. 29.
[118]Asbury, I, 469 (Oct. 24, 1784) and 615 (Dec. 16, 1789).
[119]Duke, *State of Religion,* p. 33.
[120]Asbury, I, 49-50 (Nov. 1, 4, 1772).
[121]Garrettson, *Experiences and Travels,* 166 (June 17, 1780).

[122]Haskins, Journal, July 8 and 12, 1783.
[123]Wesley to Colby, *et al.,* Sep. 10, 1785, *Minutes of Methodist Conferences,* p. 22.
[124]*Ibid.,* p. 12 (Apr. 24, 1780).
[125]*Ibid.,* pp. 15-17 (May 21, 1782).
[126]Hughes, p. 273.
[127]Wesley to Dromgoole, Sep. 17, 1783, Sweet, *Methodists,* p. 14.
[128]*Ibid.*
[129]Sweet, *Methodists,* p. 18.
[130]Asbury, I, 472-473 (Nov. 26, 1784).
[131]Hughes, p. 279.
[132]Asbury, I, 206 (Dec. 9, 1776).
[133]Wesley to "Our Brethren in America," quoted in Hughes, p. 277.
[134]Wesley to Colby *et al.,* Sep. 10, 1784, *Minutes of Methodist Conferences,* pp. 21-22.
[135]*Ibid.,* p. 22.
[136]Hughes, p. 287.
[137]*Ibid.,* p. 278.
[138]Thomas Coke, *The Substance of a Sermon on the Godhead of Christ, Preached at Baltimore, in the State of Maryland, on the 26th day of December, 1784, Before the General Conference of the Methodist Episcopal Church* (New York, 1815), p. 3.
[139]*Ibid.,* pp. 3-4.
[140]Quoted in Hughes, p. 284.
[141]Asbury, I, 474 (Dec. 18, 1784).
[142]*Ibid.,* p. 65 (Jan. 1, 1773).
[143]Haskins, Journal, Feb. 6, 1783.
[144]*Ibid.,* June 7, 1783.
[145]*Ibid.,* Dec. 22, 1784.
[146]Hughes, p. 287, 285.
[147]*Ibid.*
[148]Note the improvement in financial support of preachers under May 28, 1784, report, *Minutes of Methodist Conferences,* pp. 20-21. Subscriptions and public donations were now allowed.
[149]Ware, *Methodist Magazine,* XIV, 99.
[150]Asbury, *Journal and Letters,* I, 733-734 (Oct. 30, 1792); see also, M. Simpson, *Cyclopaedia of Methodists,* "James O'Kelley."
[151]Ware, p. 99.
[152]Asbury, I, 538 (Apr. 28, 1787).
[153]Sweet, *Methodists,* pp. 28-29.
[154]*Minutes of the Methodist Conferences,* pp. 63-64 (1795).
[155]Journal, Jan. 21, 1787; Aug. 11, 1790; Dec. 4, 1791.
[156]Duke, Journal, Dec. 8, 1790; Dec. 26 ,1791.
[157]Duke, *State of Religion,* pp. 28-29.
[158]Duke, Journal, Feb. 10, 1792.
[159]*Ibid.,* Apr. 16, 1793.
[160]*Ibid.,* July 21, 1792.
[161]*Ibid.,* July 15, 1792.
[162]*Matthews,* p. 34.
[163]Paul Sanders, "The Sacraments in Early Methodism," *Church History,* XXVI (1957), 360.
[164]Robert C. Monk, "Unity and Diversity Among Eighteenth Century Colonial Anglicans and Methodists," *Historical Magazine of the Protestant Episcopal Church,* XXXVIII (Mar. 1969), 63-5, 51-61, 65-7. See use of letter, John Andrews to William White, Dec. 31, 1784 (William White MSS, Archive of Church Historical Society, Austin, Texas), pp. 63-65.
[165]David C. Shipley, "The Ministry of Methodism in the Eighteenth Century," in Gerald O. McCulloh, ed., *The Ministry in the Methodist Heritage* (Nashville, Tenn., 1960), p. 23.
[166]Frederick A. Norwood, "The Americanization of the Wesleyan Itinerant," in *ibid.,* pp. 35-6; 33-65.

VI

REFORMED AND OTHER PROTESTANT GROWTH

On the eve of the American Revolution, there were many varieties of Protestantism in addition to what has already been noted. The Revolution clearly contributed favorably to their growth. Their aspiration to a fuller life in a Christian society were also fulfilled according to their own standards. More numerous than Methodists. Presbyterians composed the largest number of these religious groups, far surpassing Baptists, who were in the same strict Calvinistic tradition. Quakers, according to some historians derived from the Puritan sources of these two dissenter Calvinsitic groups. They had long found sanctuary in Maryland and grew considerably in the eighteenth century. Under the favorable policy of the empire in the early part of the same century, German Lutheran and Pietist settlements took root in Maryland. The latter were a reform group, which sought greater simplicity in their Christianity from what orthodox Lutheranism in Germany held for them. In America they developed into the United Brethren under the leadership of Phillip Otterbein, who was very active in Maryland. Moravians had similar origins. In general, it can be said that the evangelical piety of the Great Awakening in one way or another touched all of the reformed and pietist groups, the case of the Quakers being somewhat different. The Revolution and the era which it brought on answered the needs they had to fulfill their denominational and evangelical ideals.

The Great Awakening left a profound mark upon Presbyterianism, inspiring it to discover a distinctively American spirit and structure. The Revolution brought this development to completion. Puritanism in old and New England gave rise to Reformed Protestantism and this tradition was reared on a foundation of strict Calvinism, to which Presbyterians and Baptists adhered. Presbyterian congregations joined in a presbytery as the local source of church structure and authority allowed for affiliations at a synod level, and in time in a broader general assembly. Baptists, on the o t h e r hand, adhered to a local congregational authority which ruled out these Presbyterian practices. The situation was similar in the case of Congregationalists, who were not significant enough in Maryland for consideration in the present discussion. The conflicts and vision among Presbyterians at the time of the Great Awakening, however, arose from another source.

The itinerant preaching of George Whitefield, noted earlier in connection with Methodism, played a significant role in the creation of these Presbyterian tensions. Whitefield because of his very Calvinistic view of predestination broke with Wesley. It is not surprising that he found welcome company with such "New Light" preachers, as they were called, in the ranks of the Presbyterian congregation. They accepted the notion of experimental religion, "warm preaching," and revivalism as advocated by Whitefield. In 1739, Gilbert Tennant, in particular, collaborated with Whitefield, who proved a great support in Tennant's contest with more traditional Presbyterians, called "Old Lights." In the spirit of the Great Awakening, Tennant believed that religion was a matter of experience as much as received teaching from well-instructed ministers. The emotionalism implied in this view and the revivalism which fostered conversion to it brought attacks from the Old Light ministry. Francis Allison of Philadelphia was particularly influential among this party as far as Pennsylvania and Maryland were concerned. A student of his at the College of Philadelphia, Patrick Allison, came to Maryland and served as minister of First Presbyterian Church, Baltimore, during a significant part of the Revolutionary era. [1]

Between 1750 and this time, the very important theological differences between Old and New Lights came to focus in the question of who qualified to be ministers and preachers. New Lights tended to demand as much from personal holiness and religious experience as from the doctrinal knowledge of the candidate. Their opponents stressed orthodoxy, some to the point of demanding the candidate's rejection of religious enthusism in principle. By the time that a compromise had been reached on this matter, the Revolution was under way. If the New Light view had entirely prevailed, a greater abundance of preachers would have been available and growth similar to Methodism would conceivably have resulted. Tennant's Log Cabin College, with very minimal requirements in education, would have created a larger body of preachers, suited to the itinerant style of preaching. Nevertheless, this partial victory of the New Lights in demanding the strong place of the religious experience and revivalism combined with the power of the local congregation and presbytery to set American Presbyterianism significantly apart from the Scottish tradition reflected in Francis Allison and other extreme Old Light partisans. A distinctively American church was thus awaiting final formation with the event of political independence. The generally felt aspiration toward this religious form, therefore, attained fulfillment with the period after 1776. [2]

The transitional condition from Great Awakening days of Maryland Presbyterianism appeared in the 1760's. At the beginning of the

eighteenth century, Francis Makemie and others planted several congregations, particularly on the Eastern Shore; and it was on this that
the awakened preaching of the Tennants and other Log Cabin College
ministers developed religious life. There is evidence that some of this
New Light impetus still remained in the 1760's, but the more restrained efforts under compromise with Old Lights soon became acceptable. The numbers of preachers were now restricted under requirements advocated by Old Lights. "The Presbyterian religion gains
ground & seems to flourish;" Thomas Claggett noted of this transitional period, "& most probably the whole continent will be presbyterianized . . ." [3]

After 1770 Presbyterianism moderated "warm preaching" and
revivalism. Claggett's expectation of spectacular numerical growth did
not come about. Judged by prevailing Presbyterian standards in Maryland, which was under Old Light influence, such growth was not sought.
Competent clergy and integrated ecclesiastical structure was more important in the aspiration for qualitative improvement. Great efforts were
needed on these terms. Eastern Maryland was under the Lewes Presbytery in Delaware and from here came less optimistic reports. "Necessity of the times," said the minutes of 1776, prevented many from
attending the presbytery. "As the confusion of them are over," it was
reported more favorably eight years later, "the members promise in
future more punctuality." Still the congregations were not meeting the
troubles of the times. "Infidelity and vice greatly abound, as moral religion is manifestly decaying, and Vital Piety almost vanished from
many parts of the Land." [4] It is admitted, however, that these signs
were merely evidence of penalty for an earlier guilt. The Revolution
itself was regarded as an act of God's mercy, turning a new page of
the book of life. In time some came to believe greater emphasis on
the New Light evangelism was needed. Not the presence of gross immorality so much as the absence of "divine Influences," accounted for
the defects in religious life. The remedy proposed was "to preach
warmly." The new generation evidently had not experienced this hall-
mark of the Awakening period, but their elders reminded them of it.
Warm preaching and the desired amount of it needed to be reconsidered. [5]

There was other evidence that the old form of vitality had passed
and had not been revived. Patrick Allison, the most successful minister
of these new times, presented a different image from that of the log-
cabin graduate. "His discourse was quite systematical and amusing,"
Asbury adversely observed, "but if he had studied to pass by the con-

science of his hearers, he could not have done it more effectually." [6] Garrettson, perhaps judging by these implied standards favoring revivalism, said he found no power in Presbyterianism. [7] One of Allison's successors did not deny him his kind of achievement but noted it had a different quality. "At the close of Dr. Allison's pastorate the congregation was large, wealthy, fashionable, strong in all the elements of material and social strength, but waiting for power on high." [8] Elsewhere, too, people seemed to want what came from Allison's Baltimore's pulpit, and this became a source of discouragement to the "warm preacher." "There are instances also of Presbyterian congregations," Duke said, "that grew too much interested in the world to mind the business of the meeting and consequently they were left without ministers." He found an "entire indifference about both form and substance," in such people. [9] Ministers of New Light style did not desire to serve such unawakened congregations.

A veiled dilemma thus seemed to hamper more extensive growth. Old Light preaching like Allison's had appeal in some areas and with some groups. Yet many members longed for awakening days and passed this desire on to their children. The limited number of preachers as well as the difficulty of placing them with the right congregation, whether New or Old Light, compounded the problem. Undoubtedly Methodism made inroads into New Light Presbyterian ranks by default. Duke said that some Presbyterians came over to Episcopalianism for want of ministers at their churches who suited them. [10] One observer of Somerset and Worcester Counties in the 1790's confirmed Duke's impression. He found the old resentment for the Church of England "much worn off" in recent times. The loss of preachers was a factor in this since some of these would probably have kept alive the Presbyterian animus for the old church. [11] The Presbyterian minister James Muir took note of this situation and in one place remarked that one minister became an Episcopalian. [12] Patrick Allison, however, continued to manifest this traditional cleavage with the established church and its successor.

Baltimore marks the focus of persistent vitality during the 1780's, which contrasts with the foregoing evidence. Its story is a transition into the 1790's when the policy of a better-educated clergy brought its rewards. So, too, a greater balance in Old and New Light Presbyterians was established. The First Presbyterian Church came into existence in 1763, born out of a reform movement by members in a parish of Establishment. [13] Impetus was given to this by an influx of Scotch-

Irish, principally from Pennsylvania. "The advantageous Situation of the Town for Commerce," Allison related, "induced a few Presbyterian Families from Pennsylvania to settle in it, about the year 1761, who with two or three of the same Persuasion, that had emigrated from Europe, soon formed themselves into a religious Society. . ."[14] For about a decade after this, records showed that membership in the First Presbyterian Church of Baltimore increased at the rate of 17 %.[15] The vitality, organization, and growth here, then, was significant and eventually stood to benefit Presbyterianism elsewhere in the state.

Things were not well outside of Baltimore at the beginning of the Revolutionary period. In addition to the critical condition on the Eastern Shore noted above, James Muir stated that this was true of the area around Baltimore. Here there were few Presbyterian congregations. "Those which did exist," he wrote, "were in an Infant, and unorganized State, some of them had no ruling-elders, but were under the direction of a Committee . . ."[16] Things were no better farther west. "There is a small Presbyterian congregation in & about Frederick town," said one report. "They are as yet unable to support a Minister among them . . ."[17] Elsewhere remained the churches which were planted before the Revolution, but their situation did not seem to be any better than what these reports of other places indicated, since the supply of ministers was critical before and during the war.[18]

There was, however, a clear sign of vitality and growth revealed in the desire and acquisiton of ministers in these areas. As early as 1771 Queen Anne County Presbyterians petitioned the Newcastle, Pennsylvania, Presbytery for a minister.[19] "Seriously considering [the] very destitute situation of many vacant Congregations," read one report of the Lewes Presbytery, "their great Distance from the few remaining Members and Mr. Lewis's Removal from our bounds, agreed to *send a Request*, by one of our Commissioners, to the Presbytery of New-Castle, for assistance in supplying our important vacancies . . ."[20] The petition and importunities of Snow Hill, Maryland, on the Eastern Shore, also had much to do with this action. The war had not yet concluded when Samuel McMaster was dispatched to Snow Hill and began a long period of pastoral work here and in the surrounding area.[21] Another man was also eventually assigned and Queen Anne County soon became capable of supporting a minister.[22] Jacob Kerr was appointed minister at Menokin and Wicomico.[23] Another minister was sent to Dorchester County in the 1790's[24] In 1800, a synod was held for the first time at Wicomico for ministers of the Maryland

Eastern Shore and Delaware. It was a sign of the recovery made during the Revolutionary period. [25]

Progress on the Western Shore was symbolized by the formation of a new Baltimore Presbytery. At the Synod of Philadelphia in 1786, all congregations of that area of Maryland were detached from the Presbytery of Donegal, Pennsylvania, and organized into their own unit. In that year several ministers were available for the vacancies in Maryland. Notable among them was Stephen Balch, who began a long career in Frederick, Georgetown, and other places in the western part of the state. [26] He and others in this area gave leadership that soon produced results. In one instance they brought long-needed repair to the house of worship. "There was no convenient House in the town for public Worship," it was recorded. "A war with all its Disadvantages was general upon the Continent . . ." When the war was over, work was begun on a substantial brick church. Upon its completion more than four hundred could be accommodated for its services. [27]

The Snow Hill Church Presbytery Minutes tell a similar story. In 1771 its minister resigned and nothing was recorded until 1778, when Samuel McMasters arrived. During this period members were struggling to build a church, and the absence of meeting records suggests that the efforts were aimless. [28] By 1782, the church was open, provision was made for a suitable pulpit, and arrangement was made to have someone regularly clean the church. [29] In the 1790's the minutes showed an impressive regularity of contributions which were a token of the orderly progress the church had attained. [30]

Maryland leadership was evident in the larger organization of the church. This was particularly true of the Baltimore Presbytery. Patrick Allison, its representative, was highly regarded by the assembly held in Philadelphia in 1786. Together with the distinguished Jonathan Witherspoon, he was assigned to the committee for rules governing the synod. It demanded considerable learning of Allison to qualify for this appointment, which called for adaptation of various Scottish and Protestant theological positions. He was also designated to assist in the revision of the liturgy. [31] The Presbytery of Baltimore itself the following year seems to have become the object of special examination by the synod in an effort to seek guidance for the larger organization convened at Philadelphia. [32] The good record which the Marylanders had in catechizing the various congregations was called to the attention of the national synod at this time. [33] On the Eastern Shore, which belonged to the Lewes, Delaware, Presbytery's jurisdiction, Marylanders

were identified with the Presbytery's reform efforts at the close of
the war. [34] One of these called for the formation of associations in each
congregation which would devote one hour each week to prayer for
the civil and religeous improvement of society. [35]

Maryland Presbyterians took steps to assure continuance of leaders
and discipline in the state. The Baltimore Minutes tell of the acquisition
of four ministers in 1792, possibly due to Allison's position of influence.
Of these, three were from the College of Philadelphia and the other
from Dickenson College. [36] Lewes Minutes present a similar sign of
improvement in clergy education. McMaster was from Newark Academy; and another studied at College of Philadelphia. Allison had once
taught at the former institution. [37] A high standard of leadership was
evidently emerging with these appointments. In addition, theological
competence and responsibility was sounded by official inquiries from
time to time among those already holding appointments. [38]

In a general way, this competence and responsibility became a
matter of church discipline. Members on occasion would question the
views which a minister might express in a sermon and their presbytery
would look into such a complaint. [39] Misconduct led to some dismissals
from the church and members were known to make apologies to the
presbytery. [40] At the higher levels of Church organization measures
were taken to strengthen discipline "and promote the principles of the
gospel" in such a way as to remove dissentions. [41] Allison's church seems
to have succeeded very well in attaining this objective. [42] Occasionally,
however, political considerations became involved in church discipline
and disrupted the religious life of the congregation. In one such disturbance at Abington, it was the minister Balch "that did take some
pains to restrain those unhappy proceedings from going so far as they
did . . ." [43]

When consideration is given to the spirit and structure of Presbyterianism as relating to the political bent of the times, one is not
surprised that it progressed under the influence of the Revolution.
Presbyterians had a long-standing grievance against the Church of
England. When the Maryland Constitution separated that church from
the state, Presbyterians rejoiced. While they held much in common
doctrine with those churchmen, they nevertheless attacked confessional
chapters which gave civil magistrates authority over religion. "The
Presbyterian Church in America," their National Synod stated in 1786,
"considers the Church of Christ as a spiritual society, entirely distinct
from the civil government, having a right to regulate their own c

clesiastical policy, independently of the interposition of the magistrate." [44] This was the reason why the Eastern Shore Presbyterians could say that the conflict was a "mercy of God, so greatly remarkable, in the present war and American Revolution." [45] These providential events awakened gratitude, which in turn led to that zeal for the church noted during the period. These members were also jealous of their own local autonomy, as were the members of the Continental Congress. They did not wish to be over-involved in the Synod and General Assemblies; nor see their power attain the proportions of the church in Scotland. "They have found in many years Experience," the Lewes Minutes stated, "that there Presb. of a few associated churches is fully adequate to all the Duties & Difficulties that happen in Churches without any further appeal." The General Assembly responded deferentially, appealing appropiately to freedom of conscience, which they hoped would still allow a given local member to carry a grievance or other matter to its hearing. [46]

This idealism of freedom resounded in the General Assemblies and became the work of the Church. "It is especially the duty of those who maintain the rights of humanity," the Assembly said in 1787, "and who acknowledge and teach obligations of Christianity, to use such means as are in their power to extend the blessings of equal freedom to every part of the human race." This was becoming children of that same family which came from the hand of the Creator. In language similar to the Declaration of Independence it said "that the rights of human nature are too well understood to admit of debate . . ." The delegates were willing to go the full measure of these truths and face the reality of slavery as a living contradiction of revolutionary idealism.

> The Synod of New York and Philadelphia recommend, in the warmest terms, to every member of their body, and to all the churches and families under their care, to do every thing in their power consistent with the rights of civil society, to promote the abolition of slavery, and the instruction of negroes, whether bound or free. [47]

Patrick Allison of Baltimore had a leading role in the deliberations of this body and, as could be expected, members of his congregation participated in the first emancipation societies of that city.

The war, then, brought the impetus of revolutionary idealism to Presbyterian progress, but it also brought prestige to its members.

Earlier reference has been made to the military honor won by Presbyterians which redounded to their church. Prestige also went with wealth in aristocratic Maryland and in this respect Allison's parishioners particularly benefited from the War. Colonel John E. Howard, for example, in addition to honor in the field brought that of wealth with his attendance at First Presbyterian Church. He had, in fact, given property as a site for a church. [48] Even more important were those resourceful Scotch-Irish and other Presbyterians who in the 1760's projected the imaginative design for a city of commerce at the head of Chesapeake Bay. By thrift and hard work their dream was well on the way to realization when the war broke out. There is no doubt that the war brought wealth to Baltimore and much of it came into the hands of such Presbyterian families as the Starrets, who built the Revolutionary vessels of commerce and war. [49]

Benjamin Franklin's *Way to Wealth* had not been an impractical treatise in Presbyterian hands. Among the oldest Presbyterians in Baltimore endeavors and those who read their gospel, a religious ethic underpinned Franklin's secular wisdom. One of Maryland's first missionaries, Francis McKemie, had at the beginning of the century left *A plain Persuasive to the Inhabitants of Virginia for Promoting Towns and Cohabitation*. Thanks to God's war for freedom, it had not proven a false gospel. The importance of these wealthy and civic-minded citizens to Presbyterianism in Baltimore was frankly admitted by Allison. His fashionable sermons catered to them. When he took account of what had curbed the growth of Presbyterianism in the nearby area of Soldiers Delight, he said that this was caused "particularly by removal of some serious public spirited Members." [50] Baltimore, the nucleus of progressing Presbyterianism, did not suffer such a deficiency, thanks to the Revolution.

How then, explain Duke's pessimistic judgment of Presbyterian benefits from the war, for he believed that they had "derived very little visible advantage from the late exhoneration"? [51] Surely if the Revolution was an exoneration for Presbyterianism which wholeheartedly supported it, it benefited that religion in the way they anticipated. Presbyterians wanted a distinctively American church, more integrated, and served by an educated clergy. They wanted some of the Methodist evangelical enthusiasm, but not at the cost of these other elements. Duke would not seem to deny this. He doubtless saw the progress described here, although he evaluated it differently. Compared to the Methodists, however, qualitatively and quantitatively Presbyterianism may have indeed seemed to have "derived very little visible advantage." Not all would accept Duke's standard of quality for judging the degree of Presbyterian vitality. Undoubtedly there was no notable continuance of the Great Awakening spirit of "warm preaching," nor was there the visible evidence of "divine influence." But consideration has been given here to what Duke by the limitations of his time and circumstances could not have been expected to know. These added considerations have led one to conclude more favorably, that there was considerable "advantage from the late exhonoration." [52] Leonard J. Trinterud is in general agreement with what has been found here in more detailed evidence. His view is more general and estimates Maryland growth as inferior to that in Pennsylvania, Virginia, and some other regions. Like Duke, he tends to judge quality by the evidence of awakening preaching and the theologocal positions supporting it. The point of analysis here, however, is what Maryland Presbyterians put down as their own aspirations and measure of vital religion and church life. [53]

The Baptists did not occupy so important a place in Maryland as did Presbyterians. Yet, what standing they had at the beginning of the War they did not lose and even experienced some growth during the Revolutionary period. Possessing the same general Calvinistic and Puritan origins as the Presbyterians, they also had internal tensions regarding predestination and Great Awakening theology. These differences, as in the case of Presbyterians, were resolved by compromise in 1787. There were, however, some who went over to the Arminian theology of predestination, which American Methodists followed regarding reprobation. On their own terms, Baptists continued the warm preaching of the Great Awakening as seen in an evangelical convention in 1770. As in the case of Presbyterianism, this spirit and emphasis, however, did not dominate Maryland Baptists. Moreover, the theology behind the limited amount of Baptist revivalism during the Revolutionary era, rendered it less attractive than what Marylanders found in Methodism. Yet there was growth and stability. The specific Baptist aspiration for a Christian society was attained and its strong support of the Revolution vindicated.

The Baptist evangelization of Maryland originally developed out of Pennsylvania and Virginia congregations not many years before the war. Pennsylvania Baptists established a church at Harford County in 1754. [54] Among the letters to the Philadelphia Baptist Association in 1774 were requests for a minister for Baltimore, which were soon met. [55] Official legal incorporation was made by the state during the pastorate of a David Shield in 1798.[56] A more important and earlier preacher in this area was John Davis. At the close of the war he reorganized the Sater's Baptist Church which had been in existence since 1754 and was located on Chestnut Ridge near Baltimore.[57] The Church in this part of the state also included a location at Fells Point.[58] Thus the foundation for the Baltimore Association was laid during the Revolutionary period. There were also developments farther west. As early as 1773, Frederick Baptists had provided for proper care of their own church and membership. Taneytown by 1785 began to record the orderly proceedings of the church there.[59] Charles County and the country bordering the Potomac to the north was evangelized by the Ketocton, Virginia, Association.[60] In time many of these congregations were drawn into the Baltimore Association, together with Frederick.[61]

All of this showed that Baptists grew in numbers during the Revolutionary period in Maryland. Duke was indeed aware of a great initial impetus. "When the stream of anabaptism had barely reached us on the north as its *ne plus ultra,* it assailed us on the south with the rapidity and violence of a flood."[62] Even before the Revolution there was a notable growth recorded at Harford County.[63] The Episcopalian Bend, writing about the same time as Duke, found a large number of Baptists at Garrison Forest near Baltimore.[64] Minutes of the Philadelphia Association for this area, however, did not show any significant increase in membership after 1786.[65] Frederick, in the west, would seem to have a similar status of growth, for the membership number was considerably lower proportionately to the number of churches listed. This, however, was not the case with regard to Seneca, Reisterstown, Taneytown, and Tuscarora, Their common pattern of members, distributed over seven churches in the 1790's, did not indicate that any outstanding growth had taken place after the initial onset of which Duke spoke.[66]

"In general," Duke concluded of the Baptists, "they did not keep pace with the other sec [Methodist] just mentioned. . ."[67] He had a specific impression of what the situation was between these two sects in those western parts of the state, where so many Lutherans were found. Here he noted that Methodists made few converts and believed that Baptists made fewer. It is safe to conclude, then, that the Revolution did not adversely affect the Baptists or prevent their progress in Maryland.

Some analysis of the appeal of the Baptists to Marylanders in these times throws light on the extent and nature of the Church's structure and growth. When the Virginia Baptist came in Maryland he brought a revivalistic preaching, an evangelical theology, and a dissenting view of the church. He had also suffered imprisonment for his preaching against the *status quo* of the Church of England, for Virginia dissenters were driven by hard terms in the law courts. When he came to Maryland, however, he found an audience that had witnessed no dissenter martyrs under the easy-going Establishment of Propietary Maryland. He also was faced with revivalistic preaching by Presbyterians, Methodists, and even some Episcopalians, all in competition with himself. The large number of Lutherans whom he found across the Potomac had with satisfaction always heard an evangelical theology from their pulpits, and everywhere were always to be found some Quakers living the simplicity of congregational government. The old diatribes against prelacy, too, no longer had validity with reference to the Episcopal Church; and, if not against them, only with difficulty against Roman Catholics. Marylanders had notably lost the inclination to jibe at episcopacy as being in league with popery.

In addition to all of this, the Methodists demonstrated by their success that the Maryland climate of opinion was not favorable to extreme forms of Calvinistic predestination as a focus for the issues of salvation. Initially, this problem was not an obstacle to Maryland Baptists but would become so later. The congregation at Chestnut Ridge near Baltimore provides an example. It was formed in the 1750's under the influence of awakening sentiment and amid criticism of the confessional state. A stricter form of Calvinism prevailed, it would appear, than what John Davis brought to this church during the Revolutionary era. [68] When Duke noted in his journal how well received were Davis and his associates at Baltimore, these liberal theological considerations explained his progress. [69] In Frederick, by contrast, conservative views collided with Methodists, who rejected rigorous predestinationism. [70] Debates of other ministers with Baptists on this matter were not uncommon, even in casual Maryland. [71]

Jeramiah Moore of the Ketocten Association was one such conservative Baptist minister out of sorts with the times. He was a familiar preacher on both sides of the Potomac for more that forty years. As early as 1774 he had been stationed at Seneca, and later at Frederick and elsewhere. [72] Robert B. Semple, who had been an associate of Moore and others of the Virginia Association, wrote a memoir of those days. Among other things, he reflected upon the way rigorous Calvinistic theology had adversely affected the popularity of Baptists. The defections to Methodism had especially provoked such reflections. In the final analysis, he believed that the high Calvinism which was preached with such vehemence did not appeal to all and did not withstand the challenge from more liberal positions, in an age that lyrically spoke of freedom. [73] Yet, the counterbalance of liberal and conservative theologies within the Church brought a preaching which won many. Vitality and stability continued without any spectacular growth in numbers. That usual complaint of "deadness and lukewarmess" was made in 1773 at the Philadelphia Association and there is evidence that something was done about it in these days when a new lease on life came to minority religions. [74] When Baltimore was found to have subscribed for more Bibles than any other place in 1790, the Association clearly saw the signs of progress in Maryland Baptists. [75]

While Congregationalism, like Presbyterianism and the Baptists, was in the Calvinistic tradition, there were few adherents in Maryand. Quakers, on the other hand bear consideration here because of their numbers in Maryland and the way in which they were historically related to Calvinism and Puritanism. The evangelical spirit as described in reference to the enthusiastic preaching of the Great Awakening and prevalent during the Revolutionary era might be ascribed to Quakers analogously and with modifications. The Quakerism of George Fox in the seventeenth century, according to some historians, grew out of Puritanism in the Cromwell era. When Puritans failed to establish the godly society by force of arms, many Puritans turned to the peaceful, less-organized style which became known as Quakerism, in order to bring about the Christianization of society. Even the more simplified community of Christian church life under congregational form did not suit them. They consequently drifted farther away from original Puritan connections and even departed doctrinally from Calvinistic theology. The humble meeting house and emphasis on silent worship took root in Maryland even in the seventeenth century and Quakers continued to develop others in the eighteenth century. The direction of the evangelical impulse inherent in Puritanism took a distinctively different form which until recently has been overlooked by historians. Early in the eighteenth century greater strictness regarding membership and disengagement from concern with the state in Penn's "Holy Experiment" of Pennsylvania threatened to terminate the growth and influence that had marked Quaker presence in that province.

All the same, Quakers never lost their awareness of service to society and zeal in pursuing it without offense to their conscience.

Resolution of this conflict came about by the evangelical spirit in which they turned to philanthropy for those outside of their own religious community. They have become most famous for efforts at removing the blight of slavery from American society; but this was only one area, for they also reached out into effective works for the poor, their welfare and education. There is evidence that their necessary abstention from the war and from enthusiastic commitment to Independence for reasons of conscience, as described earlier, left their energies free to serve benevolence. The emerging Christian state in Maryland gave full scope to this inspiration, which by analogy resembled the evangelical activity of Methodists. The Revolution, therefore, was a fulfillment of this aspiration, even if their earlier decision on membership qualifications restricted any growth in numbers that would resemble the Methodist experience. Representative records of meetings show that the vitality of Quakers was enhanced by the Revolution and on their own terms they experienced moderate growth. They also enjoyed greater freedom in expressing their evangelical concern for society and benevolent efforts in its behalf. [76]

The Cecil Monthly Meetings of Kent County once complained of "The State of Society" during this period. [77] The case of a Samuel Maslin gave evidence of genuine zeal: he was censured for departing from evangelical simplicity in speech and dress and for absence from meetings. [78] Delinquents responded to admonitions and even made public confession of their failings before the meeting. [79] The stable development of congregational structure and government was further witness to the inner vitality of Quakerism in Maryland. Men were found available, qualified, and willing to become elders. [80] Support of the Cecil Meeting was so generous that it undertook in 1788 to subsidize a Chester Meeting House. [81]. In 1791 Nottingham property was acquired with the intention of further providing for Quaker growth. The Fund of the Meeting for Suffering, as its was called, made available substantial funds for building construction. [82] This fund was primarily to aid Quakers who were victims of discrimination or poverty, and secondarily for other good works and Quaker congregational needs. All of these considerations indicate a more favorable situation than it ascribed to Quakers in general before the Revolutionary period.

The Quaker official *Book of Discipline* also reflected a spirit of zeal rather than relaxation. In tune with the humanitarian impulses of the time and with their own religious tradition, Maryland Quakers were directed in 1794 to give special attention to the care and education of the poor. [83] They were reminded of temperance in drink, warned of the dangers during the vintage season, and discouraged from owning taverns. [84] The spirit of what has been called the "Middle Age of Quakerism" continued to control the official policy, admitting of no mitigation in the demands set down by the Book of Discipline of 1759. The provision on membership requirements prevented any outburst of proselytizing, such as Methodism experienced during the Revolutionary period. "Birthright membership" was emphasized. The evangelical austerity of members was exactly scrutinized by monthly meetings. [8f]

The psychology of Quaker appeal in these days, then, was circumscribed and limited the possibility of conversions. It affected non-Quakers in a different way. Garrettson, for example, was drawn by something more than curiosity to Quakers. He conversed with them and read their books. But, he concluded, "it appeared to be too easy a way for me," which would seem to say he found no impulse to proselytizing in Quakerism—a religious feeling quite common at this time, as Methodism itself showed. [86] Duke noted that Quaker simplicity and austerity awakened no resentment, even as found in exaggerated form among Shakers in Maryland. This group originated in a Quaker revival of 1747 and grew in America during the Revolutionary era, practicing communal life and celibacy. Duke told of the other extreme of the movement. "They have emancipated themselves," he wrote, "from the formalities of Quaker-dress, and probably can be as pleasant as other people, upon the subject of silent meetings and the movings of the Spirit." [87] These people of West River were shortly before the war less sophisticated about their faith and more faithful in attending meetings. "But opulence has metamorphosed them," Duke believed. [88] It is revealing that there was this type of adherence to Quaker faith, however imperfect it may have been in the eyes of some, and that it held a greater openness to society by more moderate requirements.

With such a varied impression and interpretation of Quaker belief, members continued to be retained, and others arrived with each generation. Adult conversions may not have been in striking numbers as a general rule, but there is one example at Easton, in Talbot County, where one hundred at one time became Quakers. A sect called Nicolites in that vicinity came under the influence of a Friend meeting there, which was distinguished in the person of Mary Barry, a member who did much for the manumission of slaves. [89] The austere manner and simplicity of worship logically inclined Nicolites to this decision, but it was indicative of Quaker vitality in the Eastern Shore that the conversion came in the wake of the Revolutionary War.

While all of these considerations support the conclusion that there was vitality and progress during this period, there were others which explain why this was limited in a way not found in other denominations, particularly among Methodists. One of these was the severity of marriage discipline. Monthly meeting records are filled with instances where members were expelled or otherwise disciplined for departing from the ideal union between Quakers solemnized in the meeting house. "For want of giving heed to the Dictates of Truth," condemnation of one woman read, "which would have Preserved her from Evil [she] has so far deviated as to Let out her Effections on a man not in membership with us and accomplished marriage by the assistance of a Priest therefore for the Clearing of the truth and Our society we Disown her from being a member thereof untill her future Conduct may Condem Same and she make Suitable Satisfaction to Friends. . . ." [90] Condemnations were recorded [91] which in some cases were not marriages before a priest. [92] Where marriage to a Catholic was involved the fact seemed to have been specifically noted, and the same would seem to be true with regard to a Catholic priest as distinct from the general designation *priest,* which probably referred to an Episcopal minister of a marriage ceremony. [93] The whole situation could not but be an occasion of membership leakage. In the several instances, for example, where Quakers married Catholics before a priest, they would not likely be inclined to return, even though Catholic discipline did not require acceptance of its faith by both parties for such marriages. [94] Strict Quakers required more than this. The Catholic party that had sufficient influence to prevail in the choice of a Catholic marriage ceremony would not likely meet subsequent Quakers requirement to join the faith of the spouse. There was further loss in this situation, since the children would not become Quakers. Neither Catholic nor Quaker discipline made this likely. In fact, children from such a mixed Quaker and Catholic marriage had to await the time when they would come of age and then petition it themselves. The alternative to this, according to practices at Cecil Monthly Meeting, seemed unlikely, for both parents must petition acceptance of their children by the Meeting. [95]

Another social situation important to Quakerism during the Revolutionary period was slavery, which—unlike its marriage rule—became a source of gain in numbers and influence as well as loss. Even before the humanitarian impulse of the times began to stir in other denominations, Quakers had already been crusading. In 1768, after a series of meetings at Third Haven on the Eastern Shore and at West River on the Western Shore during the preceding years, the Baltimore Yearly Meeting required the manumission of slaves for membership in Quakerism. [96] A committee began in 1772 to implement this decision. In 1776 it was entered in the Book of Discipline and was renewed again in the 1794 version. Moreover, legislation in 1778 forbade Quakers from hiring slaves where an overseer would receive the money for their labor. [97]

It was not hard to understand how the heroic implementation of these decisions won the respect of Negro slaves. The growing number of Whites who were responding to the humanitarian implication of political natural rights were also impressed. In the year of the Declaration of Independence certificates of emancipation were being made out. [98] There also seems to have been assistance to Blacks from the resources of the Committee on Suffering at this time. [99] Ten years later one finds references to a special committee for Negroes. [100] Quakers were always concerned with the subsequent lot of the slave and in some cases on the Eastern Shore undertook large-scale hiring of those who were manumitted. The rapid increase of manumission was said to be a great force in putting an end to the slave trade. [101] The faith which inspired such acts of justice and charity undoubtedly won acceptance of Quakerism among large numbers of the manumitted. Such an outcome seemed likely, for example, when a Prince George's County Quaker emancipated forty-two of his plantation. Yet, difficulties with manu-mission and emancipation were the subject of much controversy at yearly meetings between 1785 and 1792. [102] Many masters lost their membership, but there is reason to believe that these were offset by a harvest among Blacks, and Whites espousing the idealism of emancipation.

The Quaker attitude toward government also limited their influence, attractiveness and growth. As early as 1689 they were advised by their *Book of Discipline* to avoid controversies, "to give no offense, or occasion to those in outward government. . . ." [103] Circumstances emerging from the Revolutionary War, where this was applied, created a problem in the social status of Quakers which Presbyterians, Baptists and Catholics did not experience. The Quakers' whole inclination was to draw back from the exercise of public and political leadership, "to submit to the divine power, which rules over the kingdom of men. . . ." [104] Thus political prestige passed through their hands to other denominations. Appeal to new members consequently was not based on any religious identification possessed of patriotic overtones, as was the case with Presbyterians and others. The earliest discipline restricting political life continued and was upheld in the 1794 version. [105] In fact, if one considers the oath and declaration requirement of the Maryland law, it was not until the 1790's that Quakers would seem to be able to hold office. Evidently, through lack of initiative and political leadership among them these oversights were not corrected until that time. [106] Quakers, then, were not able to play a prominent role in the creation of the Christian state at the political level. Nor was a type of evangelical zeal to be displayed in proselytizing and forming new congregations as Methodists did. If this was a limitation, it should be placed along side of the great social impact of their evangel of emancipation and works of benevolence for the poor. In this light Quakers were reflecting in a distinctive way a general picture of vitality in the Christian state and society that the Revolution brought about.

In the United Brethern, and to a lesser extent in the Moravians, the evangelical impulse outstanding in the Methodist experience found place in the German communities in Maryland. German Lutheran Church life in general, however, was not directly concerned with the same evangelical spirit as expressed in these groups according to the tradition of the Great Awakening. Yet it is important to see that the Lutheran aspiration was furthered during the Revolutionary era and that the war and independence helped them cope with problems unresolved before that time. In general the emerging Christian state provided them a better environment for their idealism and the church was strengthened.

Maryland Lutherans owed their original foundations to the Ministerium of Pennsylvania, which was established by the Hanoverian immigrant, Henry Muhlenberg (1711-1787), in 1748. By the time the Revolution was over Maryland Lutheranism possessed in this foundation an effective means of stable growth, as seen in the ministerium's control over the training and placement of clergy. Candidates were examined and voted upon with great care; instances of serious offense in ministers led to dismissal. [107] Maryland drew its ministry from this solid source and from time to time Muhlenberg, the patriarch of American Lutheranism, made supervisory visits. The swift and disorderly course of events in the 1770's and early 1780's did not prevent Maryland Lutherans from successfully organizing their congregations. Duke had no doubt of the large numbers of Germans who had come into the western part of Maryland in the eighteenth century, which he said was "chiefly inhabited by Germans." [108] Available statistics of Lutheran records and the evidence of small numbers among other German pietist sects make it clear that people of this stock were largely Lutheran. [109] The number of congregations grew and so did their membership. As early as 1773 four were found in the vicinity of Canegoschick. [110] Even under the difficult circumstances of 1779 Maryland was represented at the synod of that year in Pennsylvania; one of the delegates being Fredererick Muhlenberg, the son of Henry. [111] Hagerstown provided evidence of this vitality and growth when it became an established congregation at this time. Jung, its representative at the Philadelphia Synod in 1781, told of the great need for readers and ministers among Lutherans in this part of the state, where the growing membership required them. It is noteworthy of progress that a minister from these parts was asked to give the opening sermon to the synod of the following year. [112] A pastor had been stationed at Frederick as early as 1772; and after serving Baltimore as a visiting minister for several years, Zion Church, Baltimore, was finally established in 1785 with its own minister. [113] New congregations came into existence again in the latter 1790's. Petitions for ministers were made before this, but for the first time in several years a group of four were granted in 1797. [114]

There was nothing sensational in this, as there was not in the earlier period of growth. [115] However, the church was clearly progressing in the Revolutionary period, and a token of this fact is found in the convening of a major synod at Baltimore in 1797, while Hagerstown was on that occasion striving to bring the body to Western Maryland the following year. [116] In the assessment of progress one properly puts considerable value on improvement of church organization, for membership statistics of the ministerium were not regularly reported and the meaning of categories such as "communicants" not always exact. The tendency for some figures to decline, as in the case of Hagerstown, also has an explanation in the creation of new congregations which included members from the older ones. [117] It is more indicative, for example, that the new congregation of Middletown's confirmations and communicants increased by more than thirty-five per cent in a single year, shortly after its establishment. [118] A clear leveling-off of such statistics in Baltimore in the 1790's tells how a final division of congregations in an area has been made; and how real loss of membership from the whole church cannot be inferred from loss to a newly created congregation. New congregations continued to be formed, showing a process of growth and progress.

Equally evident with these signs of progress in Maryland Lutheranism was the recurring fact of tension and conflict. While the causes of these were not always clear, the fact revealed an important condition of religion during the Revolutionary period, in which there was a general striving after liberty in a multitude of forms. The most evident feature of these various chapters of local history was the power of the membership of the congregation in determining who should be their pastor.

As early as 1770 Baltimore made complaints against its pastor. [119] Two years later they were sent another man as replacement, who had experienced a similar fate at Canegoschick. [120] Although both men resided at Frederick during this period, the incidents showed that a vocal group could evidently exert strong influence in the removal of pastors. When Baltimore Zion Church was established in 1785, the first resident minister was charged with lying, drunkenness, and stinginess, and this probably occasioned his removal in favor of Daniel Kurz. Kurz, who had earlier been removed from Canagoschick under complaint, also became a target of criticism at Baltimore; but in this case it proved unfounded, or at least unsuccessful. [121]

At Frederick, a disagreement among the members of that congregation led to an arrangement whereby two pastors ministered to the church. Immediately before this incident, Jung—a minister who had been found in good standing by the ministerium—was dismissed as a result of pressure from the congregation. In 1788 many again complained of the next incumbent named Krug. [122] The ministerium tended to attribute responsibility for the new dissatisfaction to "the disordered state of the congregation itself" and sympathized with his declining health. It was decided in 1793 that Krug should stay on but that the father of Kurz should minister as a visitor from Baltimore. The ill effects of these disorders may have been reflected in the fact that the congregation was not represented in the ministerium in some of the years following this settlement. [123]

When Jung, whom Krug had replaced at Frederick, went to Hagerstown, the congregation found him very satisfactory, but apparently he was not satisfied. His departure for Virginia shortly after 1787, brought a ten-year period of unsettled conditions for that group. A temporary successor soon left for York, Pennsylvania. [124] It would seem that at this juncture a man named Carpenter could not satisfy all parties, and the church had a period when it was dependent upon visiting pastors from Pennsylvania and Baltimore. In 1794 things had not proven much better as far as pastoral care was concerned, since the congregation was petitioning the services of a minister who had experienced difficulties in another place. [125] These problems over ministers may have explained the decline in communicants noted previously, or they may also have indicated adverse qualities in the clergy. It would seem safer, however, to ascribe it to the peculiar force of congregational power in a form which was emerging among Maryland Lutherans. One does not feel that revolutions in the congregations during this period were out of sorts with the times but rather a manifestation of them. Lay authority provided a force for reform, even if it failed at times in the direction it took. The democratic spirit of the Revolution was itself involved in this dilemna, which it resolved in favor of federal power in 1789.

Using the term *evangelical* in an analagous sense, as was done in the case of the Quakers, the broader base of Lutheranism possessed a kind of revivalistic spirit during the Revolutionary era. It is noted that in Moravian and United Brethern activities among them, the Great Awakening was being renewed among a significant number. But even beyond this, the intensification of lay activity in the life of the church in the democratic spirit of the times showed signs of a genuine religious movement at work. If one considers another facet of this impact of secular trends, the condition becomes clearer. Historians agree that at least some nationalism was stirring and taking shape during this era. It had more immediate implications for these people recently arrived from Europe or being one generation removed from immigrant status. From this particular standpoint a general picture becomes clear. In their increasing contact with people of English stock, German Lutherans became aware of their ethnic diversity and sought through their church life to narrow the division. Pressure from English-speaking Marylanders prompted this. Several sources bring to the surface some of the psychological evidence of this condition.

It is well to represent the English mentality which German Lutherans confronted in the emerging Christian state of Maryland. William Duke in his usual candid and probing manner revealed, somewhat autobiographically, his own Englishman's reaction. He had traveled through the heartland of Maryland German country and experienced their hospitality. All the same, the appreciation for these people did not offset that common play of national feeling so real to the social process of what is now called the Early National period. "Their seriousnessess," he remarked, "is as much owing to their national gravity, as to a sense of divine things." He is loath to grant much influence to the divine.

"They attend upon religious duties more seriously than other societies of equal age and worldly interest." "Very few," he said with reservation, "are not gradually reduced by these two circumstances, to that indifference and stupidity, in which religion first found them." [126] The feelings of national pride in Duke and the uneasiness it must have produced in the immigrants are not hard to imagine. The spur to become "Americanized" was evident. Those given to less reflection than Duke must have also experienced the conflict of nationality. Thomas Haskins, for example, found Germans "a loving simple people, but of great warmth of passion. . . ." [127] That warmth was displayed in congregational disputes.

One of the clearest ways in which Lutherans responded to American nationalism was found in their policy for increasing the number of clergymen. Germany had trained and bred the first ministers of Lutherans in Maryland. This seemed likely to continue, since the European stamp would not allow of self-made native American preachers becoming ministers, as Methodists were inclined to permit. In answering the early petitions for ministers the tendency was to look to Germany and its long-established schools. [128] William Kurz, however, who with his son served as ministers in Baltimore, was something of a compromise version of adherence to the older tradition of training. His education began at Halle and was completed in America under Henry Muhlenberg. [129] Others would take all of their training in this Lutheran version of Tennant's "log cabin college." Kurz in time saw his own son pass his theological examinations and ordained to the ministry on American soil. The great landmark of this transition to a native clergy came with the foundation of Franklin College in 1784. [130]

The counterpart of this rising feeling of nationality in the laity centered in the movement for English-speaking schools. "In Friedrischtadt [Frederick, Maryland]," Krug told the Ministerium in 1795, "there was a German school with 40 or 50 children, and in his country congregations several smaller schools;" but Krug also complained that many parents prefer to send their children to English schools. [131] The distress and tension of Krug's position was seen in his request for a new American order of things to replace that in which he himself was reared. In 1796 Hagerstown proudly registered that it had one English school and Baltimore complained that it had none. The following year, however, Baltimore had joined the movement in education which was being carried forward by the growing spirit of nationalism in Maryland. [132] The nostalgic feeling for recollections of Halle and its traditions was receding; the passing thought of loyalty to the Hanoverian benefactor had long ago been forgotten.

In the decades preceding the Revolution, many Germans came to Maryland. They were predominantly in the Lutheran, rather than the Calvinistic tradition, and established settlements in the northwestern quarter of Maryland. During the Great Awakening itinerant preaching among them created an evangelical reform group. In some cases this movement originated in Europe. This was the case with the Moravians, who came among German Lutherans in the Monocacy Valley in 1749. Already organized as a society, some of their preachers such as Jasper Payne and Christian Frolich evangelized the area, bringing many Lutherans into Moravian congregations. The firmest foundations were found at Graceham. Although the war created special problems for these religious people, the emerging Christian state and its constitution fulfilled their aspiration. As with the Quakers, however, they chose to stand by strict membership requirements and in general departed from the wide preaching and evangelical conversion that characterized the period of the Great Awakening. [133]

The Moravian journalist Amadaeus Thrane wrote: "We live in a country, where various opinions are to be found, on behalf of which men are ready to go to the limit . . . for conscience sake." Because Marylanders fought the war from conviction, they did not force conscientious Moravian pacifists to join them, as has been shown above. A number of Moravian volunteers for the Continental Army who were not strict pacifists relieved the pressure of public opinion and so did the reputation of Moravian hospitals during the war. [134] The Moravian demand that Christianity be recognized explicitly in the state constitutions was another way in which they found satisfaction in Maryland political life. [135] Moreover, they had personally experienced the benevolence of one of the Maryland constitution-makers, Charles Carroll of Carrollton, who had originally given them property for a chapel and otherwise cooperated in land arrangements for Moravian settlements. [136] The unusual requirement for a Moravian town won recognition from the assembly which provided for its legal incorporation. [137]

It was not strange that Moravian-American roots went deeper under these conditions. The need for this became evident during the war, when they experienced how difficult it was to retain ecclesiastical ties with Europe and depend on her to supply their clergy. A representative to a European synod was prevented for there years during the war from returning to America. [138] Located as they were among German people who were involved in a similar process of nationality adjustment, they were saved much of the distress of transition during these difficult, formative years. The reception of their minister John. F. Schlegel by other denominations was indicative of this favorable circumstance. [139] The choral aspect of their worship, distinctive of their European culture, attracted Americans of all national stocks to their churches, particularly at Christmas services. [140]

The upshot of all these favorable conditions, however, was not a widely scattered growth such as the Methodists experienced. Although this conceivably could have taken place in some degree, Moravians were more determined to deepen their vitality within rather than disseminate it. This tendency developed only during the war and in contrast to the Great Awakening preaching of Jasper Payne and Christian Frolich. [141] Just before the Revolution Joseph Powell resided as minister at Carroll Manor, but the main hardship during the ten years following his return to Pennsylvania in 1772 was the absence of a resident minister. The stability of the Church was maintained, however, helped in great measure by the ministrations of the distinguished John Ettwein. [142] The pattern of preaching and membership growth between 1749 and 1779 was about to change. During this period a liberal interpretation of the meaning of full membership played an important role in the spread of Moravianism outside of Nazareth and Bethlehem, Pennsylvania, and accounted for the growth in Maryland. The Ministers Conference of August 5, 1779, at Lititz, Pennsylvania, however, reversed this trend and put emphasis on internal discipline through stricter demands on full members. Formerly itinerants such as Payne and Frolich "awakened" persons and formed them into societies after a brief experience of Moravian preaching. Such groups could no longer be regarded as properly prepared to become congregations. "Membership in these societies," it was declared, "does not at all carry with it communicant membership or preparation for it." [143] The earlier appeal to Germans resembled the Methodist type of evangelization and would not be found after the war.

The effect of the 1779 decision on the quality of Moravian growth in Maryland was revealed in the period following the Peace of Paris. Between 1784 and 1790 Graceham's congregation grew from 136 to 209. However, of that total perhaps no more than half were communicants or full-fledged members. There were other signs of this type of intensified growth in quality rather than numbers. Suitable provisions were made for a church and even an expensive organ. [144] By 1797 a brick school house was in operation with seventy-five students enrolled within ten years. [145] From all of this it cannot be concluded that the Revolutionary War and the spirit of this period adversely affected Moravians and other pietests like them in the Monocacy Valley and elsewhere in Maryland. That the times affected their growth in this particular way was their own choice. "Had Ettwein and his associates received a freedom of operation," one critic of the 1779 policy decision noted, "even measurably corresponding to that enjoyed by Asbury and Coke, or Seabury and White and Provost, the future of the Moravian Church in America would have assumed a different form." Surely the free methods of the itinerant Garrettson and others suited the movement of the times. "The tendency to ultra-concentration in the Moravian Church," on the other hand, "caused it to ignore the boundless opportunities in America. . . ." [146] But there are assumptions here which Moravians of this time did not accept.

There were other evangelical sects which also derived from Central European sources. Mennonites, for example, were in a condition similar to Moravians. They would seem somewhat less favorably situated, however, in view of their stricter pacifist position on war. [147] German Baptists, Dunkers, and other such groups, now archaic terms but then found in assembly records, were not inclined toward the severer legalism of the Mennonites. Out of this trend of European pietism transplanted in Maryland came the United Brethren under the leadership of Philip Otterbein (1726-1814). He did not "ignore the boundless opportunities in America." Unlike the Moravians, the Brethren avoided "ultra-concentration" by taking on the pastoral methods of the Methodists and with some of their success. They also followed the theology of Wesley as it related to evangelical Christianity, for Otterbein rejected the reprobation doctrine of the more orthodox Calvinists. It is not surprising, then, that the United Brethren had an effect among German Lutherans which Methodists had among other Marylanders in the Calvinist of Anglican traditions.

Otterbein came to America from Dillenburg, Germany, in 1752 as a member of the German Reformed Church. In 1768 he became associated with another German evangelist, Martin Boehm; and together with six laymen eventually formed in 1789 the beginnings of the United Brethren of Christ, which officially came into existence in 1800 at the First Annual Conference. The whole process was an evolution away from those characteristics which have been seen in the Moravians. [148]

Conditions of the Revolutionary period in Maryland played no small part in these developments, which manifested a type of growth not found in other pietist sects in Maryland at this time.

Otterbein's society during this period began to display that power of multiplying congregations, which characterized the Methodists and which Moravians had given up. Indeed, Francis Asbury and other Methodists played an important role in the formation of what became the United Brethren denomination. "They agreed," Asbury wrote in 1774 of Otterbein and Benedict Schope, his Baltimore associate, "to imitate our methods as nearly as possible." [149] The reason for this may have been emulation on Otterbein's part, who saw that the German Reformed groups were not experiencing the growth with he ambitioned, and was even found to be losing members to other denominations. [150] The itinerant method was taken up and less emphasis was put upon theological differences, while putting aside the teaching of rigorous Calvinism. Asbury saw large numbers in the German Lutheran Church, particularly in Frederick County. [151] It was clear how Otterbein might work within this denomination as Methodism had done within the Church of England. The times more and more lent themselves to such revolutionary activities, even leading Otterbein's followers to an independent existence, as had happened with Methodism.

The possibilities of growth and independence were borne out as the period went on. Zealous disciples such as George A. Geeting carried the spirit of this enlivened gospel into the area around Antietam. As early as 1774 six such ministers came together and within fifteen years rules of faith and discipline had been drafted, so well had their hopes succeeded. The regularity of these meetings produced the good results which led to the establishment of the United Brethren of Christ. It was also significant that four years before this there was legal incorporation of Otterbein's Church in Baltimore, from which the original inspiration developed on the eve of the Revolution. Unlike the Lutherans, the ethnic and language factors operated to achieve these results. There was reason to believe that Otterbein would have joined with the Methodists had he not adhered to the preference for preaching in German, which Methodists tried to discourage. After the first wave of nationalism had moderated, Otterbein restored the "German" prefix to the official title of his church in Baltimore. At the same time, these folk of German and other non-English stock did not lose the respect of Methodists in maintaining their cultural identification, which had thus proved a factor in creating their autonomy. [152]

Because the Great Awakening impulse has been described so fully in historical scholarship it has been useful to relate these understandings analogously to denominations and groups not strictly within its theological framework nor the strict unity that has been found by historians heretofore in the movement. This approach emerges on the broader ground of what might be called a general revival or vitalization of religion, in some cases different from the Great Awakening form. It is in this setting that two religious elements in Maryand can best be understood during the revolutionary era. In the first place the provision for profession of Christianity by office holders and other features of the Christian state cannot be understood as an attack on Judaism. By legislative action, a Jew could become qualified to hold office without an affirmation of Christianity. [153] The same was not possible for an open professor of atheism or infidelity. To take one's stand with Diderot in a general attack on Christianity, not only put one outside the ranks of those free to participate in the Christian state but made him a target of zealous attacks by professors of the various denominations. Indeed the provisions on Christianity in the Maryland Constitution were there largely intended to keep such persons from influence. Marylanders felt justified in this by the militancy of professors of infidelity, which threatened to subvert the religious element of their state and society if infidels usurped any branch of the government. While there undoubtedly was anti-Semitism among some citizens, Jews were not the target of the constitutional provisions but lapsed Christians. Thomas Jefferson was a popular type of such infidelity, but Elhanan Winchester, a Baptist preacher turned leader of Universalist congregations, was a more accurate example. In written message, Ethan Allen gave the fullest expression of infidelity as Maryland Christians saw it.

In terms of the religious ferment described in this and the preceding chapter, there were two sides to infidelity as a center of agitation. The natural law impulse behind the American Revolution and the exaltation of reason caught hold of liberal elements within Christian congregations. Some passed beyond the minimal requirements of orthodox Christianity and into the ranks of Diderot and Winchester. The zeal of these professors of infidelity did not lag behind the orthodox and they left their mark on the latter. They made the orthodox reexamine the reasonable grounds upon which they would practice their doctrines. All of the denominations, on the other hand, were intent upon preventing among their ranks any drift in the direction of infidelity. It became a common device to label men as crypto-professors of infidelity if they espoused liberal theological positions. Infidelity also became a convenient dragon at which an attack could be launched; this enforced unity not only of denominations individually but of the Christian people collectively. [154] Their state and society was geared to meet the challenge. In this context, it is clear that the degree of infidelity found in Maryland was naturally exaggerated and historians have been confused by this fact. They have often ascribed infidelity and its formal philosophical classification as Deism to men and groups who were actually Christian but attached to certain liberal positions in their faith.

There is difficulty in fixing a definition of *infidelity,* and for present purposes this need not be done exactly. Suffice it to say that at least it implies any extreme tendency away from traditional beliefs of Christianity. There would be great variety in how men viewed what was extreme. The fact, however, of religious experience in Maryland under the impact of the revolutionary period was that the notion of extreme, the name called *infidelity,* awakened a response. The response was directed against some kind of entity as though it were a religious denomination or heretical group whose emanations tainted the denominations they saw. In some cases the philosophical system of Deism seemed to embody the evil that was under assault by citizens of the Christian state. In this complex consideration, at least this can be established: that there was a general awareness and fear of infidelity; a personal experience of its influence by the clergy; and an intellectual response to it as a challenge.

The Revolution removed state religion from Maryland, and with it any restraint on those forces which worked against the formerly sanctioned articles of belief. "Infidelity on the one hand," Duke said, "and schismatic innovations on the other, as might be expected, make some use of the opportunity which the indifference of government affords. . . ." [155] Even before the Revolutionary War was over, Lewes Presbytery expressed the fear "that especially of late, infidelity and vice greatly abound. . . ." [156] Shortly before the close of the century, Baptists continued to repeat their warnings against infidelity. There is little doubt how general was the concern for infidelity and its dangers to religious life. Duke and William Smith did not think that infidelity had taken deep roots. "Such attempts." Duke said for those spreading infidelity unhampered under the new conditions without a state religion, "are not likely to succeed to any dangerous degree, whilst they are checked either by a sense of religion, or a settled attachment to a religious profession." [157] Yet he found many who were moving in the direction of infidelity. "What a vast number of people profess to be Christians without believing in the Bible," he noted in 1790. "I find these to be the most zealous opposers of sectaries and the soonest unarmed of enthusiasm." Such persons tended to dampen the reform spirit, which was clearly awakened during these days. [158] Even mild forms of scepticism could kill zeal. [159] Smith agreed with this analysis of what was considered the fact of infidelity in this incipient form. [160] These were not symptoms of an organized group professing extreme infidelity, and wielding significant influence. "It is not from such that *our Church* receives her chief Wounds," Smith said. "It is from the Luke-warmness and growing Indifference of our own professed Members who are supplied with the *Word and Doctrine,* but know not how to value the Things that belong to our Peace until they are now almost hid from our Eyes!" [161] Increase of *potential* infidelity, then, did not imply that extreme infidelity was making inroads during this period. Rather, it was a manifestation of tepidity, just as more crass forms of delinquency were. Infidelity promised to be an effect rather than a cause.

The result of this appraisal was to make infidelity of this type a single object of the total pastoral effort. The revival of religious earnestness, now so evident in the denominations, through zealous preaching and teaching would prevent infection. Infidelity outside the churches served in its extreme form to be a stimulus to these exertions. Asbury, for example, did not avoid preaching to a "deistical" congregation as part of this routine itinerancy. [162] Duke made careful distinctions between those who manifested a tendency of infidelity in practice from the less commonly found theoretical professor of infidelity. The former, he found, came under routine pastoral care and the latter by God's special grace could also be helped. [163] Coke cited a personal experience of this latter instance. [164] One cannot help but feel, in addition, that persons with a somewhat secular turn of mind but of solid religious belief were not entirely understood when they discouraged measures of religious zealots to control public morality. Some of these may have been mistakenly branded professors of infidelity.

Much of the fighting spirit aroused against infidelity during this period was due to the clergy's own personal experience of its attacks. At various points in his journal throughout the revolutionary period, Duke noted his own effort at a synthesis of reason and faith. He read Voltaire and entered passing criticisms of the philosophe. [165] Other

Episcopalians such as Addison and Jackson discussed their reading of the Universalist Elhanan Winchester. [166] A Methodist of simple belief like Richard Whatcoat was not above feeling "a strong conflict between faith & belief." [167] Even crotchety Boucher felt such soul stirrings as these and dared to describe them. [168] Out of these personal experiences of leaders of the denominations came a crusading spirit against the evil abstraction of extreme infidelity and its visible emanations. "The Influence of rational religion on the Interests of Society," Bishop Claggett wrote, "has effects on the eternal happiness of mankind, & these Sacred Obligations we have come under, All call loudly upon us (especially at this time) to exert every nerve in its [Society's] service." [169] Duke held up the "easy rational Firmness of Mind" of certain adherents of infidelity as a challenge to the true Christian. [170] As the war against the enemy England was drawing to a close, the Lewes Presbytery demanded the "utmost exertions to baffle the malignant deism of infidelity," urging all "to unite in this great design of discountencing deism . . . [171] Baptists at the same time warned that the religious goals of a true Christianity lay beyond "notional religion" and called forth pursuit of "experimental knowledge of Christ [that] can bring us to heaven" [172] "The increase of *Arianism* and *Socianianism* throughout Christendom," Thomas Coke told the assembled Methodist Christmas Conference of 1784, "is so manifest to every close observer, that it calls for the greatest exertions from the true lovers of the Lord Jesus, to stop the growing plague." [173] Francis Asbury surely met that call. "I was led to strike at Deism," he wrote of one occasion when there was only one professed Deist present in his audience. He spoke on the text of St. John's Gospel 7:17 about learning that was according to God. On another occasion he took Romans 8:7 as his text in dealing obloquy on that natural wisdom which was perversely put at odds with God. Asbury's evangelical approach thus seemed to judge the tree by the fruit of observance of the law. He did not always relish such combat, but he continued with such attacks as the times demanded. [174]

The vigilance thus awakened manifested itself in the supervision of the clergy. Lutherans carefully examined candidates on their preparedness to deal with the objections of rationalists. [175] The Catholic priest John Carroll once censured a fellow clergyman for his views of infidelity. [176] The Lewes Presbytery rejected a Dutch Reformed minister seeking affiliation with them, because his views were too similar to those of the Deist Priestley. All candidates were examined on such

matters. [177] Positive efforts were also made by an initiation of beneficial intellectual activity. Bend, for example, was stimulated to read
Newton. "His dissertations are an almost inexhaustible fund of knowledge," he wrote enthusiastically to Duke, "well able to confirm believers, & to convince gain-sayers ... I wish I could prevail upon
our Free - Thinkers to read him." [178] He wrote to the sober Thomas Claggett with excitement and a revealing mock seriousness:
"I send you by this opportunity "B'p Ogden's . . . answer to Thomas
Paine, which I hope may help to preserve you from apostatizing . . ." [179]
Such remarks revealed that there was no grim crisis such as hortatory
literature of those days and Enlightenment scholars of our own tend
to attribute to these times. Asbury had humor enough to read Tobias
G. Smollett whose fiction satirized his own brand of Christianity. "I
have thought it may be I am safer to be occasionally among the people
of the world," he noted while reading Thomas Jefferson, "than wholly
confined to the indulgent people of God. He who sometimes suffers
from a famine will the better know how to relish a feast." [180] A more
constructive side of this encounter with infidelity was seen in Duke.
He saw certain valid elements in it which could be harmonized with
traditional Christianity. [181] William Smith spoke somewhat lyrically of
this realization Duke so much desired:

> A time will come when whatever is intemperate and new-
> fangled in Religion will be done away, or lost and swallowed up
> in *Christian Charity* and those who have been tossed upon the
> Ocean of Doubt and Uncertainty, will again seek for Rest and
> Comfort in the Bosom of the true Church of Christ. [182]

There were certain clear lines of intellectual growth produced in
religious thought under the challenge of infidelity when the Revolution
released it upon the scene in Maryland. "Such an unlimited Toleration," John Carroll remarked shortly after the Peace of Paris, "giving
open Field to the Display of Truth and fair Argument may greatly
contribute to bring mankind to an unity of Opinion on matters of
religious Concern." [183] This attitude, in a sense, undid the premise of
many extreme infidels, that Christianity will not willingly examine the
objections against it. The new experience of natural knowledge was
viewed by Carroll as potentially compatible with and supplemental to
Christianity. Finally, Christianity had not killed curiosity, even if some
Christians had done this in times past. Duke surely provided an
example of what Carroll meant on this point. When he explored with

a Presbyterian the problem of predestination, he spoke with reverence of "every acquisition of real science;" he inveighed against superstition in Swedenborg, carried on constructive theological controversy among his denominational associates. [184] This inquiring and critical spirit applied itself to the creative new experience of the revolutionary generation, exploring the new dimensions of Christian belief. In the case of nearly all of the denominations it has been shown how they probed into the divine character of the Church. They adjusted to the situation of a new state created out of the Revolution, providing it an intellectually Christian dimension.

The reflections of White and Carroll in this era were in some measure brilliant, passing in depth beyond the romantic over-simplification of secularistic terms, to a profound grasp of both an ancient church and an emerging society. The problem of the nature of man concerned Duke, and his journal revealed that the divine inspiration of scripture was being analyzed in the light of these new considerations. At one point he subjected Hume to an uncomfortable analysis on the consequences of the English philosopher's concept of cause and effect. [185] There were instances where Asbury succeeded with converts from Episcopalianism by his views on predestination. [186] This same topic was under extensive examination by those of the Calvinistic theological traditions and was widely discussed in Maryland. [187] Everywhere "enthusiasm in religion" was debated in terms of an alternative that seemed to lead to infidelity. [188] Adjustments of concepts led to a richer theological understanding and Christian practice. The attacks of infidelity arising out of the new liberty of the day provoked reflection on all of these major problems of Christianity and in this way indirectly contributed to the vitality of the denominations and Christianity generally.

This intellectual response was manifested in yet another way when some leaders ordered their reflections toward a synthesis. Thomas Coke's sermon to the Methodist Christmas Conference of 1784 provides a good example of the fruits of such integrated reflection. "No man" he said "is obliged to believe what he cannot comprehend." Yet this did not force him to give up the mysteries of Christian doctrine. "The incomprehensibility of the mystery lies not in the *reality* or truth of the thing," he explained, "but in the *mode* of its existence." He would remind his contemporaries of a knowledge that was higher than science. There were those truths which men with faith possessed in a far higher form (or "mode") in God. In such ways a synthesis of faith and reason was at work in these times. [189] Reflections were found in less formal philosophers, such as Haskins among Methodists. [190] Similarly, William Smith found consolation not only in Christianity but also in "Reason and the Nature of Things." [191] John Carroll's education had proceeded in terms of conscious synthesis. [192] There was abundant evidence of synthesis at work in Duke who applied it to the lowest levels of intelligence in his church. "Religion," he wrote in his journal, "seems to have been [the] repository and conservator of learning and to employ it for the promotion of infidelity seems to be a species of parricide no less criminal than the most heinous violation of humanity . . . Hence I can't avoid thinking several of our modern deists as deficient in gratitude as they are in faith." Without being an iconoclast or source of scandal to the less educated, he opposed superstition and encouraged a greater role for reason in the life of religion. His careful objections against the positions of infidelity gave grounds for doubt among "infidels" more than equal to what these had sought to sow among the faithful. [193] Duke carefully applied the spirit of synthesis to those whom he taught. "I should adopt a medium between the two," he wrote regarding the extremes of intellectualism and pietism, "that children might be instructed both rationally and religiously, and furnished both with a form of sound words to rule their opinions, and a deep sense of divine things to govern their temper." [194]

All of these considerations teach that the amorphous religious entity known in these times as infidelity and Deism cut across all of the denominations without being a denomination and without the deleterious effect sometimes noted by writers of the times and afterwards. As an abstraction, infidelity alarmed and awakened zeal. So it was used by leaders of the day. It likewise provoked reflection. In turn these cultural elements spurred vitality and growth which have been noted in varying degrees in the denominations of Maryland. This conclusion conflicts with current generalizations about the inroads of infidelity, Deism, rationalism, republican religion, and liberalism during the revolutionary period. [195] One answer would be to point out the weakness of these generalizations on the basis of their confusion of terms. Deism was a systematic school of thought, but liberal theology was ever present in the historic Christian Church and in its denominations. Hence liberal Christians were not necessarily Deists. [196] The case is all the more true in regard to infidelity.

A second answer to the difficulty could be directed at the monographs which have given rise to these estimates of Deism commonly reflected in general studies. In addition to confusion in the use of terms, these monographs have not been comprehensive in the way general studies would lead one to believe. Herbert M. Morais in his *Deism in the Eighteenth Century* has drawn his material from the Middle States. Neither in this study nor that by Adolph Koch has Maryland provided evidence.[197]

Finally, the type of sources employed in the present study stresses the professional eyewitnesses of religion in their more personal observations. Morais and Koch, on the other hand, make proportionately greater use of tracts, newspapers, and magazines. On these scores, then, generalizations on the inroads of Deism do not stand proven in reference to Maryland. Evidence stands to the contrary.

REFERENCES

[1]Leonard J. Trinterud, *The Forming of an American Tradition* (New York, 1949), pp. 162-63, 153.
[2]*Ibid.*
[3]Claggett to Butler, Sep. 19, 1769, in Utley, p. 24.
[4]Minutes of Lewes Presbytery, pp. 116-117 (Oct. 15, 1782).
[5]*Ibid.*, pp. 162, 179 (Oct. 2, 1783 and Aug. 13 and Apr. 1, 1794).
[6]Asbury, I, 153 (Apr. 2, 1775).
[7]Journal, Book I, 17 (1775).
[8]Joseph T. Smith, *Eighty Years: Embracing a History of Presbyterianism in Baltimore, with an Appendix* (Philadelphia, 1899), p. 15.
[9]*State of Religion*, p. 16.
[10]*Ibid.*
[11]Dashiell to Claggett, May 16, 1796 (Maryland Diocesan Archives).
[12]A Brief History of the Presbytery of Baltimore, 1786-1804 (Presbyterian Historical Society).
[13]Gardner, pp. 244-245.
[14]The Rise and Progress of the Presbyterian Church in Baltimore Town, 1761-1793... (Presbyterian Historical Society). See Gardner, p" 245.
[15]Alison, Presbyterian Church in Baltimore. *Laws of Maryland,* Nov. 1796, chap. lviii, records church incorporation. On membership increase, see Gardner, 256-261, which gives the list upon which the present writer's estimate is based.
[16]History of the Presbytery of Baltimore.
[17]Anon., The Rise and Progress of the Presbyterian Congregation in George Town and Frederick Town, 1793 (Presbyterian Historical Society).
[18]James W. McIlvain, *First Presbyterian Church in Baltimore,* Maryland (Baltimore, 1906).
[19]Minutes of the Lewes Presbytery, p. 225 (May 8, 1770).
[20]*Ibid.*, p. 95 (Oct. 19, 1773).
[21]*Ibid.*, pp. 36 and 111-112 (Oct. 20, 1778; Apr. 25 and June 19, 1779).
[22]*Ibid.*, p. 162 (Oct. 2, 1793).
[23]Presbytery of Lewes to General Assembly, April 1, 1794 (Presbyterian Historical Sociey).
[24]Minutes of the Lewes Presbytery (*ibid.*), pp. 166-168 (Aug. 13, 1794).
[25]*Ibid.*, p. 188 (Apr. 2, 1800).
[26]*Records of the Presbyterian Church,* p. 523 (May 22, 1786). See also Minutes of the Presbytery of Baltimore, 1786 minister list, and entry of Apr. 21, 1790, for other clergy statistics (*ibid.*).
[27]Presbyterian Congregations in George Town and Frederick Town, 1796 (*ibid.*).
[28]Sessional Records of the Presbyterian Church of Snow Hill, Maryland, 1745-1799 (*ibid.*).

[29]*Ibid.*, pp. 217-270, *et passim.*
[30]*Ibid.*, p. 48.
[31]*Records of the Presbyterian Church*, pp. 512-514 (May 23, 1785).
[32]*Ibid.*, p. 533 (May 18, 1787).
[33]*Ibid.*, pp. 532 and 500 (May 17, 1787, and May 24, 1783).
[34]Minutes of the Lewes Presbytery (Presbyterian Historical Society), pp. 115-118 (Oct. 15, 1782).
[35]*Ibid.*, p. 120 (Nov. 30, 1784).
[36]Minutes of the Presbytery of Baltimore (*ibid.*), p. 2.
[37]Minutes of the Lewes Presbytery (*ibid.*), p. 149 (Oct. 13, 1791).
[38]*Ibid.*, pp. 110-111 (June 2, 1778).
[39]*Ibid.*
[40]Records of Snow Hill (*ibid.*), p. 66 (Dec. 13, 1794).
[41]*Records of the Presbyterian Church*, p. 520 (May 19, 1786).
[42]Alison, Presbyterian Church in Baltimore (Presbyterian Historical Society).
[43]*Records of the Presbyterian Church*, p. 537 (May 26, 1787).
[44]*Ibid.*, p. 519 (May 19, 1786).
[45]Minutes of the Lewes Presbytery (Presbyterian Historical Society), p. 116 (Oct. 15, 1792).
[46]*Ibid.*, p. 135 (June 24, 1789).
[47]*Records of the Presbyterian Church*, p. 539 (May 26, 1787).
[48]Gardner, pp. 244-245.
[49]Robert A. East, *Business Enterprise in the American Revolutionary Era* (New York, 1938), pp. 164, 170.
[50]Gardner, 244-245.
[51]Duke, *State of Religion*, p. 29.
[52]*Ibid.*
[53]Trinterud, p. 53.
[54]John Asplund (ed.), *The Universal Annual Register of the Baptist Denomination, in North America* (Hanover, N. H., 1796), p. 44, in Maring, p. 8.
[55]A. D. Gillett (ed.), *Minutes of the Philadelphia Baptist Association, 1707-1807* (Philadelphia, 1851), p. 141, 1774 session.
[56]The Baltimore Church was incorporated in 1798, see *Laws of Maryland*, November 1978, chap. xxx; J. F. Weishampel, *History of the Baptist Churches of Maryland Connected with the Maryland Baptist Union Association* (Baltimore, 1885), p. 55. Joseph H. Jones, *History of the Baltimore Baptist Association* [Baltimore, 1872]) organized and used local records in Maryland dealing with early Baptist history and Weishampel gave a general presentation of this work at a later date.
[57]Weishampel, *Baptist Churches of Maryland*, p. 24.
[58]*Ibid.*, pp. 27, 55.
[59]Asplund, *Annual Register of Baptists*, p. 44, in Maring, p. 8.
[60]Robert B. Semple, *A History of the Rise and Progress of the Baptists in Virginia* [1810], G. W. Beale (ed.) (Richmond, 1894), p. 420.
[61]Weishampel, pp. 11-12; see Bend to Claggett, May, 1796, Utley, *Life of Claggett*, p. 95.
[62]*State of Religion*, pp. 18, 20.
[63]Asplund, *Annual Register of Baptists*, p. 44, in Maring, p. 8.
[64]Bend to Claggett, May 1796, Utley, *Life of Claggett*, p. 95.
[65]*Minutes of the Philadelphia Baptist Association*, pp. 267 and 226 (1790 and 1786).
[66]Weishampel, p. 14; Duke, *State of Religion*, p. 33.
[67]Duke, *State of Religion*, pp. 18, 20.
[68]Weishampel, p. 27. The terms *General* and *Particular* Baptists are not clear in application to this situation.
[69]Duke, Journal, Nov. 20, 1793.
[70]Asbury,I, 53 (Nov. 17, 1772).
[71]See Chapter VII below.
[72]Weishampel, p. 14.
[73]Semple, *Baptists in Virginia*, p. 385.

[74]*Minutes of the Philadelphia Baptists Association,* p. 255 (1790).

[75]*Ibid.,* p. 132 (1773).

[76]Sidney V. James, *A People Among People* (Cambridge, Mass., 1963), chaps. 13, 15.

[77]Kent Monthly Minutes.

[78]*Ibid.,* Feb. 13, 1788.

[79]*Ibid.,* Apr. 11, May. 9, 1787.

[80]*Ibid.,* May 14, 1788.

[81]*Laws of Maryland,* Nov. 1791, chap. vii.

[82]Kent Monthly Minutes, Aug. 10, 1785.

[83]*Discipline of Friends* (1794), p. 33.

[84]*Ibid., pp.* 37-40.

[85]Allen C. and Richard H. Thomas, *A History of the Friends in America* (Philadelphia, 1894), pp. 240-241.

[86]Garrettson, Journal, Book I(p. 17 (1775).

[87]Duke, Journal, Jan. 1, 1787.

[88]*State of Religion,* p. 16.

[89]Henry W. Wilbur, *The Life and Labors of Elias Hicks* (Philadelphia, 1910), p. 37. On Barry see St. Peter Parish, Talbot County, Report, 1797 (Maryland Diocesan Archives).

[90]Kent Monthly Minutes, Nov. 12, 1777.

[91]*Ibid.,* Nov. 8, 1788, Oct. 13, 1784.

[92]*Ibid.,* Dec. 1784 --Nov. 1786; Oct. 11, 1786.

[93]*Ibid.,* June 6, 1778.

[94]*Ibid.,* Aug. 1778; Sep. 12, 1787.

[95]*Ibid.,* Jan. 10, 1787.

[96]Thomas E. Drake, *Quakers and Slavery in America* (New Haven, Conn., 1950), pp. 65-67, 81.

[97]*Discipline of Friends* (1794), pp. 30-31.

[98]Kent Monthly Minutes. Mar. 13, 1776.

[99]*Ibid.,* Apr. 10, 1776.

[100]*Ibid.,* June to December, 1786, *passim.*

[101]St. Peter's Parish, Talbot County, Report, 1797 (Maryland Diocesan Archives).

[102]*Discipline of Friends* (1794), p. 18.

[103]*Ibid.,* p. 31.

[104]*Laws of Maryland,* Nov. 1793, chap. iii.

[105]*Discipline of Friends* (1794), pp. 31, 18.

[106]See Chapter III.

[107]Lutheran Evangelical Ministerium, *Documentary History of the Evangelical Lutheran Ministerium of Pennsylvania and Adjacent States. Proceedings of the Annual Conventions from 1748 to 1821. Compiled and Translated from Records in the Archives and from the Written Protocols* (Philadelphia, 1898), pp. 186 and 173 (1783 and 1781 sessions).

[108]Duke, *State of Religion,* pp. 32-33.

[109]See, for example, statistics for 1797, *Lutheran Ministerium,* p. 292.

[110]*Ibid.,* pp. 140-141 (1783). Hagerstown was in the Yorktown, Pennsylvania, District in 1783, as was Frederick (*ibid.,* p. 191, 1783).

[111]*Ibid.,* p. 156 (1779.

[112]*Ibid.,* p. 177 (June 1781).

[113]*Ibid.,* pp. 130-138 and 200 (1772 and 1785).

[114]*Ibid.,* p. 21 (1797).

[115]*Ibid.,* p. 287 (1796).

[116]*Ibid.,* p. 290 (1797).

[117]*Ibid.,* p. 292 (1797).

[118]*Ibid.,* p. 212, gives statistical tables for Baltimore from 1786; and p. 271, Frederick for 1794-95.

[119]*Ibid.,* pp. 130-138 (1772).

[120]*Ibid.,* pp. 142-143 (1773).

[121]*Ibid.*, pp. 200 (1785), 288 (1789), 215 (1787), 142-143 (1773).
[122]*Ibid.*, pp. 232-233 (1790), 221 (1788).
[123]*Ibid.*, pp. 262 (1793), 237 (1791), 240 (1791).
[124]*Ibid.*, pp. 214 (1787), 244 (1792), 276 (1795).
[125]*Ibid.*, pp. 240 (1791), 273 (1794), 262 (1793).
[126]Duke, *State of Religion*, p. 33.
[127]Haskins, Journal, July 17, 1783.
[128]*Lutheran Ministerium*, pp. 194-196 (1784).
[129]Lars P. Qualben, *The Lutheran Church in Colonial Times* (New York, 1940), p. 214.
[130]*Lutheran Ministerium*, pp. 210-211, 218 (1787).
[131]*Ibid.*, p. 279 (1795).
[132]*Ibid.*, pp. 285-286 (1796), 291 (1797).
[133]John T. Hamilton, p. 140; Oerter, *Transactions of Moravians*, IX, 131.
[134]Ettwein, "Short Account," in K. G. Hamilton, *John Ettwein*, p. 152. Graceham Diary, Feb. 12, 1775, and Sep. 3, 1777, in Oerter, *Transactions of Moravians*, IX, 150-153. Observances of prayer and fast for the benefit of the new government are noted frequently between 1775 and 1780.
[135]Ettwein to Towne's *Evening Post*, Sep. 26, 1776, in K. G. Hamilton, *John Ettwein*, pp. 161-162.
[136]Oerter, *Transactions of Moravians*, IX, 149.
[137]*Ibid.*
[138]J. T. Hamilton, pp. 251-252.
[139]Graceham Diary, Oct. 7, 1798, in Oerter, *Transactions of Moravians*, IX, 170.
[140]*Ibid.*, p. 162 (Dec. 24, 1795).
[141]K. G. Hamilton, *John Ettwein*, p. 197; Oerter, *Transactions of Moravians*, IX, 170.
[142]Ettwein, Journal, Sep. 21 - Oct. 17, 1774, and Sep. 3 - Oct. 29 [circa], 1784, in K. G. Hamilton, *John Ettwein*, p. 295.
[143]Quoted in J. T. Hamilton, pp. 254-255.
[144]Graceham Diary, Mary 27, 1792, Oerter, "Graceham," *Transactions of Moravians*, IX, 161 and 158.
[145]*Ibid.*, Aug. 14, 1797,pp. 166-167.
[146]J. T. Hamilton, p. 254.
[147]See Chapter II.
[148]Hardon, *The Protestant Churches in America* (Westminster, Md., 1958), pp. 108-111; Paul H. Eller, *These Evangelical United Brethren* (Dayton, O., 1950).
[149]Asbury, I, 114 (May 3, 1774).
[150]Daniel Berger, *History of the Church of the United Brethren in Christ* ("The American Church History Series," XII, 309-382; New York, 1894), pp. 331-332.
[151]Asbury, I, 53 (Nov. 17, 1772).
[152]Berger, pp. 389, 330, 333-335, and 340.
[153]Adolph Guttmacher, *History of the Baltimore Hebrew Congregation* (Baltimore, 1907), p. 21 indicates the small number of Jews.
[154]Martin Marty, *The Infidels*.
[155]*State of Religion*, p. 48.
[156]Minutes of the Lewes Presbytery, pp. 116-117 (Oct. 14, 1782). See also *Minutes of the Philadelphia Baptist Association, 1707-1807*, ed. by A. D. Gillette (Philadelphia, 1851), pp. 326-320 (1797).
[157]*State of Religion*, p. 48.
[158]Journal, Aug. 19, 1790.
[159]*State of Religion*, pp. 8-9.
[160]Convention Address, *Journal of Maryland Episcopal Conventions*, p. 32.
[161]*Ibid.*
[162]Asbury, I, Mar. 2, 1777.
[163]Duke, Journal, Jan. 30, 1787.
[164]*Extracts of Journals*, p. 112 (May 14, 1790).
[165]Duke, MS sheet (Maryland Diocesan Archives); Journal, Apr. 24, 1787, Jan. 5, 1791, and Aug. 29, 1792.

¹⁶⁶Addison to Jackson, Sep. 12, 1798 (Maryland Diocesan Archives).

¹⁶⁷Richard Whatcoat, Journal (Library of Congress, Washington, D. C.), Dec. 24, 1792.

¹⁶⁸Boucher, pp. 42-43.

¹⁶⁹Claggett to Jackson, Nov. 9, 1796 (Maryland Diocesan Archives).

¹⁷⁰Journal, Jan. 18, 1787.

¹⁷¹Minutes of the Lewes Presbytery, Oct. 15, 1782.

¹⁷²*Baptist Association*, pp. 160-161 (1778).

¹⁷³Coke, *Sermon on the Godhead*, p. 4.

¹⁷⁴*Journal and Letters*, I, 426 (June 14, 1782), 323 (Mar. 2, 1777), 199 (Sep. 11, 1776), and 97 (Nov. 23, 1773).

¹⁷⁵*Lutheran Ministerium*, p. 187.

¹⁷⁶To Plowden, Apr. 10, 1784, and Feb. 27, 1785 (John Carroll Papers).

¹⁷⁷Minutes of the Lewes Presbytery (Presbyterian Historical Society), pp. 131 (Jan. 5, 1787), 182 (Mar. 28, 1798).

¹⁷⁸To Duke, Nov. 29, 1792 (Maryland Diocesan Archives).

¹⁷⁹Bend to Claggett, July 18, 1796 (*ibid.*).

¹⁸⁰Asbury, I, 94 (Sep. 21, 1773), and 732 (Oct. 1, 1792).

¹⁸¹Duke, Journal, Jan. 30, 1787.

¹⁸²Convention Address; *Journal of Maryland Episcopal Conventions*, p. 32.

¹⁸³Carroll to Berington, July 10, 1784 (John Carroll Papers).

¹⁸⁴Journal, Apr. 11, 1791; Dec. 15, 1790; Feb. 27, 1787. Jackson to Duke, Aug. 21, 1796 (Maryland Diocesan Archives).

¹⁸⁵Journal, Jan. 5, 1776, July 28, 1792, Aug. 9, 1792, and Mar. 25, 1791.

¹⁸⁶Asbury, I, 110 (Mar. 14, 1774).

¹⁸⁷Duke, Journal, Oct. 20, 1774; *Baptist Association*, pp. 166 (1781) and 254-266 (1790).

¹⁸⁸Minutes of the Lewes Presbytery, p. 131 (Jan. 5, 1787).

¹⁸⁹*Sermon on the Godhead*, p. 4-6.

¹⁹⁰Journal, Jan. 26, 1785.

¹⁹¹Smith to Goldsborough, Jan. 17, 1791 (Maryland Historical Society); Gegenheimer, p. 206; Smith, Address to the Convention, *Journal of Maryland Episcopal Conventions*, p. 27.

¹⁹²Carroll to Plowden, Apr. 20, 1792; and Apr. 10, 1784 (John Carroll Papers).

¹⁹³Journal, Aug. 17, 23/24; July 16, 1774; and Mar. 22, 1792.

¹⁹⁴*State of Religion*, p. 46.

¹⁹⁵Evarts B. Greene, *The Revolutionary Generation, 1763-1790* (New York, 1943), pp. 110 and 369; Sweet, *American Culture*, p. 91.

¹⁹⁶For this defect in the literature on this topic see H. Shelton Smith, et al., *American Christianity: An Interpretation with Representative Documents* (2 vols.; New York, 1960), I, p. 486.

¹⁹⁷Morais, pp. 7-8, 23, 88, and 286; Koch, pp. xiv-xv.

VII

CATHOLIC EMANCIPATION

The thrust of Catholics toward independence in Maryland had much in common with their fellow Christians. Like the various traditions within Protestantism, they had a unique historical experience which set them apart from continental European Catholics. The majority of the literature on American history have taken no adequate account of the little that has been said of this feature of Catholic experience. The Maryland Catholic aspiration toward the

Christian state and society which emerged from the Revolution had a special meaning as emancipation. No religious group had been so greatly confined by discriminatory law under the confessional state of the eighteenth century in Maryland.

Catholic experience and tradition had roots in the seventeenth century both in England and in Maryland. The summation of this tradition was expressed on the eve of colonization in the apology Lord Baltimore made for his colony. Probably attributable to Andrew White as an advisor to George Calvert and his son Cecilius, this pamphlet was directed at their Virginian critics, who feared encroachment on their interests in the Chesapeake Bay country. In sum, *Objections Answered,* as the pamphlet was entitled, challenged prevailing notions regarding the confessional state. Virginians objected that there was no official religion assigned to the province over which the Calvert family would exercise its proprietership. The author in response simply commented on the confessional state's history in Europe. He pointed out that the state was ill-advised in making religious requirements of its citizens. To favor one religious group over another or to require oaths of allegiance to particular beliefs such as those found in the Thirty-Nine Articles of the Church of England, would in the end undermine religion. For then one would be religious from motives of policy rather than from conviction. The state could hope for little good from such citizens, who would not be sincerely attached to law in the matter of religion. The author of *Objections Answered* was in effect calling for equality before the law for all citizens, including non-Christians. In such a free atmosphere, the reasoning continued, a true religious life would flourish and thus provide an enduring texture to the new society that was being planted in Maryland. [1]

Traditional treatment of Maryland toleration has consistently centered in the Toleration Act of 1649, which had considerably different understandings from what was found in Lord Baltimore's pamphlet. Probably drafted under the pressure of the Puritan Revolution and the regime which it brought to power with Cromwell, this act discriminated against non-Christians and even spelled out articles of belief required of those who benefit from the act, having no doctrinal disagreement with the law. The act was therefore regarded as generally useful to assure some minumum of toleration for Christians, only a few non-Christians residing in the colony. It is significant, that following the collapse of Puritanism, the earlier more liberal provisions of the province returned, from which non-Christians benefited. Historians have generally disregarded the legal foundations for this practice of separation of church and state, which is so clearly found in *Objections Answered* but not in the Toleration Act of 1649. It is true that the Maryland Charter assures colonists that they shall not be coerced in the matter of religion; but the phrase *being Christians* loosely modifies colonists as beneficiaries. There was, therefore, some other legal basis for the broad toleration which prevailed in fact before and after the Puritan seizure of power. In this context the Toleration Act in the Maryland Ordinance of 1639 becomes of great historical importance. There was no narrowing of benefits to Christians alone in this act. It is significant that cases on toleration following the end of Puritan power in England and Maryland referred back to this act in reasoning about the freedom of the citizen. It is also true that a Jew was found to benefit from the same law. [2]

Catholics as well as Presbyterians and Quakers openly cherished this legal tradition, which they saw brought favorable growth to religious life. Their descendants in the eighteenth century always remained very conscious of these foundations. When events following the Glorious Revolution of 1688 came about in England and Maryland this climate of freedom was greatly reduced. Those who suffered most from an imposition of a confessional state and a suppression of the Toleration Act of 1639 were Catholics as bearers and protagonists of the earlier tradition of freedom. After 1689, the Church of England was established in the colony and laws were passed which kept Catholics from public office, public worship, and freedom of education. Restrictions were also placed on Catholic immigrants and Catholic children of mixed protestant and Catholic marriages. While Presbyterians, Quakers, and not a few Anglicans revered the heritage of religious freedom, Catholics as a group principally perpetuated it and longed for an emancipation from the unhappy conditions of the confessional state. Perpetuation of a Catholic aristocracy, in spite of these adversities, made possible a hardy and articulate retention of the traditions of freedom expressed in the pamphlet *Objections Answered* and the Toleration Act of the Maryland Ordinance of 1639. When Benedict Leonard Calvert conformed to the Church of England in 1714, the movement to restore the proprietary form of government succeeded. Prior to this Maryland functioned as a royal colony, once the Catholic Charles Calvert, Third Lord Baltimore, was removed as a result of the Glorius Revolution of 1688. Although the royal form of government ended, the establishment of the Church of England continued as well as restrictive legislation against Catholics which was passed during the royal period of rule. [3]

Eighteenth century Catholic life has often been called a *penal age,* in view of the colonial and Parliamentary law which discriminated against Catholics. It is not accurate, however, to equate the conditions of life with statements of written law. In the first case there is considerable evidence that this life, with all the legal restrictions, continued at a high level. The seventeenth century aristocratic families expanded their life, enhancing their inherited landed and other wealth, at times with the patronage of the Protestant Lord Proprietor. His proprietary party in Maryland was dedicated to safeguarding property generally and the gentry of whatever faith that owned it. Protestant proprietary interest at times coincided with Catholic interest, the power of the one serving the other. This was particularly true in the matter of Parliamentary statute laws. Both parties did not want to see the province bound by such laws. The Maryland Charter, they believed, freed the proprietary government and the people of the colony from such statute laws. On this principle, Catholics could escape harsh Elizabethan statutes; the proprietor and the provincial government could also claim greater autonomy and power. Out of this situation came an alliance of the Catholic community with the proprietary party. Both groups sought to soften the effect of penal laws and with some success. It is true that the period of the French and Indian War brought a double tax on Catholic property, but it was soon removed and worse provisions advocated by some were prevented, thanks to the alliance. [4]

The growth of Catholic life under these conditions must be properly described. To do so would indeed be far more a case of tribute to these proud aristocrats, than to the genteel forbearance of the proprietary party. Nevertheless the congeniality and inter-faith amity, which attained a respectable level, polished the relations of Catholics with Protestants; this would be seldom seen in the nineteenth century, when a non-English majority and leadership prevailed in Catholic life. A highly educated elite, Maryland Catholics were important members of the leadership which improved the economic life of the colony, while maintaining their own family fortunes and quality education abroad. As a formal educational institution, Bohemia Manor, on the upper Eastern Shore, conducted by Thomas Poulton, S. J., was allowed to exist in spite of the law. From here the Brents, Neales, Carrolls, Watlands and others, who would form the Catholic ranks of the Revolutionary generation, took their rudimentary training to France for what generally led to an extended intellectual experience few Americans then attained. [5]

It was not surprising, however, that their emergence from the great ferment of the French Enlightenment and its reflected glory in England left them quite different in their outlook from what had been the case with their fathers. They would no longer move comfortably in thought and feeling before the sufferance found in the old alliance with the Anglican gentry in the proprietary party. The seventeenth century tradition of freedom took an enlarged meaning for them. As the younger Protestant gentry became critical of the proprietary regime and the restrictions of the imperial government generally, young Catholic intellectuals such as Charles Carroll of Carrollton and John Carroll saw who their new allies were and how the traditional alliance must change. There quietly began an alliance with an anti-propietary party, composed of men like Samuel Chase, William Paca and Thomas Johnson, whose parents had formerly stood with the proprietor's governor against insurgents. [6] It is occasionally stated in the Carroll writings, as well as in those of their Protestant critics, that the young Maryland Catholic's experience with Jesuit schools constituted an education in republicanism. [7] Studies in recent times have brought out liberal features in the Carroll cultural environment which interacted with the Enlightenment. What made the process dynamic in the case of the young Carrolls, however, was the fusion of this stream of Catholic thought with their inherited Maryland tradition of freedom. There was consequently in the minds and hearts of these men an aspiration for a new society just as there was in the case of Chase, Paca and Johnson among the young Protestant revolutionaries. In particular, a natural-rights theory was coupled with Catholic philosophical writings on the legitimacy of revolution, so that active involvement in the movement for independence was spontaneous. There is no doubt that the Catholic gentry saw their religious emancipation as well as their political independence coming to realization in the Declaration of Independence. [8]

In addition to this legal thrust away from the confessional state and the proprietary party, a second facet should be noted in Catholic culture on the eve of the Revolution. The deepening and expansion of religious life had taken place before the French and Indian War, which was analagous to the Methodist experience in the period of the Great Awakening. Young Catholic Marylanders were introduced to writings of Bishop Richard Challoner of England; so too those of the Francis de Sales and Jean Croiset French schools of lay spirituality. Throughout the eighteenth century English-speaking Catholic clergy promoted the spiritual life of the laity with such sources, while relating them to the traditional ideas of the Spiritual Exercises of St. Ignatious. Judging from Maryland libraries and the pastoral practices of the missionaries, what is known as Devotion to the Sacred Heart of Jesus played another part in the vitalization of religious life among Catholics. Jean Croiset, known for his handbook for the Christian gentleman, was perhaps the leading exponent of this approach to holiness, which put emphasis on the humanity of Christ and the motivation of love in pursuit of salvation. Practices in Maryland regarding Eucharistic worship further indicate the influence of the devotion. [9]

There is a rich humanism found in this style of Christian spirituality. De Sales showed the gentry class how they might sanctify the normal routine of their life. He and Croiset were actually enlarging the secular idealization of gentility by a Christian dimension. Responsibility for leadership in society was thus richly motivated. The human qualities in Christ were the object of prayerful reflection by those who sought to imitate him in the tradition of Ignatian writings. It is more difficult to estimate the way in which religious culture among Catholic Marylanders was affected by the recollection of English Catholic martyrs. The religious combat theme in Robert Persons, S. J., who lived as a hunted priest in the late Elizabethan and early James I eras, must have had some influence in America, judging from the libraries that held his volumes. His *Directorium* was a guide to the spiritual life as seen by one who had also written treatises showing the illegitimacy of Elizabeth's claim to the throne of England. Charles Carroll of Carrollton's father, who had such books in his library, indeed reflected the militancy of Persons; the trait was more subtle in the son. Maryland Catholics certainly possessed a spirituality which left them inclined to fight for the freedom of their faith. Their counterpart in the English Catholic gentry, it would seem, were quite different in this respect. Richard Challoner's book, *Garden of the Soul,* did not carry a militant message and some commentators note that the title symbolizes a siige mentality and social withdrawal. Maryland conditions were not as harsh and Catholics had greater hopes of emancipation in America. They moved with considerable spirit, intent upon improving their religious lot. They showed a greater sense of responsibility and leadership in the role which they held as gentlemen. [10]

The manors of more distinguished laymen and, in a few cases, those of Jesuit missionaries were the focus of religious life. Here Mass was celebrated, instruction carried on. Catholic aristocrats felt a responsibility for the less educated or those with no education at all. Much like the Methodist circuit rider, missionaries paid regular visits to such centers in the course of a month. The freedom to carry out such a vitalizing activity was g r e a t l y helped by the fact that its direction was in the hands of the Jesuits, who as an exempt order had special ministerial faculties and a mission superior with the necessary powers. At least in the appointment and direction of men in this apostolic service and ministry the superior was aided by the vow of obedience, which bound the group together under his leadership. These priests with their special Ignatian spirit had the added advantage of collaborating with a laity significant numbers of whom were educated in Jesuit schools. [11]

It was against this favorable background, however, that a crises came in the structure and authority of the Catholic community. In the 1760's the Society of Jesus was under heavy attack, in large measure inspired by the Bourbon thrones in Spain and France. Its earlier conflicts with the Jansenists as well as its own form of the Enlightenment, a form free of the hostility to Christianity found in their former students Diderot and Voltaire, made enemies. The suppression of the Order in 1773 in all countries with the exception of Russia resulted. [12] The danger to church structure aside for the moment, morale of the missionaries and the laity they served was suddenly on the brink of deterioration. "Labour for our neighbour," a missionary confessed in his sadness at the supression, "is a Jesuit's pleasure; destroy the Jesuit, and the labour is painful and disagreeable . . . . For the sake of my rule, the night was agreeable as the day, forest and cold as a warm fire or a soft bed." Suddenly all is changed. "As the Jesuit is judged unfit by His H[oli]ness for a Mission," he wrote bitterly, in 1774, "I think that it is high time for me to retire to a private life. . . ." [13]

The broader features of Catholic life, beyond the ecclesiastical crises, should be seen to appreciate the impact of the Revolution. Perhaps no better sources bring out this general picture than the letters and diary of the missionary Joseph Mosley. A native of Lincolnshire, he came to Maryland in 1758 and founded St. Joseph's mission at Tuckahoe, Talbot County, in 1765. Here he served until his death in 1787. [14] While the Catholic gentry took greated account of the moderation of the Anglican proprietary party, Mosley represents in his writings the other side of Catholic feeling. He was aware of the open hostility of some

Church of England clergy, who lumped Marylanders into the Spanish stereotype of Catholicism. Thomas Bacon, for example, was unaware of the church-state tradition Catholics planted in Maryland, or if so gave no credit to them for sincerity. "Popery was undoubtedly exceedingly dangerous," the Maryland Anglican rector explained before the War, "as it must naturally wage continual War with our excellent Constitution both in Church and State." Other Maryland Protestants, however, were already attacking that constitution and would soon criticize its treatment of Catholics. [15] Mosley saw the less-publicized forms of discrimination in the lot of the Catholic indentured servant. Captains of ships that brought them to America had to pay a 5 pound tax if the Catholic servant refused, as they usually did, to take the oath. He knew of instances where men were whipped by way of encouragement to the oath. One such servant passed through this ordeal only to receive great abuse from a former Catholic. Mosley helped rescue the unfortunate man from his unhappy situation. He also found the Maryland conditions for a legal marriage a matter of distress to Catholic consciences. It was often necessary for Catholics to petition an Anglican minister for validation. [16]

At the same time, Mosley saw the great prospects for his work in Talbot County ten years before the War. Noting that the area should have had a resident missionary sixty years before, he took up its challenge with the zeal and style of the Methodist circuit rider. His arrival made it possible to divide the distances that had to be travelled by his Jesuit associate at the older Bohemia Manor mission, fifty miles away. Under the new development he could visit five congregations of 20 to 25 miles distance. Twice a year he had to go distances of 39 miles and 90 miles to other congregations. Two years before the War he saw the bright prospects of his work. He realized he had in the older English families a solid base upon which to build. "The English stock," he said, "are the glory of the flocks, edifying, virtuous, good Christians, and well instructed in the Faith. . . ." He very soon turned his attention to the Irish, Scotch, French, Dutch and "Country-born" who had some connection or interest with Catholicism. While he was not allowed to deal with the few Indians in the area, black slaves were a serious object of his concern as they were of their Catholic masters. Clergy and laity were continually urged to their obligations by church authorities. No obstacles to baptism were ever put in the way of Negroes, as happened in the case of some Christian churches. In letters to his sister in England, Mosley gave eloquent expression to his hopes of fully realizing the apostolic opportunity that stood before him on the eve of the Revolution. [17]

When the war came, Mosley reacted very much as Freeborn Garrettson and other Methodist circuit riders did. "A clergyman's call," he wrote in 1775, "has little to do with civil broils and troubled waters." In time he saw that he had to make a decision regarding an oath of loyalty to the new revolutionary state. He did not believe that he should act on this matter without consulting his fellow missionaries and hence wrote to his associate at Bohemia Manor. There was no response (if the letter ever arrived) and for some time he abstained from the oath. After refraining a while from public preaching, it then became necessary to act on his own. The local court would not authorize his acceptance of the new government, according to Mosley's explanation, and it was necessary to petition the assembly. It was not until 1778 that he was cleared on the records of the Revolutionary government. There is little evidence to indicate that Mosley, the rest of the Catholic clergy, and the Catholic laity in Maryland saw the Revolution and independence as anything but a positive means to the improvement of their religious condition. Mosley encouraged Catholics to take the oath and defended the morality of the independence movement. [18] In terms of religion and the ideology of revolution, John Carroll throws the best light on the compatability of the political with the religious consideration.

John Carroll returned from Europe in 1774, after being there for more than twenty-five years. He peacefully ministered to Catholics in Upper Marlboro, Rock Creek, and elsewhere in the west central portion of Maryland, making occasional excursions into Virginia. Toward the end of 1775 a discussion developed in the Continental Congress regarding a mission of representatives to Canada. Samuel Chase became involved in these matters, which were principally promoted by John Adams. Charles Carroll of Carrollton was thought useful to the commission to be led by Benjamin Franklin and Samuel Chase. His knowledge of French would make him effective in dealing with the French Canadians, possibly writing propaganda pamphlets. Because many peasants (*habitants*) and others had been excommunicated by Archbishop Jean Briand, Adams though that a Catholic clergyman from the colonies would accompany the expedition and bring a ministry to these particular needs. [19] Charles Carroll was used to approach his distant cousin John Carroll for this purpose. The clergyman made some difficulty in the case of the Canadians which throws light on his attitude toward the legitimacy of the American Revolution. He was reluctant to serve in the case of the Canadians because they had not, unlike the Americans, resorted to peaceful means of settlement through a series of remonstrances. Evidently Charles Carroll prevailed upon John to see that such means had been proven inefficacious by Americans and therefore not required of the Canadians. [20]

Another feature in the Maryland Catholic's thoughts about the course of the Revolution must be understood. Charles Carroll and others evidently instructed their co-religionists in Maryland on the future form of government in the state, which would be such as to guarantee the freedom of Catholics. There were some reasons to fear in this regard. The Suffolk Resolves of the Continental Congress was a protest against the Quebec Act of 1774, but it was accompanied by an attack on Roman Catholicism. Parliament now recognized the legal right of the Catholic Church in Canada and transferred the trans-Appalachian west to the political and ecclesiastical jurisdiction of Quebec. The anti-Popery outcry in New England that followed revelation of the Quebec Act was deafening. Even in Maryland two individuals were attacked amid the general hostility of American Protestants to the measure. Formal expression to this resentment was therefore clearly given in the Suffolk Resolves of the Continental Congress. [21] A good case has been made for the force of the Quebec Act in bringing on the American Revolution. Less successful is the claim that the American Protestant response to the act awakened a fear among Catholics that weakened their support of the Revolution. Such does not seem to be the case in Maryland, at least, because there was sufficient confidence in the spirit of toleration that accompanied the movement there, as seen earlier in the case of Charles Carroll's collaboration with the Independent Whigs. Confederation notions of government especially guaranteed that Maryland would be free to make its own religious settlements. However strong anti-Catholicism might be in New England, its force could not be expected to extend to Maryland and other states which thought differently under the state autonomy of the Confederation. Moreover, at the time of the commission for the delegates to Canada, a strong policy of tolerance was brought forth by the Congress to reassure French Catholics in Canada that they and their provinces could have the same hope that Maryland Catholics held. [22]

Conditions within their own church structure in Maryland greatly occupied the thoughts of Catholics and gave impetus to their aspirations for a Christian state. When a year before the Quebec Act, Pope

Clement XIV suppressed the Society of Jesus, a sudden religious and ecclesiastical crisis arose. The effect on the individual missionary has been noted. It is necessary here to see how the military conflict without was now aggravated by strife within the church. Mosley reflected the general uneasy condition. "To be sincere," he wrote in August of 1775, "bad times and inward trouble from our own affairs make me little content and less fit for my trust and business here. . . ." There was indeed grave danger of an exodus of such men from the unhappy scene, not unlike the losses experienced in the ranks of the Anglican clergy. [23] It was one of the accomplishments of the revolutionary era and Catholic leadership that heart was soon taken by such men as Mosley and the original clergy stayed at their posts. The way was difficult, however, particularly in replacing the toppling structure of the church in Maryland. For all practical purposes the Jesuit Order through its provincial in England and mission superior in Maryland had provided the authority from which came the sacramental ministry, the supply of clergy, and the unity of church life. Technically, priests and people were under the ecclesiastical jurisdiction of Richard Challoner, Bishop of London. This relationship had created precarious conditions of Maryland Catholics in the 1750's, when Challoner was working for the establishment of a bishop in the American provinces. He was unaware of the intense hostility to this arrangement among American Anglicans, and dissenters in the case of their own church. Protestant antagonism would be even greater if Catholics received a bishop. Moreover, the exercise of his office would flagrantly violate the laws of the province. Fortunately the move was averted when clergy and laity voiced their opposition. [24]

While the arrangement of a Jesuit missionary superior with powers of vicar general under the Bishop of London had proven a satisfactory alternative, there was no doubt that an indefinite continuation without a bishop was undesirable. The Catholic aspiration for a full religious life, as in the case of the Anglican community, called for a resident bishop in America. The way in which the Revolution opened the way to the establishment of a true national church with a bishop, therefore, marked the event as a landmark of religious growth. When the Christian state emerged in Maryland this expansion of Catholic life became possible. However, the way to this happy condition, ultimately attained in 1789, was a very tortuous one. The story centers in John Carroll, who returned from Europe in 1774, disheartened at the suppression of his religious order and Maryland ecclesiastical life. Challoner continued through most of the war to retain nominal jurisdiction and designated John Lewis, now a secular priest, as vicar general. Carroll would not defer to his authority. Assured that he had priestly powers and faculties deriving from other connections in Europe, he quietly exercised the ministry. He took part in the revolutionary events, ultimately accepting the commission from the Continental Congress in 1776. [25]

A man of liberal sentiment, as John Adams described him, John Carroll pursued a national vision of his church. He gradually became the leader of this cause, which was more and more shared by his colleagues, all like himself former members of the Society of Jesus. Many clergymen thought that their future was not only precarious but almost without hope. It was for Carroll to give them heart. Mosley had seriously considered returning to England and live out a life of early retirement as a family chaplain. Others did not consider the same thought dishonorable in view of their bitterness at the Pope's decree suppressing their Order, which had destroyed their elan as missionaries. By removing the Jesuit structure, religious life of both priests and laity was thrown into a chaotic condition. It has been noted that Bishop Challoner's concern had always been remote, ever anxious to be relieved of any ties he had with the Maryland Catholic community. He was also functioning within the technical framework where the province was viewed as a mission and therefore somewhat under the supervision of the Congregation de Propaganda Fide in Rome. As long as the Maryland mission was in the care of the Society of Jesus a smooth working of authority was possible. Only remote connection with the Bishop of London and the Propaganda at Rome was needed or even required. Challoner agreed that the ex-Jesuit Maryland superior John Lewis should continue on as vicar general. These arrangements were only being completed when John Carroll arrived from Europe. The Declaration of Independence then came, confounding the whole relationship of a patriotic clergy deferring to a Bishop in London. To be placed directly under the Propaganda was not an attractive alternative for men who aspired to a true national church with their own bishop ordinary.

It is understandable as well as revealing that John Carroll demurred before Lewis' jurisdiction in the midst of this weakened and confused condition. As the War continued more inevitably toward independence he and his colleagues sought to strengthen church authority, anticipating severance of the remaining ties with Challoner. The prelate's death in

1781 hastened reflection on some new form of authority and jurisdiction for the church in the new nation. The idea of mission status had always been offensive to a clergy which was fully established.

The alternative was to acquire an office of bishop ordinary directly under the Holy Father without dependence on the Propaganda Fide. But in view of the controversy regarding a bishop among Anglicans, Bernard Diderick led a movement among the American Catholic clergy to oppose a bishop. John Carroll was not a party to the initial deliberations of the group. He undoubtedly saw, as Anglicans did in 1781, that a truly national church would require a bishop. When the Catholic clergy assembled at Whitemarsh, Maryland in 1783, the problem was settled by disclaiming for the present any request for bishop ordinary from the Holy See. They were compelled, therefore, to the odious alternative of seeking a mission superior, who would necessarily be more directly under the Propaganda, the jurisdiction of London having now been removed by the Treaty of Peace and the wishes of Challoner's successor. The Select Body of Clergy, as the Whitemarsh gathering called itself in its incorporation, recommended that John Lewis be given powers of vicar general. It was also added that the body have the power to select its superior. Among the advantages of the arrangement was the power of the vicar to grant faculties to priests for preaching, hearing confessions and to assign ministries to those affiliated with the Select Body. All United States clergy were to submit to this source of authority in America. As it turned out, this arrangement was followed by Rome, but with Carroll named as superior rather than Lewis. This was due to the fact that Rome acted in advance of receiving the Whitemarsh petition. In a complex sequence of circumstances involving Benjamin Franklin, then in Paris, Rome worked out its own solution, which fortunately followed the assumptions of the American clergy.[26]

Benjamin Franklin, unaware of all of the ramifications of the problem, interested himself in resolving these difficulties. This episode in Paris throws light on Carroll's appointment. Franklin feared that an English prelate might continue as before and with political consequences. It appeared more beneficial to American clergy as well as to the governments of France and the United States to have a French bishop serve as the episcopal authority for the American church and its proposed vicar apostolic. Unaware of American notions on the separation of church and state, which Carroll and his colleagues held, the Propaganda thought it proper to seek out American sentiments even beyond what Franklin was observing in favor of French influence. Fortunately, the autonomy of the spiritual authority in an American church was asserted by Franklin, the Continental Congress and some other parties from whom word came. The United States government refused involvement in any recommendation as to a French jurisdiction as well as an acceptable vicar-apostolic in America. Turning to the wishes of the American clergy themselves, the Holy See saw that a bishop was inopportune, but that a superior as vicar general under Propaganda would meet present needs. Franklin's favorable view of Carroll evidently had an influence in the Marylander's appointment as superior. Looking to the time when a bishop would be considered for America, it is clear that considerable good came out of the confusion in the Franklin episode. It was now understood that a future bishop should possess powers ordinary, that is, without any connection with a prelate of some foreign nation. Very shortly after Carroll began to exercise his powers as superior short of episcopacy, the need for powers of bishop ordinary became increasingly evident. In other words, a movement toward a true national church under a bishop ordinary was being carried forward. It would be aided by a changing attitude among Protestants that led them to accept the idea of American bishops in their own denominations as well as among Catholics.

The experience of John Carroll in exercising his limited authority further supported this growing conviction. One outstanding incident in New York dramatized the need of an exclusive American church authority with its own bishop ordinary. Carroll wanted to remove Andrew Nugent from control of a New York City church in favor of William O'Brien, but because the former had faculties from a European prelate Carroll's action was ineffective. It was ultimately necessary to appeal to civil courts to remove Nugent and secure fulfillment of O'Brien's appointment by Carroll. [27]

While Carroll's office was gradually demonstrating its inadequacies in the 1780's the general conditions of religious life in the emerging Christian state of Maryland favored the first steps of a petition for a Catholic bishop. The acceptance of Samuel Seabury and William White as Protestant Episcopal bishops for America, as well as the sustained efforts that were leading to the episcopacy of Thomas Claggett in Maryland, cleared the air in society generally from suspicion of bishops. All were coming to see that bishops were threats only under the confessional state of colonial days. The increasing strength of the nation in its political life and national self-consciousness made Catholics see that they must honor the times by creating their own national church.[28] The persistent fear of control from Rome, found in the American Catholic clergy, naturally led to a national church with a native bishop viewed as a barrier against this danger. In doing so, they would be putting the church above the traditional American Protestant fears of domination by Rome. The success of Carroll as superior assured the recommendation of himself as the most suitable candidate for bishop, when the next meeting of the clergy turned to this question. The appointment finally came from Rome in 1789: Carroll was consecrated first bishop of the Catholic Church in the United States.

During the course of the War and through the remainder of the century various estimates were made of the benefits that came to Catholics from the emergence of the Christian state in Maryland. One was unmistakable. "Toleration granted by the Bill of Rights," Mosley wrote in 1784, "has put all on the same footing, and has been of great service to us." John Carroll had earlier taken note of this fulfillment of Catholic aspiration. Marriages, Mosley was now pleased to say, need not be subject to any Anglican ceremony.[29] To Carroll the lowering of the bar to public office-holding by Catholics had great significance, particularly as seen in the career of Charles Carroll of Carrollton and Governor Thomas Sim Lee. "To me," Carroll said of the pre-Revolutionary oath of office, "it has always appeared degrading that Catholics should find it necessary to recommend themselves to Government by renouncing tenets, which form no part of their belief. . . ." "If his mind is not great enough to raise him above the mean & infamous prejudices," John Carroll said of provincial officials favoring the religious oath, "no tests will satisfy him." The future Catholic bishop wrote with a great sense of historical context, when he spoke of religious freedom and separation of church and state. The oath and other forms of discrimination, according to him, "were inspired in the course of national education of England." It was certainly not attributable to the seventeenth century foundations of the province. He was lenient in his blame for eighteenth century Marylanders who did not effectively oppose the hostile trend that originated in the mother country. In the final analysis, the Revolution emancipated Maryland from the effect of this "education" and asserted her own tradition of freedom as found in Maryland's earliest laws.[30]

What were otherwise unfortunate acrimonious attacks by Protestant clergymen and by a former Catholic priest turned out to be useful to Carroll in presenting his church-state views. Thomas Wharton, remote in England, misread the Maryland community when he attacked its Catholics for intolerance. Few took his part. At the time of his departure from the Catholic priesthood Wharton fastened the charge on Carroll, using as his device the well-worn and confusing axiom, "outside of the Church there is no salvation." (*Extra ecclesiam nulla salus est.*) Placing the traditional Maryland Catholic emphasis upon the need of freedom in personal faith, Carroll denied that Catholics held others incapable of being in good faith. Persons faithful to their consciences were not displeasing to God, he explained, nor deprived of the hope of salvation. He also denied that his faith was alien to the notion of separation of church and state. All that he had said throughout his life added up to a case against the notion of the confessional state, where religious life and belief were under its control. In a publication of more than one hundred pages he drew upon his exchange of ideas with the English Catholic Joseph Berington and his liberal theological writings on this matter. Of less importance were two disgruntled priests who attacked Carroll not only for his ideas and policies, but also for his devotedness to the Society of Jesus. [31] It was fortunate that in the more important circles of Protestants and men in public life in Maryland, a much more understanding attitude prevailed. Little comfort was given to Wharton and other critics. This was due in no small measure to the influence and example of laymen such as Charles and Daniel Carroll. The one served on the Maryland Convention Committee for drafting a Constitution and the other on the Federal Constitutional Convention's Committee for the Bill of Rights. There was genuine Catholic concern that the First Amendment become part of the Federal Constitution. It prevented the discrimination against Catholics in New York and other state laws from affecting the favorable church-state arrangements in Maryland and Pennsylvania, where most of the Catholic population resided. An oath touching religious matters was required for the naturalization of immigrants for some time in New York. North Carolina, for example, required profession of the truths of the Protestant religion by office holders. Massachusetts and Connecticut maintained an established Congregational Church even after 1800. [32]

There is another pattern of evidence on Catholic life which shows beneficial effects of the Revolution. The successful resolution of the crisis caused by the suppression of the Society of Jesus and the acquisition of an American bishop for a national church did not fail to have a wholesome effect on the growth of Catholicism. "Their numbers are at present very inconsiderable, and their influence of no weight in public concern of the province," wrote William Eddis, a provincial official before the war. He unwittingly told the reason for this condition: "They, however, continue to be tolerated without being permitted to participate in the office of government." [33] Unaware the Revolution had considerably changed all of this, he did raise questions about the possibly unfavorable impact of the war on the Catholic population. British marauding on the southern counties attacked the center of the Catholic community. Catholic slaves were undoubtedly victims of raiding. The loss of Catholic property probably accounted for migrations to Kentucky. Moreover, the hard-hit Maryland Old Line at the Battle of Harlem Heights had large numbers of Catholics from the southern counties in its ranks. Yet the Kentucky migrants could not have been written-off as loss, for they established the foundations of what became in the nineteenth century a highly developed center of Catholic life in the vicinity of Bardstown. [34]

John Carroll, however, made it clear that these considerations did not change the optimistic picture of Catholic growth after the Revolution. While he told the Englishman Charles Plowden of Catholics seeking new land beyond the Appalachians, he made clear that Maryland still remained promising. [35] "Our hopes of spreading Religion," he wrote in 1785, "are continually increasing in the old States...." [36] Eight years later he found "Catholics being much increased in those [states], where it existed before." [37] His official census report confirmed the truth of these observations. The number of Catholics in Maryland was conservatively set at approximately 15,000, all of whom were judged members by actual contact with the Church on an official basis. [38] There were undoubtedly other areas of strength unreported by those with looser ties to Catholicism. All of this growth would not in Eddis' term be "inconsiderable." Duke, observing Catholicism twenty years after Eddis' judgment, gave the clear impression that Catholics ranked with Presbyterians among the numerically greater minorities. He also found the condition of the Maryland church's structure remarkable, considering its short period of favor. [39] This impression could have been formed only upon signs of growth.

The orderly condition of Catholicism, which Duke observed even before the Revolution, increased and led to progress of the Church. The key to the ideal pastoral condition for Carroll was the resident pastor. [40] The war disrupted parish life but did not necessarily take the pastor away from well established religious communities. [41] Maryland was better off after the war, claiming the most exemplary and qualified of the clergy. Baltimore was the center of the newly created nation-wide diocese. [42] With constitutional rights recently won, Catholics began to form new parishes and chapels. [43] "In this town," Carroll wrote from Baltimore with gratitude ten years later, "we now have two very handsome & large Churches besides the old original chapel, which was the cradle of Catholicity here. . . ." He told of the frequent reception of sacraments and attendance at worship. [44] Claggett noted a "very large proportion of Roman Catholics" in the George Town area in the 1790's, which had two churches with their own resident pastors. [45] The war and the new constitution removed another source of distress and attrition. Catholics along with dissenters and others were formerly obliged by their taxes to support the established church. They were in addition liable as a special group to penalty taxes attached to their faith, as occurred during the French and Indian War. [46] Duke attributed the decline in membership of these churches to tax assessments, which made it difficult to support their own pastors. He said that together these groups originally constituted a greater number than those of established anglicanism in Maryland but over the years after 1776 this standing was reversed. [47] Duke was using the same source of misinformation found in Eddis regarding seventeenth and early eighteenth century Catholic numbers. He was sound, however, in observing the significant growth of his own times following the war. He also took accurate account of the fact that the favorable conditions of freedom first planted in Maryland had returned with the revolutionary era.

Catholics clearly recognized that the Maryland Constitution gave the same generous benefit to their church property which was accorded the Episcopalians. John Carroll saw a similarity between the property once held by the Jesuits and that of the established church. When the Society of Jesus was suppressed by the pope shortly before the Revolution, he feared that the land and other means supporting this body of clergymen in Maryland would be removed when these priests took up a new status as secular priests. "Their succesors to the same religious functions," he wrote with assurance in 1788, "enjoy them now in the same manner." [48] When Carroll became duly established in an episcopal see at Baltimore, church property was further protected. The assembly, according to its constitutional powers, provided that the diocese be "created and erected into a body politic and corporate. . . ." [49] Individual churches, parishes, and chapels were also legally incorporated. [50] All of these protections from law encouraged the Catholic clergy and Bishop Carroll to plan for the incorporation of a school as one of "the most effectual means of promoting the welfare of Religion. . . ." [51] Catholic clergy and laymen could well recall their own extralegal education in Catholic schools abroad or at isolated places in Maryland and be further thankful for the constitution. It is also true that the protection of civil law helped prevent any threat to American Catholic ownership of these resources. The Whitemarsh conference of the clergy also secured material support to the Society of Jesus in the event of its restoration. When this happy event came about in 1804, most of its property returned to the Order, thus continuing its apostolic work and growth.

Psychological improvemens within Catholicism came to Marylanders. "This unjust exclusion," Carroll reminisced in 1790 of the old bars to office, "has always hurt my feelings." [52] "Many, whom past discouragements and oppression kept concealed," Carroll said of the weak, "begin to show themselves." [53] Carroll left no doubt that his church continued, as it always had, to be made up largely of the poor who "have few superfluities to spare." [54] At least their faith now had the consolation of allowing the small amount available to religion to go to the house of God at which they freely chose to worship rather than to an established church. Understanding and charity began to flow through the minds of many who now saw Catholics in a new light. The English diatribe against Catholicism was greatly stilled with the passing of colonial government from Maryland. That faith had been carefully defined since Elizabeth's day as inexorably political and the old "education," as John Carroll called it, had entrenched hostility among many during the Hart governorship and the period of the French and Indian War. [55] "Many here, even of their principal people," Carroll wrote of the old misunderstandings, "have acknowledged to me, that they would have crossed to the opposite side of the street rather than meet a Rom. Catholic. . . . The scandalous misrepresentations, by their ministers, increased the horror every Sunday." [56] He realistically acknowledged that there was always a "malicious or jealous-minded person" remaining who would resurrect this old spirit. [57] Yet he was sufficiently confident in the leading non-Catholic men of the state openly to profess his beliefs, even that spiritual dependence upon the pope. [58]

This was all so much evidence of recently won respect and prestige. William Duke gave witness to this new condition of Catholicism, providing an analysis of why it came about. He singled out the good use which the church made of its material means in the bad times and good. "They conduct their affairs to advantage, and by a well-contrived economy, have maintained themselves, not only without the favour of government, but under the discouragements of a public odium. [59] The remarkable thing was that church estates were used only for the religious purpose for which they were created. Duke was amazed that this was accomplished without the force of law, which was normally required if men's cupidity would not pervert the use of religious property. "We shall be tempted to think," he said with frank admiration, "that this society has discovered the secret of government, and adapted its maxims to the passions of the human heart, with a precision unknown to the rest of mankind." [60] A large number of the Catholic clergy in Maryland were ex-Jesuits who continued on after the suppression of the Society of Jesus in established spiritual works and church locations. These men also won the respect of Duke, In an age when men in both Catholic and Protestant countries were accepted for their categorical condemnations of things Jesuit, Duke called these views into question. In his journal he expressed admiration for the French Jesuit missionaries in America, [61] and in another place examined the case for St. Ignatius. "I queried with myself," he wrote soberly, "could a man found an order so respectable as that of the Jesuits without real merit in the civil sense of the word—without such consistency and propriety of conduct as shew a mind sufficiently large to grasp a design and sufficiently determined to execute it." Providence would not permit it "unless there was some real goodness in the first intention." [62] Duke found these same marks of prestige on the church of Maryland, and they were due in no small measure to the authentic spirit of the sons of Loyola. The Revolution opened the way to the frank recognition and admiration which he expressed.

Merely to narrate the public careers of the Carrolls and others of the most prominent Catholic families would suffice to establish the fact of a newly won prestige for Catholicism. They were found at the State Constitutional Convention and on its drafting committee, the houses of the legislature, the council of the governor, at Independence Hall, the Constitutional Convention, the Continental Congress, and the Federal Congress. [63] The governorship, which was one of the few high offices the family had not been called to, was early occupied by a Carroll co-religionist, Thomas Sim Lee. It was significant of the prestige of Catholicism that Lee had only shortly before this election gone over to Catholicism. [64] A publicly esteemed laity greatly helped the church. Such high public position of its lay members had once given great advantage to the established church. [65] "Under God," Bishop Carroll frankly confessed to his cousin, Charles Carroll of Carrollton, "its [Catholicism's] chief protection has long been owing to the influence and preponderance of yourself. . . ." [66]

Underlying these ingredients and signs of prestige which the Revolution restored to Catholicism was the factor of personal wealth and culture in important Catholic families. Bishop John Carroll pursued the interest of his church with great success, but this hardly could have been done had he not enjoyed the financial security his mother's estate afforded him. [67] It alone had earlier made possible his studies in Europe, which did so much to establish his respected position as a man of culture among the notables of his times. Similar men were found among the Sulpician priests who came over from France for his educational projects. [68] It was the personal wealth of the Digges, Carrolls, and other families that gave Catholics a prominent role in St. John's and Washington College and accounted for the creation of Georgetown College. [69] In civil matters, too, wealth was required to acquire high public office and devote long hours to its demands. As one of the wealthiest men in America, Charles Carroll of Carrollton's early support of the Revolution had great public importance and opened the way to the leadership which he exercised. His subsequent recognition was assured, nor could the religion which had heretofore been a liability to him be any longer subject to discrimination.

As Marylanders began to enjoy the benefits of religious freedom, they grew in appreciation for the Catholic tradition which reached back to the founding of the colony. In the years following the war, John Carroll had occasion to present a fuller view of the separation of church and state found seminally in the Toleration Act of the Ordinance of 1639. Young Protestant revolutionaries had made brief references to this tradition. Carroll's answer to Wharton had many important reflections on this matter of which he often spoke in his conversations. He once noted that the English author Joseph Berington, whose views were very close to his own on church and state, provided useful reading for non-Catholic friends. In some instances the reader joined the Catholic Church. [70] His heart very much with the libertarian trend of the times, he denied that one had an obligation to submit to an established state religion. [71] He condemned the practice, found in Catholic and Protestant countries alike, which used force to suppress heretics and other religious dissenters. He believed that weapons of religion must never cease to be spiritual. "I do not think," he wrote, "that J. Christ ever i[m]powered his church to recur to the means of force & bloodshed, for the preservation of faith against error." [72] On one occasion he attacked a Scottish bishop's writings, where they rationalized on theological grounds a system of union of church and state. The author was using the reasoning which Wharton had falsely ascribed to Carroll, that those not clearly connected with the Church had no hope of salvation. "He carries to a most alarming, in my estimation, unjustifiable length," Carroll said, "the doctrine of no salvation out of the visible communion of the Church." [73] He rejected the author's implication that the secular power can be enlisted against the ideological opponents of a religion. At the same time, Carroll did not see that the new order of freedom need dampen one's zeal to share his faith with those who would freely receive it. Appropriately writing to a Spanish bishop in this instance, he made it clear that such zeal must not be directed at taking over a government. [74] The Maryland Constitution stated that the new government was not partial to any particular church. Carroll explained this provision to an English friend, noting that the state was securing the individual's rights as well as those of churches. To accomplish this, he said, was "a matter of natural justice," apart from any particular consideration of Christianity or the faith of the individual in question. [75]

What Carroll spoke and wrote in his more official role for Catholics, others among the clergy and laity said with the same effect. An understanding of Catholicism came to those among Protestants who previously lacked the knowledge found in men like Chase, Johnson, and other Revolutionary leaders. In the letters and diary of Mosley is found evidence of the lively interest among Catholics in fostering greater understanding by Protestants. The Catholic laity evidently were striving to gain some share in John Carroll's insight into the uniqueness of their community's situation in Maryland. A great appeal for books was made by Mosley on a wide range of topics to feed Catholic interest in reading. General church history was sought but also Challoner's writings on Methodism. Protestantism's emphasis on Sacred Scripture led Mosley to request material on the Apocolypse, which Protestants often used as a basis for interpreting the course of the church's history. Undoubtedly there was an apologetic vein in the readings he sought, but it was also calculated to bring about understanding of the Protestant environment in which Maryland Catholics lived. This implied that there was honest Protestant inquiry into Catholic belief, similar to what Duke showed in his journal. [76]

A year before his death in 1787, Mosley with great consolation rejoiced at the great change that had come about in Catholic life in the past twenty-two years of his ministry. He now had a house of public worship and his flock had grown considerably, not only in numbers but in quality. "The harvest is great," he told his sister. "It has done great good," he said of the deepening interest in their faith. "These books are so beneficial to the poor Catholics, who are entirely unprovided of such information. . . ."[77] So many Catholics, for years without the careful attention of ministers because of the restricted life of the confessional state, now came under their influence. The words of this zealous missionary contrasted sharply with those of despair uttered shortly before the war. In his life and writings Mosley portrayed the full meaning and feeling of the Catholic emancipation that had taken place.

REFERENCES

[1]Thomas O'Brien Hanley, *Their Rights and Liberties: The Beginning of Religious and Political Freedom in Maryland* (Westminster, Md., 1959), pp. 74-76.

[2]*Ibid.*, chaps. 4-5; and by the same author, "Church and State in the Maryland Ordinance of 1639," *Church History*, XXVI (December, 1957), 325-41.

[3]Thomas O'Brien Hanley, "His Excellency's Council: Maryland, 1715-1720," *Records of the American Catholic Historical Society of Philadelphia*, LXXIV (1963), 137-50.

[4]Thomas O'Brien Hanley, "The Catholic and Anglican Gentry in Maryland Politics," *Historical Magazine of the Protestant Episcopal Church*, XXXVIII (June, 1969), 143-52.

[5]Hanley, *Charles Carroll*, chaps. 2-3; and by the same author, "Young Mr. Carroll Meets Montesquieu," *Maryland Historical Magazine*, 62 (December, 1967), 394-418.

[6]Hanley, *Charles Carroll*, chap. 13.

[7]*Ibid.*, p. 243.

[8]John Carroll to Charles Plowden letters during the war years bring this out. (Jesuit Maryland Province Archives, Baltimore, Md.; and John Carroll Papers, Catholic University Transcripts.)

[9]Pierre Pourrat, *Christian Spirituality: Later Developments: Part. II: From Jansenism to Modern Times*, trans. by Donald Attwater (4 vols.; Westminster, Md., 1955), III, 251-55, 271-84, 338-41; and André Schimberg. *L'Education morale dans les collèges de la Compagnie de Jésus en France sous l'Ancien Régime (XVe, XVIIe, XVIIIe siècles)* (Paris, 1913), pp. 251-55.

[10]See Michael Trappes-Lomax, *Bishop Challoner: a Biographical Study Derived from Dr. Edwin Burton's the Life and Times of Bishop Challoner* (New York, 1936), for context of Challoner's writings and titles.

[11]Thomas Hughes, *The History of the Society of Jesus in North America* (4 vols.; New York, 1910-17), *Text*, II, 550-56; and John Tracy Ellis, *Catholics in Colonial America* (Baltimore, Md., 1963), pp. 315-59.

[12]See 1773, MS. Account of the Suppression of the Jesuit College at Bruges, written by John Carroll (Jesuit Maryland Provincial Archives).

[13]Mosley to sister, Oct. 3, 1774, "Letters of Father Joseph Mosley, 1757-1786," ed. by E. I. Devitt, *Woodstock Letters*, XXXV, No. 1 (1906), 234; Mosley provides a concrete picture of pastoral life and spirit in this era.

[14]*Ibid.*, 35.

[15]Mary Augustana Ray, *American Opinion of Roman Catholicism in the Eighteenth Century* (New York, 1936), p. 72.

[16]Mosley to sister, *Woodstock Letters*, XXXV, 143.

[17]*Ibid.*, 35-42.

[18]*Ibid.*, 132-43.

[19]Melville, chap. 4.

[20]Charles Carroll's letters for this period have led to the interpretation of the mission given here. It is assumed that he gave John his own reasoning about the legitimacy of bringing Canadians into the war, which answered the difficulties John put down in a memorandum of 1776 on the matter (Catholic Archdiocesan Archives of Baltimore, Special Case C-F).

[21]Ellis, pp. 391-94.

[22]Metzger, chap. 2.

[23]Mosley to sister, Aug. 16, 1775, *Woodstock Letters*, XXXV, 237-38.

[24]Ellis, pp. 420-31.

[25]Melville, pp. 54-57. While John Lewis seems to have agreed not to hold any jurisdiction over John Carroll in terms of appointment to a parish or other ministry, Carroll clearly enjoyed faculties from Lewis for preaching, hearing confessions, saying mass, etc. As a missionary he very likely had powers to absolve the Canadians from excommunication incurred for supporting the American cause.

[26]*Ibid.*, pp. 59-63.

[27]Carroll to Plowden, Mar. 1, 1788 (John Carroll Papers).

[28]Humphrey, *Nationalism and Religion in America* gives a description of the general trend through this period.

[29]Mosley to sister, Oct. 4, 1784, *Woodstock Letters*, XXXV, 240-42.

[30]Carroll to Plowden, Feb. 24, 1790 (John Carroll Papers).

[31]*An Address to the Roman Catholics of the United States of America* (Annapolis, 1784); Patrick Smyth, *The Present State of the Catholic Missions conducted by the Ex-Jesuits in North America* (Dublin, 1788); Charles Wharton, *Letter to the Roman Catholics of the City of Worcester* (Philadelphia, 1784).

[32]Ellis, p. 437.

[33]Eddis, passim.

[34]Metzger, chap. 9.

[35]*Ibid.*, Sep. 26, 1783 (John Carroll Papers).

[36]Carroll to Edenshins, Oct. 4, 1785 (*ibid.*).

[37]Carroll, Pastoral of May 28, 1792 (*ibid.*).

[38]*Relatio pro Emo. Cardinali Antonello de statu Religionis in Unitis Foederatae Americae privinciis*, in Guilday, p. 223.

[39]Duke, *State of Religion*, pp. 34-35.

[40]Carroll to Plowden, Apr. 20, 1792 (John Carroll Papers).

[41]Carroll *et al.*, Petition quoted in Guilday, p. 171.

[42]Carroll to T. Lee, Feb. 10, 1779 (John Carroll Papers).

[43]Carroll to Plowden, Feb. 28, 1779 (*ibid.*).

[44]*Ibid.*

[45]Ralph to Claggett, Dec. 24, 1796 (Maryland Diocesan Archives).

[46]John G. Shea, *A History of the Catholic Church in the United States* (4 vols.; New York, 1886-1892), I, 414.

[47]Duke, *State of Religion*, p. 14.

[48]Carroll to White, May 5, 1788 (John Carroll Papers).

[49]*Laws of Maryland*, November Session, 1796, chap. xv.

[50]*Ibid.*, November Session, 1799, chap. liii.

[51]Carroll to O'Brien, May 10, 1788 (John Carroll Papers).

[52]Carroll to Plowden, Feb. 24, 1790 (*ibid.*).

[53]Carroll to Viar, Apr. 20, 1790 (*ibid.*). Jose Ignacio Viar was the Spanish Consul.

[54]*Ibid.*

[55]Ellen H. Smith, *Charles Carroll of Carrollton* (Cambridge, Mass., 1942), pp. 16-21.

[56]Carroll to Plowden, July 11, 1791.

[57]Carroll to Thorpe, Feb. 17, 1785.

[58]*Ibid.,* and Carroll to Penalver y Cardenas, Apr. 7, 1796.

[59]Duke, *State of Religion,* p. 34.

[60]*Ibid.,* p. 35.

[61]June 29, 1792.

[62]*Ibid.,* Feb. 3, 1792.

[63]U. S., Congress, House, *Biographical Directory of the American Congress, 1774-1949; The Continental Congress, September 5, 1774, to October 21, 1788; The Congress of the United States From the First to the Eightieth Congress, March 4, 1789 to January 3, 1949, Inclusive* (Washington, 1950), "Charles Carroll and Daniel Carroll." *Proceedings of Convention,* p. 222 (Aug. 17, 1776), indicates membership of Maryland Constitutional committee.

[64]John Carroll to Charles Plowden, June 1, 1792 (John Carroll Papers).

[65]Werline, pp. 210-211.

[66]Carroll to Charles Carroll, July 12, 1800 (John Carroll Papers).

[67]Carroll to Plowden, Feb. 28, 1779 (*ibid.*).

[68]Carroll to Plowden, Sep. 3, 1791 (*ibid.*).

[69]William Smith to West, 1784 [?] (Maryland Diocesan Library).

[70]Carroll to Plowden, Nov. 13, 1786 (John Carroll Papers).

[71]Carroll to Plowden, Sep. 3, 1800 (*ibid.*).

[72]Carroll to Robert Plowden, July 7, 1797 (*ibid.*).

[73]Carroll to Plowden, Jan. 22, Feb. 28, 1787 (*ibid.*).

[74]Carroll to Penalver y Cardenus, Mar. 31, 1796 (*ibid*).

[75]Carroll to Plowden, Feb. 27, 1785 (*ibid.*).

[76]Mosley to sister, July 20, 1786, and October 4, 1784, *Woodstock Letters,* 240-45.

[77]*Ibid.,* July 20, 1786.

VIII

EXPRESSIONS OF PLURALISM

Supporters of the confessional state in England and America had always held to ideas which would make them fear the Maryland religious settlement following the Declaration of Independence. To see so many diverse religious groups breathing with such vitality and independence led to prophecies that religious life in society was doomed. It had been the virtue of the Church of England to keep sectaries in some conformity, however loose, with broad professions of belief required from all honorable citizens. Baptists, Presbyterians, Congregationalists, yes, even Quakers, were somehow within the pale of the church and its confessional state. Many historians would say that the pretense at discipline was a fiction. More important to the purpose here, however, is to call attention to the phenomenon of diverse denominations thriving in a status of equality of all before the law; and then to note that their behavior disproved the prophecy of the pro-establishment voices. In this estimate it must be shown that freedom for groups did not breed deeper contentions than prevailed in the old scheme. It can soon be further observed that, given the legal transformation and the resurgence of evangelical piety, Maryland was no longer left with sects but denominations. [1]

The extensive scholarship on denominationalism as distinct from sectarianism throws great light on the subtleties of the Maryland religious transformation. Adding to these understandings what the records of Maryland yield, something special can be said of denominationalism *vis-à-vis* sectarianism. The former term dispenses with force of exclusiveness in a religious group or denomination, and with any claim that other expressions of belief are fundamentally false. Moreover, sectarianism under the impetus of exclusiveness carries with it the bitterness of self-righteous proselytizing. [2] Perhaps the supporters of the confessional state, granted that sects and not denominations existed within the establishment scheme, had some basis of infallibility in their prophecy of doom. Religious acrimony clearly raged before the Revolution among the religious groups who were restlessly tethered to the Anglican structure. Competition for growth came naturally with the acrimony. What was not understood was that privileged position for a theological tradition and group, once removed from the legal structure, radically changed the relations of groups toward each other. Of course some latent force of Christian love and tolerance within the groups was required before a legal change would effect a community free of the predicted factionalism. The growth of piety in Maryland during the revolutionary era clearly instilled such dispositions as a concomitant of the disestablishment legislation. While those zealous as a result of the deepening religious life might sincerely desire to spread the good news of their faith, under the new conditions they would do so in a far different spirit from what the establishment philosophers had predicted.

In the light of these considerations, the religious scene can be said to have been transformed by the Revolution into a condition of pluralism, a twentieth century term. Pluralism has the notion of apartness, which was drawn from the term's original application to the phenomenon of the immigrant populations and their respective geographical locations. Transferred to the religious realm after World War II, it meant a community of faith apart from others but not in a way to leave them alienated from the civil realm, where all shared a common equality in religious terms before the law of the land and the opportunities of secular life. Nevertheless, the ethnic ingredient of the post-nineteenth century religious scene is very real, so that apartness today in a religious group is often identified with national origin. In contrast to this twentieth century estimate of the religious meaning of pluralism, the eighteenth century condition had a much smaller margin of separation among religious groups, for their common Christianity in its broadest traditions was more fully understood and accepted. A very telling reflection of this fact is seen in the Maryland Constitution's provision for the recognition of Christianity without any preferred place for a specific group within its meaning. It is also significant that the ethnic complication was lacking, for the most part, in the Revolutionary scene in Maryland. The impulse of evangelical piety, finally, further limited the force of separatism. It will therefore not be surprising to see the effort at inter-faith amity encountering fewer obstacles than would be the case in other periods of American history. Pluralism thus understood in general and in Revolutionary Maryland provides a useful concept in the records of the times, when one estimates the quality and forms of religious expression.

One cannot escape the impression of a growing esteem for tolerance during the revolutionary period in Maryland and at least a minimal desire to develop it. At the first conventions to form an autonomous state in 1776, delegates were keenly aware of religious differences, which could destroy unity needed in defense of political freedom. County committees were strongly urged to see that religious factionalism was put aside in the interest of the common good. To do so required that men recognize and respect the fact and right of differences in religious belief and opinion.[3]

The various denominations responded to this difficult requirement. Before the Peace of Paris had been concluded, the Lewes Presbytery attributed to the war a peculiar force for Christian union and harmony. It praised those occasions when "the pious of all parties will often talk together to promote . . . Religion, on which it is promised their names will be registered in the Chronicles of heaven . . ."[4] Thomas Haskins, the evangelical-minded Methodist, did not hesitate to see wide application of this principle when he attended the preaching of the extreme liberal and Universalist, Elhanan Winchester. Although Haskins thought him a good man, he did not see that tolerance implied indifference to religious principles in which there was no agreement. "We ought to distinguish between a man and his principles," he noted, "tho' we cannot between a man & his practices."[5] Haskins honestly judged the merit of principle and practice, which in no way prevented respect for Winchester's rights.

With tolerance went the quality of benevolence, as seen in a high-ranking leader of the once-established church. "I know that a few *grains* of mutual confidence & Benevolence among different denominations of Christians," William Smith wrote shortly after the war, "will be better, than splitting & torturing . . . Christian good will is not [to]. be weighted of *Drams & Scruples* —It should be unconfined & universal."[6] From a somewhat different viewpoint but with the same spirit, Francis Asbury spoke of other denominations. "This neighborhood," he noted of Worcester County, "is supplied with preaching by the Episcopalians, Presbyterians, Baptists and Methodists. All is well, if the people are saved."[7]

William Duke, who had served under the dispensations both of Smith and Asbury, gave further analysis of the principle of interdenominational relationships. "I could not help reflecting," he said as an Episcopalian and ex-Methodist, "upon the — I don't know what to call it [—] that induces every religious denomination to distinguish itself even in the most trivial circumstances." Their conduct is "distinguishable as that of ducks and geese. . ." He found these old pre-war trivia an obstacle to good relationships between the denominations. "I hope they don't intend it for a shibboleth or anything very essential to the service of God." In time he found that this was not the case, such obstacles being removed in the interest of harmony.[8] It is significant of the change to pluralism that this zealous preacher advocated benevolence of a kind that kept attachment to religious differences in proportion. "Had occasion to animadvert with some severity," Duke recounted, "on the insolence with which some people attack opinions which they are not able to affect one way or another by real reason."[9] Duke was directing attention to the need for constructive exposition of one's own view as a proper exercise of zeal. Examination of one's own opinions at the hands of others could be done without insolence, as Duke himself demonstrated. "I told him," he wrote of one who had expressed great dislike of Methodists, "that I differed so much with him as to like them very well and advised him not to trouble his head about the Methodists but to get the spirit of a Christian."[10] He insisted on this fair-mindedness even in Hume and other authors whom he read.[11]

With greater breadth than Haskins, Duke's considered estimate of a man was inevitably identified with that man's practices. Psychologically as well as logically, it was less difficult to deal with a man from the standpoint of his conduct, which externally affected others. As Haskins said, one can in the first case distinguish principles from the man, but not so his conduct. In dealing with this second situation of a man's conduct, Duke focused attention on God and self. One must "hate only what God hates and for that only reason." Sincere but erroneous beliefs were different from immoral acts. "We should find so much matter," Duke said by way of application to external actions, "of Censure and abhorrence on our own corruptions that we should be rather inclined to excuse the Misconduct of other . . ." He assumes that acts are "Matters which do not immediately affect the Moral State." He would thus restrain evangelicals and those of stronger Puritan inheritance from external suppression of private immorality by the hand of the state. "And supposing they are avowed Enemies to the Gospel of Christ," said Duke, passing a step further, "we shall combat them only with spiritual Weapons knowing that this Cause cannot be injured but by a spiritual Opposition." [12] In this line of reasoning he found agreement with his bishop Thomas Claggett, who believed exertions in the use of the spiritual weapons of the Gospel would bring a victory over bias as well as vice. [13]

In the light of these general observations, was the principle of tolerance stated generally applied in practice? There was no doubt in the mind of John Carroll that tolerance characterized the Revolutionary period as a new experience for him. "I believe," he confessed, "that in my last letter I gave you proof of the decay of religious prejudice here . . ." He cited as evidence the election of Thomas Sim Lee, a convert to Catholicism, as the second Governor of Maryland. [14] Like Duke and Haskins, he was aware of the problem of adjusting a healthy individuality in conviction with an indulgent and tolerant attitude toward others. [15] William White called attention to the fact that out of the Revolution "arises an argument for charity and forebearance among religious societies in America, with whom the same causes of contention and mutual censure have no place . . ." This was largely as a result of disestablishment. [16] Garrettson notices a peculiar situation in Maryland which gave further advantage to tolerance. In contrast to Pennsylvania, where there were as many as fifteen sects, Maryland had relatively fewer denominations. [17] These writers tended to contrast these conditions with pre-Revolutionary days. Duke gave a more complex assent to the tenor of these favorable judgments on the practices of tolerance in general during the Revolutionary period in Maryland. "Our different societies," he stated in his qualifications, "though they do not anathematize one another, acknowledge one another's excellencies with reluctance, and are sure to catch up every scandalous story that can gratify an envious disposition, for the entertainment of their respective parties." [18] Basic agreement, however, was found with the generally favorable view of others, while indicating the areas still open for further growth. He implied that the post-Revolutionary condition was better than the preceding one with its anathemas. Duke makes a major point regarding the quality of the new condition of tolerance, for he saw virtue of a king in the pre-Revolutionary period. "We find the people of this part of America about thirty years ago," he said, "not so guilty of bigotry and furious zeal as the people of New-England; but upon the whole they were not better." He would attribute any tolerance to the virtue of "sociability" in those days, rather than to any deep conviction. "Sociability" as a motive had superseded all religious principles, according to him. "Upon examination it is found to proceed either from culpable indifferency, or a prevalent spirit of disobedience and impiety." [19] If one combines these views with what Duke had favorably observed of a revival of reform and piety after the Revolution, however, one will conclude that the absence of anathemas among Marylanders derived from something firmer than sociability and indifference.

Duke was skeptical of prospects for a harmony between the two virtues of zeal and tolerance. His estimates of the degree of tolerance, therefore, should be taken with other persons of a different viewpoint. He was often reluctant to concede evidence of true tolerance, for a divided flock of Christ was to him the gravest of misfortunes. "What makes it worse," he believed of this situation, "is, that we become the more dissonant as we become the more religious." [20] Since the true Christian had no alternative to becoming more religious, dissonance and strife among religious groups seemed inevitable. He did not see that denominationalism was not sectarianism. In his disturbed condition on this point, he did not clearly see the relevance of his other observations which showed both the progress of "vital religion" and tolerance of higher quality.

The Methodists, the most active group, had the greatest basis for good relations with the Episcopalians, the most numerous; and this situation provides major evidence of the improved relationships during the revolutionary period. Asbury, for example, had always proceeded with the greatest regard for the Church of England and its discipline. He did so to the very end of the union of the two which he likewise strove to maintain to the very eve of the Christmas Conference. That week of conferences in Baltimore, made division an accomplished fact.

"The difference between us lay not so much in doctrines and forms of worships as in experience and practice." [21] His conduct gave substance to his disclaimer of the "violent sectarian," the dissenter who could not make this statement. [22] When some preachers in Virginia were not as faithful to this policy, Asbury redoubled his efforts at fidelity to ordinances or sacraments received at the hands of Episcopalian ministers. [23] During this period he kept contact with a number of Episcopalians who were intent on retaining Methodism within their Church. Among these were William West, Secretary of the Maryland Episcopal Conventions, and John Andrews, both residents of the vicinity of Baltimore. [24] Thomas Gates of Annapolis and Mason Weems of Anne Arundel County, also consulted with Asbury in this period before the Christmas Conference. [25] Needless to say, when the conference separated Methodists from the Episcopalians, it was not easy to meet them again without some embarrassment, as Asbury found on one occasion with Duke. [26] Meetings, however, did not breed rancor or destroy the large area of theological and liturgical harmony between Methodists and Episcopalians.

Although William Duke profoundly disagreed with the decision which Asbury made to leave his church, he still maintained esteem for the separated "society," to which he had belonged before this event. Duke's Church had once commended George Washington, "who has happily united a tender regard for other churches with an inviolable attachment to his own." [27] Duke himself gave special application of this virtue. His wife was a Methodist and seems not to have been disturbed by her husband's "inviolable attachment to his own" Church. [28] With Methodists there seemed to be a similar liberality which did not exclude inter-denominational marriages; certainly not with Episcopalians, but only with those given to ungodliness and unbelief. [29] Duke's journal frequently noted association and dialogue with Methodists and their preachers. Once at the Ridgely's residence, he enjoyed the company of their Methodist minister friend. [30] He always took note of Methodist preachers in the area where he was visiting. [31] On one occasion at Frederick, Duke was mistaken for a Methodist preacher. "It was necessary," he said of his confused host, "to tell him that I was not. However he said he believed that I was a servant of God (may I justify his good opinion)..." [32] In conversations with Methodists there was none of that insolent attack on opinions of either party which Duke so much deprecated. "Spent the evening comfortably," he said of one such exchange of views. [33]

As dissenters against some aspects of the once established Church of England, Methodists now took on a more favorable relationship with Episcopalians after the Revolution. Previously they tended in the minds of churchmen to be lumped together with more violent Presby· terian and Baptist critics, to whom they would seem by their reform criticism of the Church to give comfort. Boucher, among others, testified that these sectarians disturbed the Church and its relationships with these churches.[34] Asbury described the tensions of some of these former situations. "I visited Joseph Cromwell," he noted in 1774, "a very stiff, old Churchman. But his parson, a Mr. Edmiston, disagreed with him in the doctrine of predestination, he was much displeased with him, and willing to receive us."[35] On another occasion, while he did not disagree with Samuel Chase's father, the Anglican minister, he did indulge in the reformer's judgment: "One more ignorant of the deep things of God, I have scarcely met with, of his cloth."[36] When this society moved out of the church in 1784, Episcopalians and Methodists were put in a more constructive position with its accompanying responsibility. Moreover, Methodists took much of the theology and liturgy of Episcopalianism with them, which was not the case with Presbyterians and Baptists.[37] The remaining issue of importance between Episcopalians and Methodists, to judge from the emphasis in journals and the Duke's *State of Religion,* centered on the question of "enthusiasm" in religion. "The noise and confusion of the Methodist meetings," Duke found in 1789, "has become a very common topic of conservation."[38] This was the concern among men with "a pretty good share of understanding qualified with a proportion of prudence." Such men, however, "regard the Methodists very sincerely . . ."[39] The adaptation of Methodist enthusiasm to Episcopalian hymnology and preaching was an instance of interfaith influence and adjustment. Difficulty between the denominations was thus marked by intransigence on either side.

Methodists also had a great deal in common with the dissenters — Presbyterians and Baptists— as well as the pietist groups. In the first case, Methodists had striven to accomplish many of those things within the Church of England which the Presbyterians and Baptists desired. These dissenters and reformers all applied the remedy of enthusiastic and awakened preaching together with an emphasis on evangelical piety, with which they hoped to revitalize religious life in the Church. While the Methodists did not set out to revise church ecclesiastical structure, they did after the Revolution move significantly in this direction. They modified Anglican concepts of sacerdotal powers, which brought the now independent Methodist Church to a more acceptable place in the eyes of dissenters. Methodists now stood on dissenter ground, more clearly outside the strictest Anglicanism. In addition to this better basis of understanding, it should be noted that the old case against the once established Church had now passed and with it any resentment for Methodist identifications with that church. There may have been subtler differences, such as Calvinistic predestination, but here too modification had been made by dissenters and they were moving in the direction of the Arminianism of Methodists.

There is clear evidence that Methodist relations with the Presbyterians improved. As patriots during the war, Presbyterians could not after it make a case against the native preachers of Methodism as they had against the Anglican Boucher. [40] Methodists were far less political during the war and a smaller percentage of the non-native preachers among them left the country at its conclusion. With the passing of the war, however, adjustment proceeded rapidly. During these years Methodists experienced some other tensions with Presbyterians, but there were contacts; and the situation was better than what Episcopalians found with this denomination. Asbury, for example, had great interest in Patrick Alison, and he heard him preach even though regretting the passing of "warm preaching" among some Presbyterians like Alison. [41] Garrettson also had disagreement with Presbyterians who followed this more moderate course. [42] Yet, even during the pre-revolutionary period Asbury found many Presbyterians receptive to this type of preaching even by himself in their house of worship. [43] The desire for the spirit of the Great Awakening continued strong after the war, even if it was not found among elements who were satisfied with Alison. Asbury's pattern of experience resembled that of other Methodist preachers. In 1779 Freeborn Garrettson first received hospitality in Somerset County at the hands of a Presbyterian minister and a layman. The following day, however, he reported, "one sayes my Proselites is two-fold more a Child of Hell than before. & the other showes to asperce my Caractor . . ." [44] He received similar treatment a few months later from another dissenting minister. [45] These attempts at winning adherents to his society would not proceed so adversely after the war, when Garrettson would then be appealing to Episcopalians for the most part. He would no longer appear to Presbyterians as one undoing their work, as he formerly did when he appeared to be intent on bringing their members back to the Church of England.

In the war years Garrettson preached his liberal view of predestination, so widely opposed to the Great Awakening theology and offensive to Presbyterians. Although he had controversies in Makemieland on the Eastern Shore, and around Baltimore, this pre-war situation later improved when Alison and others popularized a more liberal theology.

The Peace of Paris brought a thaw in Presbyterian relations not only with Methodists but also with Episcopalians. The results of a new outlook seemed evident. "Inasmuch as universal Liberty in Religion," declared the Lewes Presbytery, "is now firmly established thro' all the united states . . . it is hoped that all Churches pursuing their own forms of Religion, will enjoy perpetual Harmony and Charity . . ." [47] No further mention is made of those conflicts with Presbyterians which Garrettson noted in his journal during the pre-war years. The Presbyterian minister Balch had cordial association with the ex-Methodist and now zealous Episcopalian William Duke. "I spent the evening in agreable conversation with revd. Mr. Balch," Duke wrote. "How I wished for the vigour and cheerfulness which seemed to afford him a fund of constitutional happiness." [48] Accord may have been carried a little far in Claggett's eyes, when he was approached by a Presbyterian minister with a proposal for a convention between the churches. Although it was regarded by the Episcopalian bishop as "an artful overture" it was still an expression of better feeling between dissenter and churchman. [49]

With the passing of the war, the Baptists, who were a considerably more aggressive dissenting body than the Presbyterians at this time, also developed better relations with Methodists. Duke noted that they had stirred a tidal wave of proselytizing, which broke on Maryland about 1770. They were still sensitive to their greatest rival in such activities, the Methodists, when Presbyterians had receded from an earlier manifestation of such tensions. Asbury went through trying experiences as a result of this situation. "About five and twenty Baptists," he wrote of Frederick in 1772, "are the greatest enemies the Methodists have in this place." [50] Those who attended his sermons went away angry. "There are some," he also found, "who oppose the work under us, and perplex and trouble our young beginners." [51] This took place in the area evangelized by such Baptist exponents of the vigorous gospel as Jeremiah Moore. Asbury left a brief narrative of the Methodists' fortunes as evidence of these tensions. "Friend Bonham," he wrote, "was awakened by the instrumentality of Friend Strawbridge, and he told me that he had been much opposed [by Baptists]. He said they had used him very ill; but he was determined to have no more connection with them. He appears to be a solid, sensible man." [52] The year of the Declaration of Independence, however, this friction seemed to decline. Civilities among preachers of the rival evangelical denominations were in evidence on one occassion, thanks to the traditional hospitality of a Maryland gentleman and the Dutch Reformed Church, which consciously mediated among these religious groups. Asbury had been asked to preach at this church and afterward met two Baptist preachers among the Ridgely family's guests, who together with Asbury were welcomed and provided the pulpit of the Dutch Reformed Church. [53]

A year after this incident, Freeborn Garrettson began noting his own changing experiences with Baptists, which like Asbury's, passed on to better days. He boldly evangelized Baptist communities for two weeks. "Distress I met," he said with understatement, "and many very disagreable disputes . . ." Garrettson related that a conservative Calvinism which prevailed among this particular group was the nub of opposition. Yet he did not hesitate to plunge ahead with a discussion of election, predestination and final perseverance of the saints, which the Baptists felt in duty bound to confute. "I saw it my duty to preach." Garrettson said for his part, "and that strong, that Christ dyed for all . . ." In all of this "distress" appeared some light in the sky, promising a dialogue for a better day. "Among some I met with cold reception," he observed, "but with others was recd. with openness." [54]

Beginning in 1779 Garrettson had friendlier associations with Baptist ministers. He would, for example, share a Baltimore house of worship, preaching after a Baptist sermon and service. [55] They might, as itinerants, meet each other on the road as they journeyed to such a situation. Things once became so favorable, that Garrettson gave in his sermon a rebuttal of the Baptist's remarks, in order to show the reasonableness of infant baptism. No unseemly incident followed on this exchange. [56] Zealot though he was, Garrettson listened more than once with open mind and heart to a Baptist preacher. "I thought much more of his discourse," he confessed on one occasion, "than I did the day before." [57] A few days later two Baptists accepted some of his views and there was further evidence of increased good will. "I lodged with an old baptist," he recorded at this time. "I had great satisfaction, altho' we differed in regard to external spirit." [58] This situation was repeated later in subsequent years and after the Revolution one finds little or no mention of the conflicts and tensions noted in the earlier period. [59] The experience of Haskins did not seem to differ from Garrettson. [60] In fact, in testing with Garrettson, use is being made of something of an extremist compared to these other Methodists and their manner of preaching and evangelizing. A *fortiori* things were better with these others. In all of this, too, attention is called to the fact that a theology less dissonant with Methodist ideas was developing among Baptists after 1780, and that Methodists did not proselytize very much among Baptists after the War. [61]

Nothing seemed better to indicate these generally improved denominational conditions than the cordial relations in the 1790's between Duke and the Baltimore Baptist minister Roach. The first meeting which Duke's journal mentions came in 1792. He had preached at a court house one evening. "Immediately after Mr. Roach a Baptist from New England unexpectedly preached." While it was customary to share such a temporary place of worship, the dinner engagement of the two preachers which followed was not; and both friendly situations were unlikely twenty years previously. In 1793 the atmosphere had become so congenial that Duke, "after a stirring day went to hear him [Roach] preach in the evening." Earlier that same day the two had breakfasted together. [62] Further cordiality and charity was extended to Roach by Bend, another Episcopal minister, whose parish was in Baltimore. Three Sundays every month he made his chapel at Fell's Point available to Roach and out of these beginnings developed the Second Baptist Church. [63]

Methodists in earlier days had heated controversies with Presbyterians and Baptists, judging from Methodist journals. There were also Quaker-Methodist differences and out of them occasionally came subdued friction. Yet, theological developments in Methodism following the Revolutionary War provided greater grounds of agreement with Quakers.

Francis Asbury had what might be typical Methodist experience with Maryland Quakers. In the early 1770's he had been favorably impressed with William Sewell's (1654-1720) history of the Quakers. "My heart has been affected," he confessed. [64] Undoubtedly Asbury admired the exemplary lives narrated in such histories, rather than the theology attributed to the Quakers. For two months following Asbury's reading of Sewell, he made entries in his journal which unfavorably described Quaker acquaintances. In one instance Asbury found one individual "too much a Quaker in principle." Another would not allow vocal prayer in his family, which, it would seem to Asbury, was an application of Quaker views of these matters. [65] Silent prayer which would not allow "hollowing" meetings would never be adequate diet for a Methodist's soul, no matter how his heart might be affected by the good example of the Quaker. But Quakers also preached, and as Haskins found firsthand, "speak feelingly." He regretted, however, that they were a "sad people," as he observed them. [66] Garrettson shared the feelings of Asbury toward them. Like Asbury, he read their books but, unlike Haskins, Quaker sandness did not disturb him. Rather, he felt, "it [Quakerism] appeared to be too easy a way for me." [67]

As it turned out, however, Asbury and his co-religionists, after the Revolutionary War, moved closer to becoming "Quaker in principle." When the Methodist Christmas Conference of 1784 settled the matter of ordination of ministers and bishops differently from previous practice within the Church of England, and afterward in the American Episcopal Church, Quakers would view Methodists in a more favorable light. Minutes of Quaker monthly meetings had deplored marriage of members before priests according to the former dispensation. [68] There were no such "hireling priests" after the Revolutionary War among Methodists. These and other implications were reflected in an enlightening conversation which Asbury had with one Quaker. "It gave him pain." Asbury wrote of the Quaker's reaction to an ordination at the hands of English bishops, "that Joseph Pilmoor should go home for ordination. . . ." He felt, as Methodists later decided, that they should have the power of ordinances among themselves. [69] Undoubtedly, such a view brought Methodists closer to Quakers, increased good will and even attracted Quakers to Methodism. When an elderly Quaker preacher became a Methodist in 1785, it was reasonable to suppose the new doctrinal settlement of the previous year had provided a forceful motive for the decision. [70]

Good relations with Methodists did not logically bring Quakers closer to Episcopalianism, or notably improve Quakers relations with Episcopalians. The Episcopalian Jackson revealed some of this distance between the two denominations in a letter to Duke in 1796. "I should be willing almost to become a Quaker," he wrote ironically, "were not Baptism to be followed by this rite." [71] This indicated an impasse between Episcopalians and Quakers over this issue of confirmation. Nor did Duke show any particular appreciation for Quakers. In reading of them he was less moved than Asbury. "He seems to have been a man of great firmness and probity," he blandly commented on a life of William Penn. [72] In his *State of Religion* positive praise, often given to other denominations, was notably wanting in his treatment of Quakers, although he was sufficiently tolerant.

Methodist relations with religious groups of Continental European origin became as good, and even better, following the Revolution than those with the Quakers. Actual collaboration took place at one point. Moreover, for theological and political reasons, the formerly Established Church, out of which Methodism grew, generally held greater favor here that it did among English dissenter sects. This is particularly true of the Lutheran community. Reports to the Lutheran Ministerium from the western part of Maryland before the Revolution suggested that things were not always so favorable. "This district," it was noted in 1772, "is said to be very populous and to abound in various sorts of sectarian agitators." [73] From what is known of Baptist, Presbyterian and Methodist evangelizing in the area, disturbances seemed to come from them as they tried to win influence among German. When rivalries abated in the 1780's, Lutheran relationships with these denominations and particularly with Methodists could not but be better.

Lutherans after the war, however, seem to gravitate more toward the Episcopalians than toward Methodists. As early as 1781, the Ministerium record noted that "a union with the so-called High Church [was] proposed." The Episcopal bishop-to-be William White seems to have been responsible for these overtures. Because the development of American independence had faced Episcopalians in this direction of autonomy, such liberal innovations and initiative in conduct became possible. Although this design was not accomplished, it showed that the new constitution of the once established church became more favorable toward Lutherans. Another token of this improvement was the application of an Episcopalian for ordination in the Lutheran Church. [74] As these conditions continued, one finds William Duke in 1789 attending a Lutheran sermon, and afterwards discussing it in detail with the preacher. [75] There was evidently a substance of communication sufficient to offset Duke's confessed aversion for the German temperament.

These communications evidently obtained between diverse German religious groups themselves. Lutheran minister Schmucker of Hagerstown once preached at Otterbein's Reformed Church. In 1783 Lutheran meetings with other Reformed congregations took place, and evidently continued through the decade. [76] Common theological, ethnic, and cultural affinities encouraged these movements, as did the secular force of the new nationalism which had to be dealt with in common.

Methodist contact with Maryland Lutherans was not to come directly, or even through its associations by origin with Episcopalianism, which seemed to have possessed greater empathy with them. Collaboration with Otterbein and the Dutch Reformed Church provided Methodists with their only noteworthy relationship with the Lutherans. This is not to say that individual preachers were estranged, in contrast with the experience of Duke. Richard Whatcoat, the Methodist preacher, stated that he too attended Lutheran sermons, discussed them with the minister, and had dinner with a Lutheran minister. [77] Nevertheless, official reserve toward Methodists was suggested in Ministerium records in contrast to the attitude toward Episcopalians and Reformed. The Ministerium warned pastors to proceed cautiously with Methodists. [78]

On the other hand, Francis Asbury's impact on Philip Otterbein and the Dutch Reformed Church was dramatic and decisive. Indeed, he seemed to carry the revolutionary spirit of the times, on which his evangelical religion grew, into the congregations which were to evolve into the United Brethren. From Asbury's first days in America he had attended the preaching of Otterbein. Richard Whatcoat's journal in 1793 related that similar practices by other Methodists still continued to link the two religious movements. [79] Asbury's earliest probings, however, proceeded beyond this passive exercise. With Benedict Schope, an early associate of Otterbein, he discussed the theological matter of ordinances (or sacraments), their meaning and necessity. Asbury did not believe that ordinances were essential to the Church, which was far too liberal a view for Schope, at this early date of 1772. Two years later, however, the two came to greater agreement. "He appeared to be a good man." Asbury commented of Schope after this second meeting, "and I opened to him the plan of Methodism." [80] Later the same year Philip Otterbein joined the two and proceeded further with an adaptation of the plan of Methodism, but apparently without any adjustment of basic theological differences regarding ordinances. "They agreed to imitate our methods as nearly as possible." Asbury said in summary. There is no doubt that he left the mark of his influence "respecting the plan of Church discipline on which they intended to proceed." The following year Asbury, on a special occasion, urged Schope and Otterbein to his view. [81] At the appropriate moments Asbury thus played the intermediary within the Dutch movement. He prevailed upon Otterbein to accept the independent Reformed Congregation in Baltimore, thereby furthering Otterbein's leadership among Schope and other evangelicals of the First Reformed Church. Methodism thus influenced the first decisive steps of the Evangelical Reformed Church. [82]

Catholics stood in a quite different relationship with all of the
Protestant denomination from what has been observed, especially in their
interaction with Methodism. They were not, it is true, the target of nati-
vism as may have been the case with German immigrant Protestants.
Those who stood in the minds of Marylanders for Catholicism were of
English stock and many of their families were residents of America for
several generations. Unlike Maryland Germans, however, their faith was
in English thought long considered alien, which upon analysis often
seemed to say it was not Protestant. Politically, at least, for more than
seventy-five years Catholics in Maryland, and for a longer time elsewhere
in the Empire, had been stigmatized as prone to disloyalty. The non-
national nature of their faith prompted such doubts in others. As a
result of the Revolution Maryland was liberated from a lingering
domination by the official English religious and political views of
Catholicism. Possessed of full citizenship for the first time in that century,
the latent prestige of some prosperous and cultured Catholics created
a new image that was naturally more palatable to Marylanders. The
relationships of Catholics and Protestants clearly improved under the
impact of the newly won freedom.

In their writing Asbury, Garrettson and Haskins show that they
had no deep bitterness toward Catholics, even if they held great differences. The war and the combined religious endeavor to form a new
Christian state threw Catholics and Methodists, as well as other dissenters,
together in a way that brought about better relationships. It was in this
newly emerging context that these Methodists thought and wrote. Educated
as he was in the Church of England, Asbury had many understandings
that created initial difficulty in his relationships with Catholics. As late
as 1774 he stated that he devoted himself to the study of the Bible's
Book of Revelation and found therein clear prophecy of the "gradual
rise and artful progress of Popery." [83] Coke in his sermon to the Methodist
Christmas Conferences had pointed out how the Church of England
had been misled by Catholic deviation in Christianity. [84] These Methodists
disapproved of Catholic emphasis on papal and other hierarchical authority in the church, something criticized even more emphatically by
Presbyterians and Baptists.

In the hard days of the war, however, a Catholic governor in Maryland
came to the rescue of Asbury and Garrettson in an incident which
could not but leave both sides better disposed. While Asbury was in
Delaware, he heard that Garrettson had been imprisoned in Maryland
and was awaiting trial. In those times such waiting inevitably involved

a long period of discomfort and Asbury approached the Governor of Delaware to see if something could be done to bring relief to Garrettson. When the governor contacted the Catholic governor of Maryland Thomas Sim Lee he received a generous response. Lee ordered the local justices to bring Garrettson to Annapolis for a personal review of his case by the governor. After an examination of the matter, Garrettson was found innocent and set free; undoubtedly there were sincere regrets expressed by Lee for the state government's failure or inability to remove such conditions of injustice. About ten years after this experience, Garrettson had occasion to note that he was again pleased with Catholics, and implied that relations had improved. This was due not only to improvement in Methodist attitudes but also those of Catholics. Some people whom he found in 1789 to be "mild and Catholic" during his visit to a particular town, had not always been mild as their present pastor seems to have made them. "[He] did not do as some had done," Garrettson wrote, "prejudice and harden the hearts of the people against other denominations, especially arminians, as we are called." [85] The past tense and general manner of reference indicated that Garrettson, a Maryland native, was speaking from his own long experience. Having felt discrimination from Catholics, he became generous toward them when better days came. It is reasonable to explain what Garrettson saw of improvement by saying it was a happy outcome of the Revolution which made all religions equal before the law, thus removing the source of such tensions as he recalled. Under the new conditions of equality, Catholics were no longer defensive and prone to criticize Protestants as a group privileged before the law.

Thomas Haskins throws further light on Protestant relationships with Catholics, which tell of better days in the revolutionary period. He had an inquiring mind toward Catholics, as he showed in his reading of Louis Du Pin (1657-1719), the French Catholic who had written a history of the Church. "It is pretty well so far as it goes," he believed, "and it is worth reading." Yet he found this European "a rigid Roman Catholic. . . . [who] favored his own Church at the expense of every other church." Du Pin had a spirited propensity for designating other denominations as heretical. In this case, however, it was not the preoccupation of a Catholic minority spokesman in Maryland, but that of a conformist in a Catholic state. Haskins did not hesitate to regret this spirit in writers among his own fellow Protestants. In so doing he revealed his own sensitive attention to these interdenominational relationships. In one incident Haskins showed that he had attained some success with his good intentions and that the Catholic party whom he encountered had in contrast to Du Pin, shown great respect for Protestants and their beliefs. "In the morning [I] visited some prisoners under sentence of death & to be executed in a few days," he noted in his journal a short time before the conclusion of the war, "[and] they were all Romans [.] [The] Priest came in while we were exhorting them to prepare to meet their God..." The mild response by each clergyman to what would be an explosive situation under other historical circumstances spoke well of interdenominational relationships. The priest "seemed dissatisfied," and merely "desired we would retire as he wanted to be privately with them," Haskins' recounted, evidently intending to hear their confessions. [86]

On the Catholic side of these growing good relations with Methodists was the preeminent influence of John Carroll, the future bishop. The zealous activities of Methodists before the Revolution evidently awakened concern among Catholics at a time when they were insecure. Joseph Mosley requested apologetic books from England and Challoner's treatise on Methodism was specifically noted. When the condition of insecurity changed, the fear of Methodist inroads evaporated. Catholics were reassured at the sight of their own growing ranks, counting Protestant converts among their numbers. The pre-Revolutionary posture of Catholics appeared rigid to Protestants, as Methodists observed. However, in the era of John Carroll it is clear that Catholics stood in a better light, which improved relationships with Methodists. Carroll's many letters to Catholic clergymen throughout Maryland invariably carry consideration which would keep down any inclination to be the "rigid Catholic" of which Haskins spoke. The experience and personality of Carroll were poles apart from that of Du Pin. He soon made Americans understand that his view of freedom in theological terms differed from the Frenchman; and that his was the more authentically Catholic. Carroll enthusiastically collaborated with Methodists and dissenters in what they commonly believed to be a defense of religious freedom in the Maryland Constitution, when they opposed the Clergy Bill. It was "calculated to create a predominant and irresistable influence in favor of the Protestant Episcopal Church: and therefore we shall all oppose it with might and main. . . ." Theoretically grants for clergy salaries by the state were to be equal in each case. Cumulatively, one denomination stood to gain a more favorable position. In this analysis of Carroll one also finds a special bond between Catholics, Methodists, and other minority denomination in this matter of opposition to the Episcopalians. "All other denominations," he recalled, "were formerly subject to pay a heavy tax to the Clergy of the Ch. of England." [87] Not only the War, then, but the pre-Revolutionary experience and formation of the new nation created forces which united these Protestants and Catholics in certain vital areas.

The favorable relations which developed between Catholics and Episcopalians during the revolutionary period, however, should not be overlooked in the face of the special case of the Clergy Bill. These also had meaning for the Methodist-Catholic relations. Theologically and ecclesiastically, Methodists and Episcopalians had greater proximity than was the case of both regarding other Protestant groups. This fact must be related to a similar proximity between Episcopalians and Catholics, a favorable association in the eyes of Methodists. This was not the case in the Presbyterian, Baptist and Quaker views of Catholicism. These Protestants do not in the light of the sources studied here reveal any concrete evidence for exploring such aspects of Catholic interdenominational relationships deriving from theological and ecclesiastical views.

A detailed theological analysis of Methodist and Episcopalian situations with Catholics would be outside the scope of this study. However, William Duke illustrates an improved attitude of Episcopalians toward Catholics, which derived from theological elements of agreement. He expressed frank admiration for the Catholic Church, its personnel, and their management of its affairs. Like Haskins, he challenged writings which expressed the narrow Old World Protestant view of Catholicism and its history. At this early date he called in question that old wives' tale, the fable of the woman Pope Joan. Other reading took him into a discussion of Anglican ordination written by a Catholic. The author's favorable treatment of the matter pleased Duke, and reminded him of the priesthood as an ancient basis of kinship with Catholics, however difficult its recent genealogy might be. Thus it is not surprising that he went out of his way to attend a sermon by a Catholic priest. On one occasion he noted in his journal that he called at Mellwood on a priest-member of the distinguished Digges family, who "talked freely and was pretty communicative." [88]

There were other instances and persons attesting to better days between the two denominations. The Talbot County Vestry praised Episcopal and Catholic clergy together. "The Episcopal Clergy", it said in respect to their ecclesiastical affinity, "whether protestant or Papal, conduct themselves as men who fear God and keep his Commandments." [89] James Madison, returning from his consecration in England as the first Protestant Episcopal Bishop of Virginia, enjoyed the company of John Carroll as a fellow passenger. Bishop Carroll once said that some of his administrative principles for that office agreed with those of Thomas Claggett of Maryland, soon to become a bishop himself.[90] Carroll was willing to appeal to the example of the Episcopal Church in justifying his recommendation that American Catholic clergy should themselves choose their own bishop.[91]

John Carroll possessed an exact intellectual grasp and perceptive awareness of the situation in Maryland, both of which were decisive in the good Catholic adjustments with Marylanders in the Revolutionary period. In general principle he accepted the reasoning of Hugo Grotius on Christian pluralism, written in the seventeenth century during the wars of religion. The broader meaning of the Christian community must be restored, Grotius believed, even though it lacked all that unity which prevailed at earlier times in Europe. These principles, Carroll believed, would promote tolerance not only in America but in England.[92] While saying this with a favorable response from Protestants, Carroll was not unaware of the delicate position of Catholics. "More caution is required in the ministers of our Religion," he warned a recently arrived cleric from France, "than perhaps in any other Country."[93] Catholic positions could not merely be stated. They must take into account the Protestant mentality which would receive these statements and thus remove a heritage of misunderstanding.[94] When Carroll crossed out the phrase "violent opposition" in a letter and replaced it with "deep rooted prejudice," much was revealed of his grasp of the transition between 1770 and 1800.[95] Protestant goodwill was banishing violence that came from bitterness; there yet remained prejudice which would recede only before understanding carefully provided by Catholics.

Carroll and Episcopalians dealt successfully with the difficult situation of Francis Wharton, who defected from the Catholic priesthood and took up the Episcopal ministry. Duke had noted that such things more than anything else strained good feeling, and Carroll observed in February of 1785 that some Protestants exulted over the news. A doctrinal controversy followed. While Carroll decided to respond to Wharton's attack, he took pains to avert any protraction of polemics. In a chief pastoral office, he directed his remarks to his own flock in a spirit of instruction. He seems to have been faithful to the spirit of pluralism when he resisted the opportunity to reopen the controversy in June of 1785. Six years later as bishop he gave further meaning to this principle when he opposed a public debate by one of his clergymen.[97] There was a display of moderation by Episcopalians who shunned the easy opportunity of exploiting Wharton. This had the effect of inclining Wharton himself to moderation. In another case, Carroll noted that it was usually not the "leading people in this country" that gave countenance to what was unseemly in these delicate situations, thus indicating a growing stability in the relationships of Catholics with Maryland Protestants. [99] A reasonable and respected firmness prevailed in the same way in other matters, interfaith marriages, [100] arrangements for orphans, [101] and membership in Freemasonry. [102]

Another type of interdenominational relationship embraced specific situations. In some instances of worship sites, charitable works, and particularly education, several denominations collaborated in a way which shows that improvement in tolerance came about during the revolutionary period. Part of the rapid religious recovery from war-time destruction of chapels was due to sharing among the denominations what facilities remained. Where chapels were in such disrepair, or completely lacking in an area with growing numbers of worshippers, people turned to the court house as an easy solution to the problem. This not only tended to throw denominations together in a single congregation but also encouraged the preachers to attend sermons of another denomination. Nor was worship in these situations confined merely to public buildings. A Methodist chapel might be used by an Episcopalian, who saw a Baptist minister among his congregation. One denomination's school house might be made available to another at regularly stated times, in spite of the complications. [106] Some consciences may not have allowed this because of some special condition, but there was considerable reasonableness and flexibility. [107] Objection might be made to a particular preacher of another denomination but not to others. [108] In all of these situations, in spite of their difficulties, evident good will and cooperation was found.

There is some suggestion that many communities acted jointly in the matter of worship and especially in charitable efforts. Ministers were as scarce as were well-kept chapels after the war, and it was natural, particularly for Protestants, to benefit from the preaching of whatever denomination might succeed in supplying a community's needs. Both Asbury and Claggett had experienced this. [109] When a community formed a corporation for the relief of the poor and distressed it went much farther in erasing denominational lines. Legal provisions of such programs specifically required aid to all, whatever their religious profession, and this was at the request of the petitioning community. [108]

"When the real, or supposed necessity ceases of sending the youth of this continent to distant seminaries for the completion of their education," William Eddis wrote on the eve of the Revolution in Maryland, "the attachment of the colonies to Great Britain will gradually weaken." [109] It was not surprising, in the face of this, that Marylanders intensified education within the new state when they broke off from England. The period saw great development on the county level; and in instances like Charlotte Hall, three counties collaborated for a more advanced form of education. [110] More revolutionary than this activity was the broadening of the religious character of the school, particularly on the higher levels. The inter-faith approach in this is but another manifestation of pluralism.

The structure of Maryland education before the Revolution was largely controlled by the thinking of the established church. "We have, therefore, attempted to make learning the handmaiden to devotion," the Assembly wrote to the Bishop of Lincoln in 1684, "and founded free schools in Maryland to attend on their college in that colony. . . . The chiefest aim and end . . . [is] instructing our youth in the orthodox, preserving them from the heterodox tenets, and fitting them for the service of Church and State in this uncultivated part of the world." In those times it was frankly stated that schools sought "a perpetual succession of Protestant divines of the Church of England." [111] William Smith gathered up the best of this religious context of education and gave it new directions even while the Revolutionary War was in progress and religions experiencing equality before the law. "Lasting provision must be made by GOOD EDUCATION," said Smith, architect of Washington College, at its dedication, "for training up a succession of *Patriots, Lawgivers, Sages and Divines;* for liberty will not deign to dwell, but where her fair companion, KNOWLEDGE, flourishes by her side. . . ." The new education would reach out to broader areas of the new society. Special place, however, was given to the training for public and political life. "Now can GOVERNMENT be duly administered but where the principles of *Religion, Justice, Virtue, Sobriety,* and *Obedience* for CONSCIENCE SAKE, are upheld." [112]

This religious character of education was natural to Smith and to the society of his day, as it had been before the Revolution. He gave it wider significance, however, and entered upon a bold experiment prompted by the spirit of the Maryland Constitution as well as the interfaith amity of the revolutionary era. The official act of the Assembly established Washington College to train its students "for the service of their country in Church and State." Yet the "youth of all religious denominations and persuasions, shall be freely and liberally admitted to equal privileges and advantages of education, and to all the literary honors of the College." The same impartiality was required in statutes governing appointments to the college administration and faculty. [113] It is not easy to put down a term for this type of educational institution. One might call it either *multi-denominational or non-denominational.* At any rate, the experiment went on and was also found on the Western Shore at St. John's College, Annapolis. Here too was put down the "fundamental and inviolable principles," that the College was "for the benefit of youth of every denomination . . . without requiring or enforcing any religious or civil test, or urging their attendance upon any particular religious worship, other than what . . . have the consent and approbation of their parents or guardians. . . ." [114] All of these provisions for the colleges added up to an arrangement which would be religious without being discriminatory.

The bold design carried this same spirit into provisions for the administrative structure. The college became a private corporation, serving the public under the financial and legal favor of the government. Boards of trustees were made up from distinguished citizens of the state. A more important policy-making board of visitors was composed with due regard for the religious diversity of the state. [115] Three prominent clergymen —Allison, Carroll, and Claggett, for example—were members of St. John's College Board of Visitors. [116] Subscribers grouped themselves along religious denominational lines in order to make a joint contribution sufficiently large to entitle them to a lay representative on the board. [117]

With the colleges so constituted, the state proceeded to support financially both St. John's and Washington College. [118] In order to pass such legislation it was especially necessary to win the favor of Episcopalians, Presbyterians and Catholics, the chief potential sources of interest. This came about and legislation for the colleges was passed in the Assembly. The religious aspects of the college plans gave considerable difficulty, according to William Smith, but among Charles Carroll and the others he was able to find agreement upon certain fundamentals without any one party unreasonably demanding greater recognition of their particular views. [119] The religious settlement was satisfactory enough to allow all parties to approve conferring of a Doctor of Divinity degree on Bishop Carroll without any objections. [120] This seemed a needed gesture. Another tribute to the interdenominational spirit in the school venture was the strong religious quality of the academic program. While it does not seem that scientific theology was taught, religious principles as known from philosophy were, and this was apparently the basis of compromise. On the face of it, the controversial matter did not seem to come to a vapid item in the curriculum. Natural and moral philosophy were put down as subjects in which the student must gain competance.[121] He could be expected to enter upon matters close to theology. Smith's own son gave a public defense on the question whether eternal pains of hell contradicted the attributes of God.[122] It is significant to note that public opposition to the state grants for these colleges derived from resentment of the high fees and of the aristocratic tone of the schools,[123] rather than their religious ingredients. The schools, like the state, reflected the religious thrust of the Revolution and the intent of Marylanders to create a Christian society with all of these political and cultural ramifications.

The fact that John Carroll in time formed plans for his own school did not indicate objection to the religious settlement of the curriculum at St. John's and Washington Colleges. "I received additional pleasure," he confessed regarding this matter, "from the diffusion of liberal and tolerating principles." The overlooking of diversity of religious sentiment seemed to be successful.[124] "Being admitted to equal toleration," he explained by way of encouraging cooperation from one of his clergymen, "must we not concur in public measures, and avoid separating ourselves from the Community." He fully appreciated the great advantages Catholics received from these ventures. They were possible only with the help of other denominations and the state government, for by and large Catholics had not then the money to provide for such academic programs. In the beginning, when he had no funds for training future clergymen, Carroll even expected their preliminary training to come from the two new colleges. "Providence," he believed, "has ordained these as a resource for the exigencies of Religion."[125] He was also exerting himself to meet the great need for qualified teachers. "To me it appears that it may be of much service not only to learning," he thought, "but to true Religion, to have some of these professorships filled by R.[oman] C.[atholic] men of letters and virtue: if one or two of them were in orders, it would be so much the better."[126]

Only the most urgent circumstances prevented Carroll from carrying out his cooperation to the full measure of these expressions. None of these difficulties were objections to the religious conditions of the college curriculum. Rather, the pressing need for American-educated clergymen required special training in college years, which Carroll soon found Washington and St. John's could not be expected to provide. This was closely related to his determination to have America provided with such a clergy so that a bishop might be selected from them rather than Europeans.[127] Even the practice of sending college-age men to Europe for their studies was not proving satisfactory. Carroll also became over-exacting in what he required of educational conditions favorable to fostering priestly vocations. These conditions could not be reasonably expected from Chestertown and Annapolis. This explains why Carroll and the first Georgetown College board of governors tended to require a discipline more suited to seminarians than lay students. [128] By 1790 he became notably critical of the new Maryland colleges as "defective in discipline" as it affected all types of students. Under these circumstances he now had additional motives for Georgetown College which looked to the special needs of Catholic laymen. Practically speaking, such a venture was more likely to succeed in getting sufficient numbers if it could draw from both lay and seminary students. Carroll always understood that this enlargement of purpose would make possible educational benefits to non-Catholics. [129] Georgetown, therefore, held a kindred spirit with Washington and St. John's. The latter two, like Georgetown, held a special attraction for some on the basis of their religious identity. Episcopalians and Presbyterians often found them more suitable.

The Methodists, like Catholics, undertook their own independent school—Cokesbury College. Initially their problems and understandings were similar to those of Catholics. The institution, however, eventually put itself under multi-denominational auspices, in order to qualify for grants from the state, as Washington and St. John's had done. At the time of its founding, Cokesbury set a very demanding standard for itself as a denominational and religious institution. "We are determined to have a College," said Thomas Coke after whom the college was named together with Asbury, "rich in religion and learning; hand in hand together, or not at all." He understood this objective in strictly Methodist terms rather than in the broader statements of Washington College statutes. In testing high achievement of this Methodist objective, Coke looked for "what is best of all, [that] many of them [students] are truly awakened." One boy was expelled for ridiculing "experimental religion." [130] Two years later Richard Whatcoat thought Cokesbury succeeded very well in promotion of true virtue and a few were "under gracious impressions," thanks to excellent spiritual guidance. [131] William Duke took similar note of these good conditions at Cokesbury. [132]

It was evident to Duke, however, that the college was approaching a serious financial and managerial crisis in 1793. He had previously observed that the "whole institution is in an infant state." [133] The college authorities clearly saw that they would have to look in the direction of the state, as Washington and St. John's had done, for the collaborator needed to keep their endeavor alive. This would require a radical change in the philosophy and procedures of the school. The larger student body would include non-Methodists; this in turn would limit much more the possibility of spiritual influence on Methodist students. In addition the selection of Methodist teachers and the requirements made of them would be more difficult to accomplish. These were not unlike the obstacles Carroll found in pursuing seminary objectives for some Catholics in Washington and St. John's Colleges, young men he had hoped would come under "gracious impressions."

Asbury was unwilling to make the change to a multi-denominational foundation for Cokesbury. He reasoned somewhat differently from Carroll. It seemed clear to him that the strictness of Cokesbury could not continue under the new arrangement of collaboration with the state. This prospect promised to be unworthy of his efforts. "If we cannot have a Christian school (that is, a school under Christian discipline and pious teachers)," he said on the eve of the decision, "we will have none." [134] It would seem that the Christian content of religious teaching at state-related colleges did not entirely please Asbury. The discipline and piety in teachers and students, to which he referred, derived from a clear and specific religious teaching. He required that the quality and amount of that teaching be what it had been at Cokesbury. In this he would be going beyond Carroll, who at least made a distinction between what was demanded for potential seminarians and other students. General Christian teaching and average virtue in teachers seemed adequate in the latter case.

Whatever Asbury's conservatism and reservations on the new arrangement for Cokesbury, other Methodists went ahead with the interdenominational venture. Some trustees and governors were taken from other faiths in accord with the new law of incorporation of 1794. [135] Students and faculty were not limited to Methodists. All of these good intentions and imaginative plans, however, came to a tragic end when fire destroyed the college and creditors closed in on Cokesbury's decimated resources. [136] Nevertheless, this whole chapter of the Methodist college gave convincing testimony of the good relationships which obtained between the denominations, and of the willingness to enlarge them. The common religious aspiration of Marylanders for a Christian state and society left its mark on all of these academic foundations. They adjusted to their difficulties with a discerning spirit of pluralism here as they had in other expressions of it.

REFERENCES

[1]Ernst Troeltch,*The Social Teaching of the Christian Churches* (2 vols.; New York, 1960) gave a full development to the sect-denomination topic.

[2]William Duke in *State of Religion* indicated that he was testing the new system. See Thomas O'Brien Hanley, "Reluctant Witness to Pluralism in Early America," *Theological Studies,* XXXVI (Sep. 1965), 375-92.

[3]Silver, *Provisional Government of Maryland (1774-1777)* (Baltimore, 1895), p. 12.

[4]Minutes of the Lewes Presbytery (Presbyterian Historical Society), p. 116 (Oct. 15, 1782).

[5]Haskins, Journal, July 29, 1783.

[6]Smith to West, 1784 [?] (Maryland Diocesan Library).

[7]Asbury, I, 655 (Nov. 3, 1790).

[8]Duke, Journal, July 29, 1789.

[9]*Ibid.,* Apr. 21, 1792.

[10]*Ibid.,* Nov. 9, 1790.

[11]*Ibid.,* Aug. 17, 1790.

[12]*Ibid.,* Feb. 1, 1787.

[13]*Ibid.,* Jan. 12, 1787.

[14]Carroll to Plowden, June 1, 1792 (John Carroll Papers).

[15]Carroll, sermon on possession of See, Dec. 1790 (*ibid.*).

[16]White, p. 26.

[17]Garretson, *Experiences and Travels,* p. 181 (Feb. 26, 1781).

[18]Duke, *State of Religion,* p. 31.

[19]*Ibid.,* pp. 16-17.

[20]*Ibid.,* pp. 14-15.

[21]Quoted in Hughes, p. 285.

[22]Asbury, II, 323 (Nov. 22, 1779).

[23]*Ibid.,* I, 346-347 (Apr. 25, 1780).

[24]Sweet, *Methodist Sources,* p. 25.

[25]Asbury, I, 441 (June 2, 1783); 473 (Nov. 30, 1784).

[26]Duke, Journal, Aug. 12, 1789.

[27]*Episcopal General Convention Journal,* pp. 131-132.

[28]Duke, Journal, Oct. 21, 1793.

[29]Haskins, Journal, Jan. 26, 1785; Whatcoat, Journal, Dec. 7, 1792 (Library of Congress).

[30]Duke, Journal, Jan. 16, 1792.

[31]*Ibid.,* Nov. 2, 1793.

[32]*Ibid.,* July 8, 1789.

[33]*Ibid.,* June 21, 1792.

[34]Boucher, p. 47; Utley, p. 11; Duke, *State of Religion,* pp. 18 and 20.

[35]Asbury, I, 110 (Mar. 14, 1774).

[36]*Ibid.,* p. 99 (Dec. 14, 1773).

[37]Hughes, p. 287.

[38]Journal, Aug. 27, 1789.

[39]*Ibid.,* July 8, 1789; Bend to Claggett, May 1796, in Utley, p. 95.

[40]Boucher, p. 105.

[41]Asbury, I, 153 (Apr. 2, 1775).

[42]Garrettson, Journal, Bk. I, pp. 48-49 (1777).

[43]Asbury, I, 97 (Nov. 13, 1773).

[44]Journal, Jan. 18, 1779.

[45]*Ibid.,* July 8, 1779.

[46]*Ibid.,* May 29 and June 14, 1799.

[47]Minutes of the Lewes Presbytery (Presbyterian Historical Society), p. 116 (Oct. 15, 1782).

[48]Duke, Journal, July 2, 1789.

[49]Claggett to Duke, June 19, 1786, in Utley, p. 50.

[50] Asbury, I, 53 (Nov. 19, 1772).
[51] *Ibid.*, p. 52 (Nov. 11 and 12, 1772).
[52] *Ibid.*, p. 54 (Nov. 21, 1772).
[53] *Ibid.*, p. 190 (June 15, 1776).
[54] Garrettson, Journal, July 6, 1777.
[55] *Ibid.*, June 18, 1779.
[56] *Ibid.*, Apr. 3, 1779.
[57] *Ibid.*, June 22, 1779.
[58] *Ibid.*
[59] Garrettson, *Experiences and Travels*, p. 108 (Apr. 4, 1779).
[60] Haskins, Journal, Sep. 19, 1783.
[61] Semple, p. 385.
[62] Duke, Journal, Oct. 7, 1792; Oct. 28, 1793.
[63] Weishampel, p. 55.
[64] Asbury, I, 65 (Jan. 1, 1773).
[65] *Ibid.*, pp. 68 (Feb. 2, 1773), 71 (Mar. 1, 1773), and 54 (Nov. 21, 1772).
[66] Haskins, Journal, Sep. 19.
[67] Garrettson, Journal, Bk. I, 17 (1775).
[68] Kent Monthly Minutes, Mar. 10, 1779.
[69] Asbury, I, 109 (Mar. 11, 1774).
[70] Coke, *Extracts from Journals*, p. 24 (Jan. 7, 1785).
[71] Jackson to Duke, Aug. 21, 1796 (Maryland Diocesan Archives).
[72] Duke, Journal, Nov. 23, 1790.
[73] *Lutheran Ministerium*, p. 3.
[74] *Ibid.*, p. 178 (1781), 187-91 (1783).
[75] Duke, Journal, July 8, 1789.
[76] *Lutheran Ministerium*, pp. 289, 187-191 (1791).
[77] Journal, July 10, 1789.
[78] *Lutheran Ministerium*, pp. 187-191.
[79] April 9 and 10.
[80] Asbury, *Journal and Letters*, I, 54 (Nov. 21, 1772), p. 103 (Jan. 4, 1774).
[81] *Ibid.*, p. 114 (May 3, 1774), p. 153 (Mar. 28, 1775).
[82] Berger, pp. 329-330.
[83] Asbury, I, 113 (Apr. 23, 1774).
[84] *Sermon on Godhead*, pp. 3-4.
[85] Garrettson, *Experiences and Travels*, pp. 170, 235-36.
[86] Haskins, Journal, Jan. 22, Dec. 11, 1782; Dec. 12, 1784; Oct. 28, 1783.
[87] Carroll to Plowden, Feb. 27, 1785 (John Carroll Papers).
[88] Journal, Feb. 3, 1792; Apr. 25 - Jun. 10, 1791; Feb. 10, 1794; May 5, 1792; June 10, 1971.
[89] St. Peter's Parish, Talbot County, Report to Claggett, 1797 (Maryland Diocesan Archives).
[90] Carroll to Charles Plowden, Sep. 25, 1790; Nov. 12, 1788 (John Carroll Papers).
[91] Carroll to Farmer, Dec., 1784.
[92] To Plowden, Oct. 21, 1791 (John Carroll Papers); see also Guilday, John Carroll, pp. 172-173, for discussion of papal authority in this connection.
[93] To La Poterie, Apr. 3, 1789 (John Carroll Papers).
[94] Carroll to Thorpe, Feb. 17, 1785 (*ibid.*).
[95] To Gardoqui, No. [March ?], 1795/6 (*ibid.*).
[96] To Plowden, Feb. 27, June 29, 1785 (*ibid.*).
[97] Carroll to Plowden, Feb. 22, 1791 (*ibid.*).
[98] Carroll to Plowden, Dec. 22, 1791 [1793 ?]. In 1798, after his wife's death, Wharton again renewed his attacks (see Carroll to Plowden, Dec. 13, 1798) (*ibid.*).
[99] To Plowden, Apr. 27, 1780 (*ibid.*).
[100] Carroll to Charles Carroll, July 15, 1800, and to Beeston, Nov. 16, 1791 (*ibid.*).
[101] Carroll to Charles Carroll, Nov. 11, 1783 (*ibid.*).
[102] Carroll to McElhine [e] y, Jan. 7, 1794 (*ibid.*).

[103]Duke, Journal, Oct. 20, 1792; July 25-26, 1789.
[104]*Ibid.,* Dec. 30, 1793 - Jan. 2, 1794.
[105]Asbury, I, 597 (May 2, 1789).
[106]Duke, Journal, July 26, 1789.
[107]Bend to Claggett, May 1796; Utley, p. 95; Asbury, I, 471 (Nov. 7, 1784).
[108]*Laws of Maryland,* Nov. 1792, chap. liv.
[109]Eddis, pp. 148-150.
[110]*Laws of Maryland,* Nov. 1789, chap. xcii.
[111]Oct. 18, 1694, quoted in Thomas Fell, *Some Historical Accounts of the Founding of King William's School and Its Subsequent Establishment as St. John's College* (Baltimore, 1894), pp. 8, 10-11.
[112]Horace W. Smith, *Life and Correspondence of Rev. William Smith* (2 vols.; Philadephia, 1880), II, 67.
[113]*Ibid.,* p. 72.
[114]*Laws of Maryland,* 1785, p. 4.
[115]Utley, *Life of Claggett,* p. 45.
[116]Carroll to Plowden, Feb. 24, 1790 (John Carroll Papers).
[117]*Laws of Maryland* (Green), 1785, pp. 4 ff.
[118]*Ibid.;* Bernard C. Steiner, *History of Education in Maryland* (Washington, 1894), p. 13.
[119]William Smith to West 1784 [?] (Maryland Diocesan Archives).
[120]Gegenheimer, p. 86.
[121]L. Wethered Barrell, "Washington College, 1783," *Maryland Historical Magazine,* VI (June, 1911), 164-179, discusses subjects taught and indicates there were clergymen on the faculty.
[122]Steiner, p. 77.
[123]Crowl, pp. 85-86.
[124]To Visitors and Governors of Washington College, July 1, 1785 (John Carroll Papers).
[125]To Plowden, Feb. 27, 1785 (*ibid.*).
[126]To Edenshins, Oct. 4, 1785 (*ibid.*).
[127]Carroll to Plowden, July 11, 1786 (*ibid.*).
[128]Minutes of the Board of Directors of Georgetown College, 1797 to 1815, entry for April 24, 1799 (Georgetown University Archives, Washington, D. C.). See John M. Daley, *Georgetown University: Origin and Early Years* (Washington, D. C.: Georgetown University Press, 1957), p. 3 and chaps, ii-iii for a more general discussion of the College's beginning.
[129]To Plowden, Feb. 24, 1790 (John Carroll Papers).
[130]*Extracts from Journals,* pp. 111-112 (May 6, 1790).
[131]Whatcoat, Journal, Oct. 23, 1792.
[132]Journal, Aug. 16, 1792.
[133]Ibid., Dec. 7, 1793; Aug. 16, 1792.
[134]Asbury, II, 30-31 (Oct. 21, 1794).
[135]*Laws of Maryland,* 1794, chap. xxvi, quoted in Leo J. McCormick, *Church-State Relationships in Education in Maryland* (Washington, D. C., 1942), pp. 69-70.
[136]*Laws of Maryland,* Nov. 1798, chap. lx.

IX

WORKS OF A CHRISTIAN STATE

The Maryland Constitution of 1776 made it clear that Maryland was a Christian state, intent upon fostering religious life in society without imposing the confinements of the confessional state which had preceded it. The story of the various religious groups showed that they had been released by the new order and underwent constructive growth according to their own terms. But what about the good works of a Christian people under this new dispensation? Did they flourish? Did these Christians, their state and their society give these visible signs of the faith that was in them? The composite picture of the denominational parts, of course, provides a positive answer to these questions. *Good works* as a term encompasses the deeds of Marylanders in building up their respective churches and vital worship. What must be added here to the earlier treatment of those deeds is a broader religious context and a more specific meaning for *good works*. Care of the poor, emancipation of slaves, educating the young, and other good works had their inspiration in the religious spirit of Marylanders. These good works marked the Christian, his church, society, and state as authentically as the sublimest act of worship itself. It is important in measuring the good works of the Christian state in Maryland to consider later developments in the Protestant Episcopal Church. In a sense, the pluralistic spirit of other groups was tested by that church's well being. Defenders of the confessional state had often said that any other order would give rise to bitter sectarianism and jealousy. Did the Episcopal Church now become the object of spoliation? If in the later period leading up to 1800 it thrived, then the progress of other groups did not come at her expense, and the Christian state of Maryland proved to be free of that dreaded sectarian spirit. It has already been shown that there were many manifestations of a spirit of pluralism and inter-faith amity. Further evidence is provided here, but with a different emphasis in terms of Christians achieving good works. In addition to the usual meaning of the term, it is well to include the exercise of a zeal free from sectarianism, without the intent of undermining the largest religious body in the state. *Good works* in this sense will be examined first.

Two critics in the Anglican tradition underscored the challenge which the Episcopal Church and Maryland generally as a Christian state met. Jonathan Boucher said that the concession of equal status to a dissenter Protestant group, as had been long the case in New England, doomed the whole religious life of the new state of Maryland. Sectarian jealousy and conflict would spawn on the new ground formed in 1776. William Duke, on the contrary, held hope. The old confessional order was difficult to defend, as it imposed a confinement on the religious spirit of Maryland. At the same time, Duke did not feel that the provisions for Christianity in the new constitution were substantial enough to assure a flourishing Christian life. Vague professions of belief in Christianity by office-holders were not enough. Though he knew not how to accomplish it, the state should somehow more effectively foster evangelical Christian virtue and worship, perhaps prescribing profession of specific creed and ritual—Biblical belief, for example. This may have represented the thinking of many members in the Protestant Episcopal Church, who at the same time stood against the establishment and confessional state notions enunciated by Boucher. Yet Duke seemed to be saying that a clearly stated evangelical form of Christianity must be favored by the state. Otherwise, sectarian jealousy would swarm on the amorphous Christian state. But this was only a fear, and Duke admitted that he might be wrong, which would please him in this case.

Methodists, on the other hand, were inspired by the constitutional arrangement and desired no further descriptions in law of the Christian state. By their own evangelical preaching, they were producing visible results in society which Duke expected to be accomplished by further clothing the constitution with Christian legal garb. Presbyterians, Catholics, and probably all other groups concurred in the Methodist view. In general, therefore, all felt that the Christian nature of the state opened the door wide enough to bring about a renewal of society, not only immediately in the growth of organized religious groups, but also in broad social works which manifested a Christian inspiration. A healthy zeal, free of sectarianism, was already evident to confirm their hopes. [1]

There was a more divergent view of the Christian state than any of these that have been considered. Its advocates were not concerned with sectarian animosities which might arise from the way the constitution referred to Christianity. They denied that there should be any such reference and, most of all, that there should be any religious test for office holders. Luther Martin articulated the thoughts of this apparently small group of absolute separationists. In discussing the Federal Constitution at the time of ratification, he considered naive those who demanded profession of Christianity by office holders. "There were some members," he said of such persons at the Federal Convention, "so unfashionable as to think that a belief in the existence of a Deity, and of a state of future rewards and punishments would be some security for the good conduct of our rulers, and that in a Christian Country, it would be at least decent to hold out some distinction between the professors of Christianity and downright infidelity of paganism." [2] William Vans Murray, once a diplomat of the United States to France, spoke in much the same vein and saw any constitutional gestures such as Maryland had to be contrary to the spirit of religious freedom. [3] The subtleties of their views were not examined. In their minds, it would seem, a truly Christian country or society need not have a state identified as Christian by constitutional provisions. The majority of Marylanders on the contrary, saw an unnatural condition where a Christian people did not manifest their social reality by constitutional references to this faith. The antagonistic voices of Murray and Martin accounted for majority militancy for the 1776 constitutional arrangement.

Samuel Chase posed a very different challenge to these defending the religious settlement. He asserted the power of the state over the churches in a way that was unacceptable in 1776. Prior to the Revolution he stood with those who saw the assembly as the proper supervisor of the then Established Church. As the politics of that period show, however, this policy was prompted by the lay vestries in the hope of strengthening their authority. The prospect of episcopal power expanding in their area of authority was very real. Chase's views from 1776 onward were not fully developed, certainly not expressed carefully enough to see what church-state arrangement he originally wanted. After 1790 the success of his own Episcopal Church both within and in its relations with the rest of Maryland society vindicated the constitution. [4]

In understanding why all of these critics won no substantial following, it is necessary to see the success of the Protestant Episcopal Church from 1790-1800. This will show that it was not the object of sectarian animosity and spoliation; thas as the largest religious group it flourished in the Christian state. When this is added to the general story of good works in the era, a final dimension is given to the religious scene that emerged from the Revolution. The vitality to which Maryland religious life aspired before the Revolution was attained.

The Protestant Episcopal hopes for great benefits from an American bishop were visibly fulfilled in the 1790's. The political danger of a bishop now past, Bishop Thomas Claggett took up his important powers and used them vigorously. He unified the process of clergy supply to the parishes and stimulated their zeal. Lay vestries, so strongly established as a result of the colonial experience, were properly consulted. Duke's appointment to St. Margaret's parish in 1796 bore this out. In one of his regular visits with the vestry he learned that a rector must be appointed. He suggested Duke, but the vestry was to offer the appointment directly. [5] The basis of good government, Duke found, was the laity in the Church. "I have long been of the opinion," he said, "that if left to the prudence and direction of its members[,] provided the doctrines of

Christ are rightly taught and applied[,] the names or arrangement of offices cannot be very material [cause much difficulty]." [6] Others admired the effectiveness and promise of these Maryland ingredients of the church. "The future comparative growth of the Protestant Episcopal church in the rising metropolis of America," Ralph wrote to Claggett, "may be much influenced by the bigger and manly features of its infant constitution." [7]

Most Episcopalians did not want favored financial support from the Christian state. They wanted all clergy salaries of whatever denomination paid by the government, as the new constitution allowed. Joint action by the other denominations prevented this. Was the result financially disastrous for the Protestant Episcopal Church? Surveys by Claggett and vestry records in the 1790's show that it was not. When the official reports were circulated in 1790, West expressed confidence in the new arrangement. "It shews fiscal progress of our Ch[urche]s," he wrote, "forming itself into stability." [8] Claggett's relationship to the whole structure was far more complex, and he more clearly saw the Church's problem. Subscription was now used to replace the government grants of former times. "How are we poor Parsons perplexed by this Subscription business," he wrote to Duke in 1794. [9] He expressed similar sentiments to gentlemen in Washington County regarding their financial plight; but here church life was least established. St. Mary's County was a less critical case. [10]

West's optimistic view can be reconciled with Claggett's deprecation if it is understood what was involved in the adaptation to voluntarism and subscription. [11] Pew rents were lowered and some of the properties of parishes were rental. Subscriptions of outright money gifts were added to these customary sources of income. It can be seen beneath these records that the vestries were energetically refinancing parishes in a remarkable spirit of zeal. In some cases they postponed getting a clergyman until debts had been cleared away. Glebe land was sold in order to improve churches already in existence and land acquired for additional ones. [12] This clearly called for a long-term involvement of parishoners as subscribers, who no longer left the church dependent upon its inherited property for support. [13] There were significant instances of these activities in Kent, Dorchester, and Talbot Counties. [14] The story of progressive improvement stood out quite plainly in the minutes of St. George's Vestry from 1776 to 1796. Pew rent arrangements especially showed the vitality of religious life. One could no longer pay a substantial rent and rest complacently as a churchman; it was now necessary to subscribe additional amounts of money. Fees were lowered within reach of all and subscription was a more authentic challenge to zeal. Final resting place in the parish cemetery required some kind of fidelity to subscription according to one's means. [15]

With such responsibility in the laity, it was not surprising that the quality and numbers of the clergy were secured. One instance showed the reputation of the Maryland church was good and attractive to idealistic young ministers. A young man from New York was anxious to receive an appointment to a Maryland parish. [16] Many noted the great improvement in the quality of the clergy. "The ministerial duties were more faithfully performed by the clergy in general," wrote one observer in 1797, "than they probably ever were before in Maryland." Their zeal carried over to concern for undeveloped regions. Some at this very time prepared for a missionary career in the trans-Appalachian country. [17]

In spite of this picture of growth and stabilization of church life, Claggett and others feared that a loss in numbers would inevitably follow the revolutionary change in the state. Methodists especially appeared likely to win Episcopalians to their congregations. The St. George Parish vestry minutes noted in 1796 that many "families have either left the Parish or joined themselves to other religious societies." [18] A report from St. Mary's County was more definite, but indicated that only a few families had joined Methodist congregations. There are only vague pieces of evidence to justify Claggett's fears. While Anglicans no longer constituted a group numerically larger than all others together, this could be explained by the migrations out of the diocese rather than by leakage.

It is important to note that leakage to Methodists, or even other similar vital religious groups was not viewed as hostile to the religious life of Marylanders as a Christian people. Jackson, for example, who was reserved about taking up awakening features of religious practice and preaching, saw that he must be concerned even as a good Episcopalian with the general improvement of religion as more important than growth of his own denomination. The Baptist Rippon's collection of hymns, he felt, should be used by the Episcopal Church. This might "afford Proof of our Liberality; & Christian Attention to what seems to have originated in a benevolent Design to serve the best Purposes with the Religions of *all* Denominations." Duke, who was an admirer of Wesley, Coke, and Asbury in these matters, was ultimately commissioned by Bishop Claggett to compose a hymn book which drew upon Methodist and other sources. [19] This means, therefore, that even allowing for leakage to the newly formed Methodist Episcopal Church, that group redounded favorably to the growth of piety generally and within Episcopalianism. All of this showed that any Episcopal fear of spoliation following the emergence of the revolutionary Christian state was unfounded.

From reports which Claggett received it is possible to further confirm that the Episcopal Church in the 1790's experienced no spoliation. Religious life, in fact, had grown in quality in the parishes. It is therefore possible to pass beyond the evidence developed earlier, which showed that the new constitution of the state and of the Protestant Episcopal Church emancipated religious life from the confinements of the confessional state experienced before the Revolution. In the spring of 1793, Claggett discussed with the clergy convention plans for a survey of religious life in the parishes at that time. [20] To the ministers and vestries together he addressed "interrogatories," which tested the health of the church and religion in general. "Do virtue and piety gain ground among you?" he asked. "Has infidelity made any progress among you? What danger do you apprehend from it?" He also wanted to know if "other religious denominations gain ground;" and whether this was due to the zeal of these groups, or "the influx of strangers." [21] As the study progressed a general picture of religious life within the Episcopal community took shape. In addition to written inquiries on these matters, Claggett also sent visitors to several parishes and their dependent congretations. There was, however, a reluctance to cooperate with visitors. [22] Yet if these reports that did succeed are added to other communications to Claggett, there is sufficient evidence that religious life was improved and that the once established church was not an object of spoliation by sectarianism.

Profiles of the various counties and regions can be constructed from these records. Joseph Bend's observation on the congregation at Custis' Creek as a generalization sums up very well the condition of the several congregations and their related parishes in Anne Arundel County. "Affairs . . . rather prosper than decline," was his comprehensive comment. [23] This territory stretched from Annapolis northward to Westminster in what is today Howard and Carroll Counties. St. Anne's ancient parish in Annapolis was well served under Higgenbothom, who requested permission to preach in the afternoon. He expected greater nembers at services as a result of this modification in parish practice. The parish also successfully maintained a school during this period. St. James, under Compton, a much younger congregation, showed signs of orderly growth in fidelity to subscriptions which would help the bishop in acquiring land for the maintenance of a rector. While it was considerably smaller than St. Anne's, St. James was soon very well established. [24] All Hallows at Moscross was even more striking. Bend found that the numbers here were growing and there was no leakage to other denominations. A large congregation attended his sermon service and the vestry was zealously making provisions for a new rector. Farther north at Westminster was St. Margaret's Parish, where Williams Duke ministered very effectively and to the admiration of Bend, Claggett's appointed visitor. Bend was distressed, however, at the Elkridge congregation, which was not very attentive to Sunday observances, and at Queen Caroline, which was without a rector. [25]

Baltimore County and Baltimore City proper, with its St. Paul's Parish, rated very well. "The state of my own parish," Bend wrote to Bishop Claggett, "is flourishing; & . . . I hope soon to call upon you to consecrate another building to the service of God." A similar condition was found at St. James on My Lady's Manor, several miles from Baltimore, "where virtue & piety are increasing . . ." Owings Mill and Farrison showed how handicapped a congregation was without a resident minister. A lay preacher conducted services and instruction was greatly lacking. St. Thomas Parish in this situation was coming under the influence of Calvinism, some parishioners going over to other denominations. There was no evidence of hostility in this, nor defection to irreligion. [26]

The Eastern Shore of Maryland had many long-established parishes. It was clear that this condition continued after the Revolution, as seen in the case of St. George's Parish, Talbot County. Vestry reports for 1790 indicated vitality. Catechizing activity was carried on in the face of the challenge of infidelity rather than from sectarian competition. The growth in numbers called forth plans for a division of the parish. At Easton in Talbot County, Jackson also saw great signs of progress. "In my parish & School," he wrote to William Duke, "I find all the Encouragement which I could reasonably expect." Nearby preachers of the Calvinist tradition gave occasion for emphasizing the Anglican doctrine on baptism, when he preached or catechized. St. Peter's Parish was planned in the face of growing numbers. Services were already being conducted on a visiting basis at the Court House in Easton. Militant catechizing began, awakened by the threat of Thomas Paine's *Common Sense* in the hands of some of the citizens. [27]

The western fringe of the state had never come as greatly under the influence of Anglicanism as the central and eastern portions. Here fifty percent of all Catholics were centered in Charles and St. Mary's Counties in the south. They constituted more than thirty percent of the population. In Frederick and Washington Counties to the north and west, denominations of the Calvinist and Lutheran traditions had grown up as a result of migrations in the first decades of the century. William Duke as an itinerant Methodist within the Church of England had noted the sad conditions of religion in the central area of Prince George and Montgomery Counties in the 1770's. He did, however, see promise from his evangelization, his journal in the late 1780's confirming his prophecy. [28]

The reports on St. Peter's Parish, Montgomery County, from 1790-1800 show a thriving church. Growth of the congregation made necessary a gallery. Thomas Read the rector of St. Peter's also ministered to Hagerstown in Washington County and Frederick in Frederick County. The last seemed to make the least progress when he reported in 1798. Bower, another minister located in Frederick, regularly attended to communicants in the area and experienced the same difficulties. Lutherans and Catholics seemed to gain numbers from among those who held no religious connection or only a slight one with the Episcopal Church. "They are so scattered about this extensive parish," Bower explains of his Episcopal flock, "I have found it impossible to make out." From a general religious standpoint, however, it should be noted that the Christians were aided in these situations by other denominations. [29]

Perhaps more than in Montgomery County, the parishes in the southwest counties prospered, having been longer established. Reports as late as 1807 show, however, that parish life here had not attained the strength found in the central and eastern parts of the state. There were some instances of membership leakage to Catholicism and Methodism. Since St. Mary's and Charles Counties were never under the ascendancy of Anglicanism, these few losses in numbers were not caused by sectarian spoliation. In general, then, reports said that the condition of Episcopal parishes and congregations in certain areas appear less favorable because they are seen beside the thriving counties and regions. [30]

For a summary view of the once established church in the 1790's, William Duke's Journal serves very well. At the end of the era he was convinced that the old order deservedly passed; and that his church and religion in general benefited. "The principles of reformation" rather than the principles of rigid stability under a confessional state were succeeding. He was fully aware of "the usual risque of quarrelling about means and methods" to the evangelical renewal of religion and society in the new Christian state. It is true that he wanted the state to be more explicitly evangelically Christian. All the same, his journal said the results of change were good. His own church was not the target of any prosely-tizing zealots. He rejoiced at the large number of adult baptisms, and crowded congregations. Laymen requested his preaching outside of his own official pulpit. He attended a sermon by a Baptist preacher in a Methodist church, which stood symbolically for what he reported of the good conditions of his own church, free old Sectarianism. [31]

The Anglican vestry had been the official organ for the good works of Christianity, as the confessional state viewed religion. There was clear evidence that within the new form of the Revolutionary Christian state this aspiration was successfully pursued and in collaboration with other Christians. With them the Episcopal community saw that the Gospel held a message of social as well as personal transformation. Duke clarified this point by paraphrasing Thomas Hutcheson, author of *Moral Philo-sophy*, where the philosopher distinguished the love of benevolence from other expressions. It is this love, wrote Duke regarding the true Chris-tian, "whereby he is led to contribute to the good of society." He would have the true Christian citizen soundly versed in secular knowledge, but accompanied by religious reading which would give it depth and "savour." Not all would agree, however, with his application, when in 1793 he succeeded in getting the Episcopal Convention to pass a canon against gambling. In more general terms, Fergusson believed that the Episcopal community and Maryland had succeeded in pursuit of this deal of Christian works in the new state, prompted by a love of benev-olence." "The Representatives of the People are so numerous, the different departments so vigilant over each other and our Officers so often changed," he estimated in 1798, "that nothing short of universal Depravity of Manners and Corruption among the people can introduce Oppression among us or suffer the continuance of it." [33] Released from the confinements of the confessional state by the Revolution, the Chris-tian pursued good works without the danger of political repression. The new government by its mechanical features helped produce this effect, as Fergusson noted. The majority of the Marylanders believed that the removal of corruption resulted from men of virtue in the government and a religious-minded constituency electing only such men.

The spirit of the Social Gospel, as the religious spirit of Seventy-Six, took hold of other denominations in the general ferment of the times. Public thanksgiving was decreed by the Methodist Conference at Balti-more in 1783, not so much for independence but for "temporal and spiritual prosperity, and the glorious revival of the work of God." [34] The year before, the Lewes Synod of the Presbyterian Church proposed to influential members of the different congregations that they devote themselves after sound education to promoting moral public reform. [35] An historian of the Lutheran Church significantly called attention to this same preoccupation of the age. He noted the large number of works published during this period which dealt with religion; they were substantial when compared with the writings on the revolution and other secular matters. [36] John Carroll corresponded with Benjamin Rush regarding the social implications of Christianity and the good works which it inspired. [37] It would not be possible to do justice to the great number of ways in which the good works of the Gospel came about during the era. There were three categories, however, into which the writings and activities along this line emerge. The broad concern for human welfare by the state and private groups was unmistakable. Secondly, the striking enlargement of education manifested the Christian spirit at work. Finally, a conscience troubled by the condition of chattel slavery labored at the difficult task of rooting out this institutional growth, the first significant attempt in the region of Maryland.

The Maryland legislature during the revolutionary era intensified its concern for the poor. The war, of course, caused considerable destitution for the families of those bearing arms and especially when a father lost his life. In the 1770's petitions to the assembly called attention to instances of this pressing need. [38] Servants and others were also in dire need. [39] In 1785 an act for the relief of widows of officers who died in the war was enacted. Various county programs for the poor were criticized in 1785 by the assembly, which extended additional subsidies to counties which were unable to provide adequately for their poor. There was always danger that the vagrant or indigent would be thrown in with criminals in the jails. It seems, however, that adequate measures were now being taken to avoid this. Between 1785-1790 the following counties were objects of grants for these and other improvements: Kent, Dorchester, Somerset, Montgomery, Harford, Caroline, Queen Anne, Talbot and, somewhat later, Calvert County. [40]

Zeal and imagination were also shown in adjusting welfare financing. Property was converted into subsidy. Private benefactions were commuted into grants to public alms houses. Pensions were arranged for indigents living apart from the alms houses. Provision was made for special cases, such as the retarded and deaf mutes. Some counties were overburdened with care for illegitimate children originally under the jurisdiction of another county. The state government concerned itself with resolving this difficulty. The threat of poverty among Indians was not overlooked. Choptank Indians in Dorchester County were individually given one-hundred acres of land, which would pass to their heirs. This law of 1790 and related legislation declared invalid any sale of such land to white citizens. All of this care called for substantial levies, as much as three shillings on every property holding of £ 100 ([.] 100 pounds). [41] A reading of the laws for the period showed that the Christian state was not a token designation.

The records of Christian ministers show that they attended to the needs of the poor. Garrittzen, the Methodist preacher, said that the poor especially found his preaching profitable. He had no inclination to favor the wealthy. [42] Francis Asbury had a similar experience. He told the poor that once they possessed a vital religion they could then pursue material things without being corrupted by them. [43] Haskins and Duke told of their visits to prisons, where they also found Catholic ministers on visits. Duke's journal notes his ministry to alms houses. [44]

In more organized and effective ways, however, the denominations dealt with the problem of human suffering. There was systematic collaboration with the Christian state. A member of St. Stephen's Parish, Cecil County, left the church funds for the poor. The vestry decided to commit the contribution to county trustees for relief of the poor, to be dispersed at their discretion. [45] Continuing a practice of colonial times now on an unofficial basis, the vestry concerned itself with the problem of illegitimate children. It maintained social pressure against cohabitation by bringing the irresponsible parties to vestry hearings. [46] Perhaps the most striking endeavor by Episcopalians came when they established by Maryland law in 1784 a fund for the relief of the widows and children of their clergy. [47] This became important as a model of future philanthropy, which would be on a sustained basis. William Smith had initiated this idea before the Revolution; but it was received with hostility by dissenters, who understandably saw political motivation in it. This association served as a device for bringing together the laity and clergy of several provinces. It promised greated organizational unity, serving to some extent as a substitute for an episcopal see and preparing for one. The Revolutionary severance from the mother country removed any political odium for the relief association, thus allowing, it to pursue its original philanthropic purpose. [48]

It has been shown how dissenters came under a similar mixed motivation in their own philanthropy before the Revolution. They undertook the Christianization of the Indian with greater zeal, for example, when they saw the Society for the Propagation of the Gospel to Foreign Parts enter this field under the auspices of the Church of England. The Revolution changed this sectarian atmosphere. [49] A refreshing change in mood was also seen in the Baptist Association, when in 1788 it turned to an interdenominational approach to Christian social reform and philanthropy. A temperance crusade, for example, was undertaken on this basis. [50] Methodists responded to the imaginative leadership of Asbury in charity for the poor and the benighted. Care of orphans was joined to the general development of Cokesbury College; and he organized services to children of the poor or wayward. He envisioned a utopian movement of impoverished young couples of the Eastern Shore to the more unsettled and promising westward regions of the state. [51]

The Society of Friends enlarged their horizonts of philanthropy during the revolutionary era. In addition to their relief funds for victims of the war, monthly meetings assumed direct responsibility for their own indigent members. [52] In Baltimore could be seen the expansion of works of Christian charity on a highly imaginative scale. A Charitable Marine Society was incorporated, in order to maintain funds for the support of the widows and children of seamen who, it would appear, had affiliated with the society in their lifetime. In this growing city there were always citizens living on the edge of poverty, but outside of the alms house. When sickness came, they were beyond the reach of existing programs. In 1796 a private group launched a hospital to meet this need, which envisioned collaboration with the state programs. Nor were existing state provisions left without continual concern for their effectiveness. Eager Howard, whom Duke styled "The Philanthropist," made prison reform one of his chief concerns. [53] This was a sign that the emancipation of the American involved something more than the political victory in the Peace of Paris. The emancipation from poverty was a process of continual revolution in the Christian state.

The question of slavery before the Civil War and of racial injustice thereafter has been taken as a barometer of the depth of Christian conscience and perception in American society. Applied to the Christian state of Maryland in the era of the American Revolution, it indicates a growth of religious life. The religious achievement was not an elimination of slavery, but an emancipation from the myths which had long obscured the Christian conscience. There were in addition positive works which testified to reform and mitigation of evils in the institution. That a significant number sought at great personal sacrifice the emancipation and manumission of slaves testifies to the vitality of the Christian life. The same is true in the case of many more who candidly saw slavery as a violation of principles inherent in the Declaration of Independence and Christianity itself.

In the seventeenth century Negroes were in many regions indentured servants, attaining freedom after five to seven years of service. The intrusion of the slave trade into the southern colonies after 1650 undoubtedly accounted for the institutionalization of permanent servitude as the only legal condition for Negro life. With a large black population present in the eighteenth century, many responsible whites generally believed they could do nothing about this servitudes without worsening the life of the Negro. Colonists could plead not guilty to the spread of slavery because the mother country permitted the inhumane traffic. In a structured society with indentured servants, the permanent servitude of blacks seemed better than that of the poor freeman in London and superior to his African environment. The human tendency to attach congenital inferiority to a people continually in an inferior status took root in a pseudo-philosophy of racial superiority. The superficial observation of this phenomenon led many early Americans to see verification for ancient classical themes justifying slavery.

The Revolution, as expressed in the Declaration of Independence, reexamined human nature as a basis to claims of political and economic freedom. The optimistic estimate of man justified extreme claims to independence but immediately galled the rebel statesmen with the unexplained chattel slave condition of thousands of Americans. Henry Laurens of Virginia, a slaveholder himself, enunciated these distressing corollaries. Yet few saw any promise for the Negro in the immediate act of independence. Many argued the danger of greater harm to the slave in emancipation. The Revolution did, however, confront the founding fathers with the colonial myth, that outside conditions caused the evil institution. The country was now their own and the slave trade could be forbidden by law. Furthermore, in particular regions and in specific local instances it was clear that immediate emancipation would not work the destructive disorder which the myth predicted. These forces, operating generally in the united colonies following the Declaration of Independence, led Americans to confront their own version of the myth. The Christian reckoning required less of New England than of Maryland as far as emancipation was concerned: the former had no economic institution of slavery, as planter states did. The point here is not to prove that the Christian state of Maryland met the requirement of justice with great generosity. Rather, in the legislation touching emancipation and the general treatment of slaves, it is clear that there was an attack on the myths which confined the Christian conscience under the old order.

Since legislation is in many ways a barometer, it is also a common denominator of attitudes. In estimating quality in the Christian conscience, it is therefore necessary to pass beyond this average scale to show Christians whose conscience attained more than the median reflected in legislation. A considerable amount of effort at a removal of slavery and a vital agitation against its continuance would certainly reveal the vigor of religious life. Using assembly legislation together with the considerable amount of denominational sources, a fair estimate of the extent of Christian works in this important area of human freedom will be found. It will be noted that both levels of evidence contribute to the general estimate of religion beyond what has thus far been established.

William Eddis in 1776 sensed a liberal spirit in Maryland regarding slavery, which contrasted with the attitude in the Caribbean Islands. He also believed that the numbers of slaves in Maryland had doubled since the close of the French and Indian War, due largely to natural increment rather than slave trade. Large numbers had been taken by raiding British forces in Southern Maryland and Virginia. The future of agriculture in the former region was altered. Boucher himself was zealous in the Christianizing and catechizing of Negroes, but these works would now be done in the greatly modified atmosphere regarding slavery of the revolutionary era. These conditions goaded the Christian conscience to pierce the mythology which had enveloped the institution. The Negro was now not merely a factor in the planter communities elsewhere. [54] It is significant that in 1787 the assembly had to curtail the inroads of Negroes into the piece employments of freemen, such as ferry-boat pilots. A leniency with slaves developed, many masters permitting their slaves to do such work. The importation of slaves and the obstructions to the manumission of individual slaves could no longer appear justified by appeal to traditional rationalizations. Immediately upon signing the Declaration of Independence Delaware outlawed slave trade and three years later Massachusetts declared slavery unlawful. The Government of the Articles of Confederation, once approved in 1781, gave promise of an end to slave trade and honored the pledge with the Northwest Ordinance, which outlawed the institution there. It was not until 1795, however, that Maryland legislated against it. Yet the earnestness of the assembly was shown in the related provisions. While respecting inter-state comity, allowing slave holders to bring their servants to Maryland, careful prescriptions prevented anything passing as a slave-sale transaction. The act of foreign importation was more readily detected and prevented. [55]

The manumission of slaves was safeguarded and liberalized. The laws of 1715 and 1728 allowed no manumissions of those under thirty-one years of age; children of a parent who had been convicted of a crime or immorality were not to benefit from legislation in favor of manumission. A law of 1796 struck down these obstacles to freedom. Since there was always danger that slave merchants might prey on manumitted Negroes, careful provision was made for punishing such acts. There were many other special provisions made in the same spirit. Capital punishment had been dealt out with ease before the Revolution. A law of 1793, however, implied that this had been especially true in the case of slaves; and it was therefore necessary to stipulate that certain crimes by Negroes could be commuted to imprisonment and hard labor. Until a law of 1789, it was apparently possible to "manumit" a disabled slave, which under the circumstances would have been an act of cruelty rather than of liberation, opening the door to great abuse. This legislation put an end to such injustice. While thus exploding the two myths of Colonial times—slave traders were to blame and freeing slaves creates a greater evil—the fundamental inequity in the political and juridical orders remained. At the same time, it was inconceivable that one in a condition of chattel servitude should vote, hold office, or act as judicial witness against a white man. Although the assembly received a petition for full emancipation in 1791, it upheld in 1795 the law of 1783 which imposed these political and judicial restrictions. This then was the reading of the barometer of the Christian state and the slight respect for the alienable rights of blacks by the white possessors of inalieanable rights. [56]

Beneath this surface, however, was a continually erupting ferment of a deeper Christian conscience, which would be satisfied only with the total elimination of slavery. If there were no urgency about it, no active agitation, then the revolutionary era in Maryland experienced only a desire for gradualism, hardly a sign of Christian vitality and concern for such an important work of the Gospel. As in Colonial times, Quakers now shone as a burning light in this cause. Under the emancipated political conditions of other Americans, the light burst forth more brightly and cast sparks about in what developed into a movement. The Quakers, of course, had much to do with the laws that actually improved the condition of Negroes and limited the effects of slavery; but members in good standing were strictly bound to manumit their own slaves. [57] The financial contribution of a slave holder to the meeting was spurned.

and a member might even be condemned for serving as an overseer of slaves. Quakers understood that the manumitted had problems fitting into society, but this argued not tolerance of the institution but zeal in aiding the Negro's adjustment. Minutes of monthly meetings frequently told of this Christian work. Those who still held slaves were visited in brotherly fashion and were admonished. In Kent County, James Barry served on a committee for this purpose and enlarged its scope to a general crusading effort for the emancipation and manumission of slaves. [58]

The authenticity of the Methodist crusade against slavery during the revolutionary era spoke clearly in word and deed. They saw that the ideals of the Declaration of Independence, as well as their Christian faith, inspired urgency in the elimination of slavery. "We view it as contrary to the golden law of God," the Christmas Conference of 1784 stated, "on which stand all the law and the prophets, and the inalienable rights of mankind, as well as every principle of the Revolution, to hold in the deepest abasement . . . so many souls that are all capable of the image of God." [59] Francis Asbury frequently preached to slaves and had a deep respect for their growth in the Christian life. With a touch of sarcasm he narrated in his journal how a wealthy Christian cursed when a Negro earnestly prayed shortly before his execution for theft. On another occasion he told how a slaveholder was so galled by the devout Christian life of a Negro that he manumitted him. His compassion for their sufferings was ever present in his writtings. [60] Haskins upbraided a Christian for his treatment of a runaway slave. "He was a part of God's creation," he said, "that he was not to use him so. . . ." He was able on occasion to help in the emancipation of slaves. Garrettson provided refuge for a slave who had been severely beaten. For a period during the era official church laws demanded that members of the society emancipate their slaves if they would be in good standing. Had not pressure from growing church numbers in Virginia prevailed, Maryland Methodists would probably have succeeded in making this a permanent provision of church discipline. [61]

Presbyterians spoke in this same revolutionary spirit. "It is more especially the duty of those who maintain the rights of humanity," the Philadelphia Synod decreed for Marylanders and others in its jurisdiction, "and who acknowledge and teach the obligations of Christianity, to use . . . means . . . to extend the blessing of equal freedom to every part of the human race." Yet here too there was pressure from those still laboring under the old myth, suggested by those who emphasized preparation for emancipation, saying that there was possible danger to the community in wholesale emancipation. On the other hand, the sincerity of the protest for freedom was seen in the fact that the synod felt responsible for removing that danger. The day of freedom would be hastened. when Christians educated slaves in work skills and other needed knowledge. The Synod honored the person of the Christian slave in regard to baptism. Some Presbyterians had thought that black children should not be baptized if their master was not a Christian, being thereby incapable of instructing his slaves. The minister should baptize them, it was decreed, implying that instruction was the burden of the church in such a situation. [62]

The spirit of the Baptists resembled that of the Presbyterians. The Baltimore congregation brought the slavery question before the Philadelphia Association meeting of 1789. They were determined to take action against people and conditions which led to re-enslavement of manumitted Negroes. Local congregations were to form societies for this purpose and also for promoting emancipation. [63] Maryland Lutherans with their leading layman John Hanson, President of the Continental Congress, were part of this general ferment for emancipation. In the Congress, Hanson attacked the institution of slavery. It is true that Lutheran farmers who migrated to Georgia left this mentality behind and followed Muhlenberg's classical notion of slavery in a hierarchical society. Even these, however, advocated an end of the slave trade. [64]

The Catholic community from its beginning in Maryland had a conscientious concern for Negroes, without being free of the myths that supported the institution of slavery. With a clergy and laity thoroughly educated in philosophy and theology, they could not support it theoretically. Francisco Vitoria and some other Spanish theologians of the sixteenth and seventeenth centuries had exploded the classical theory, which had been used to mythologize the institutions of the Spanish-American empire. Joseph Mosley, the Maryland Jesuit, explained how a moral life within the system was extremely difficult, even though he found Christian life firm in his parishioners as well as others elsewhere in Maryland. "I am as far as you," John Carroll wrote in 1794 to John Thayer, "from being easy in my mind at many things, I see and know relating to the treatment & manners of the Negroes." He encouraged Thayer to speak out freely against the evils of slavery. Aware of the prevailing mentality, Carroll reminded him how his achievements of reform would fall short of his idealism and aspirations. The efforts of the Carrolls, Taneys, and other Catholic families at emancipation at a later date is further indication that the ferment described here was experienced by elements of the Catholic community. [65]

Episcopalianism in Allen produced an abolitionist who was very active in the 1790's. He drew up a program for the emancipation of slaves and promoted popular acceptance of the doctrine. Joseph Bend believed that Allen was very much under the influence of the Methodists and that he had misrepresented Bishop Claggett by claiming ecclesiastical approval for his crusade. Bend was very critical of the Methodists as well as Allen. [66] St. Peter's Parish, Talbot County, at this time had a running battle with the Quaker James Barry who carried his abolitionism to the ranks of Anglican parishioners. The vestrymen were also imputing charlantry to Methodists, who made their members believe that all of their sins would be blotted out by the act of manumitting their slaves. They appealed in old style to the scriptural justification of slavery. In any event, the Anglican conscience was clearly agitated about the inconsistency of defending slavery. The emancipationists indeed suceeded in promoting sentiment for manumission in Episcopal ranks. [67] Yet the references to Negroes and slavery in Duke's journal and elsewhere show that he and Claggett were still very traditional. There were others, however, who were very clearly under the influence of the Christian ferment of the times which sought not only an end of the slave trade, but also urged emancipation and manumission.

Taken in general, then, this fostering of a Christian attitude of opposition to slavery was growing after 1776. The colonial myths that had rationalized the evil condition were badly eroded by it. The measures of the assembly to safeguard the environment of the manumitted slave were calculated to remove any justification for delay. The churches similarly were saying that disorder in emancipation came from the condition of white society, and they therefore fostered reform and education here. Individually masters were now responsible for educating their slaves for manumission.

Following the Declaration of Independence there was a great enthusiasm for the development of education. Marylanders regarded this as a great Christian work. Both church and state felt a strong obligation to enlarge a work that was only rudimentary before the Revolution. Seventeenth-century education greatly stressed training ministers of the gospel, but this view was modified in the eighteenth century. Education was seen as a need of all men. Influenced by the Enlightenment as well as an expansion of the gentry class, Governor Eden had made a serious effort at beginning a college in Maryland. Legislation was passed only after much delay and never actually created an institution. Public enthusiasm and the interest of religious groups was thus greatly lacking before the Revolution. [68]

The new Maryland government showed its earnestness about education from the beginning. Masters and students were regarded as so important to society that the assembly deliberated about exempting them from military service. [69] New dimension was given to the Christian notion that education was preparation both for civic and religious life. [70] John Carroll expressed this general sentiment very well when he spoke of "virtuous education" and "moral, religious & literary improvement." [71] Duke clearly understood how such education would improve the general religious climate in Maryland, about which he was optimistic. [72] The great collaboration among the denominations in fostering education has already been told at length to establish the interfaith harmony that the Revolutionary War brought about. The purposed here is to present evidence of the Christian zeal manifested by the promotion of education. The Christian state and the religious people, whom it served as an instrument, together revealed their vitality here, marking an improved condition of religious life from what had prevailed before the war.

The founding of Washington College best indicated the Christian spirit which animated Maryland's activity in the development of education. In the Act for the Founding of a College at Chestertown of 1782 the religious purpose was clearly stated. Subjects which were to be taught should be useful "for the service of their country in church and state." "Youth of all religious denominations and persuasion shall be freely and liberally admitted to equal privileges. . . ." "The principles of virtue," it said, "are of the highest benefit to society, in order to raise up and perpetuate a succession of able and honest men, for discharging the various offices and duties of the community, both civil and religious. . . ." Divinity as well as other subjects were to have a proper place. Although interdenominational sources provided considerable funds for this college, the state in 1784 added its own share of assistance, in order that the endeavor might clearly be "under the care and patronage of the State. . . ." In this way it hoped to provide a "most effectual means of disseminating the principles of religious and civil liberty." [73]

William Smith, who had been a moving spirit behind the founding of the College of Philadelphia, was most enthusiastic about the Maryland response to his proposal for Washington College. In 1784 he reported that £ 2000 were subscribed within a twenty-four hour period in Baltimore. The growth of the institution by 1790 under the "nursing Hand" of the state justified his optimism. He felt that Maryland was more promising than Philadelphia. Were he not so advanced in years, he would have accepted the headship of Washington College.[74] Smith, however, served on the Board of Directors of Washington College and also of that of St. John's College, Annapolis. The enabling legislation of both colleges was similar in stating the purpose of the Christian state. The act of incorporation assured that the state would provide funds to be added to those brought together by private denominational subscriptions.[75]

These developments in higher education encouraged others. John Carroll, like Smith, came to be another moving force. From the beginning he served on the board of visitors of Washington and St. John's Colleges. In his liberal spirit, he successfully encouraged Catholics to financially support and attend these institution, including those who would go on to higher education for the priesthood. He hoped to establish an advanced seminary in Maryland. The assembly praised the endeavor as "highly beneficial to many of the citizens of this state. . . ."[76] It would seem that a general college similar to Washington was necessary to support an ecclesiastical seminary as an adjunct. A practical consideration, there-fore, led to the founding of Georgetown College in 1789. The plan was altered shortly after this, when some members of the Sulpician Order came from France to develop an entirely ecclesiastical institution for the training of priests. Georgetown thereafter continued as a private lay-college, but unlike St. John's and Washington, carried on without state financial aid.[77] Its doors were open to those of all faiths, with the result that the original endeavor ultimately led to the development of the life of the laity in a "virtuous education." A much-needed native clergy became a greater possibility, now that the number of young men with academic prerequisites for admittance to such a seminary was growing with the advancement of Georgetown College.

Francis Asbury had the chance to see the growth of Cokesbury College at Westminster at first hand. His journal left no doubt about his enthusiasm for education and the good results that were coming from it at the college. "God was working among the students," he said in 1788 after he had been less favorably impressed the year before. He served as an examiner of the students on one occasion, with an eye to the standards of a "virtuous education." Methodist ministers took on much responsibility in financing the college. While Asbury had some difficulties with the program of studies at Cokesbury, his writings manifest his general zeal for education. In 1790, for example, he was promoting the foundation of a school for women. [78]

Higher education catches the historian's attention because it was a striking innovation and rapid development in the revolutionary era. The earlier stages of education, however, gave similar evidence of zeal in the Christian state and its citizens. Particularly in the 1790's a large number of new institutions came into existence. In Kent County, George-town School was founded. Eden School in Somerset County was reorganized and moved nearer Worcester County, so that students there could benefit. Anne Arundel County sought funds from the assembly for a similar project. A new academy was formed at Easton, Talbot County, in 1799. Frederick expressed the desire for a public school before the Revolution and ultimately realized it in 1795. The year before, Joseph Cresap, with the collaboration of Lutherans in Washington County, obtained an enabling act to establish their school in this western region. The Christian state had made its own zeal clear regarding such causes. "The happiness and prosperity of every community depends much on the proper education of youths," it said in 1789, "it being the interest and duty of the state to assist legislative complements. . . ." [79]

Imagination and innovation was seen in all of these efforts. Undis-persed funds of St. John's College were applied to King William School by the legislation of 1785. Reverend Joseph Bend and prominent laymen of the Episcopal Church organized The Benevolent Society of the City and County of Baltimore in order to make possible the education of girls. By 1796 Francis Asbury could boast two-hundred scholars and five teachers at his Baltimore Academy. "The interests of virtue," the assembly said, were served by the encouragement of libraries. The Bal-timore Library Company was incorporated that year. Somerset County formed a similar organization at this time. [80]

This study appropriately draws to a close with these considerations of what today is called the "social gospel." By their works you shall know them, seems a common scriptural bond between the eighteenth and twentieth century religious value systems. Joined to the many other vital manifestations of religious life in Maryland after 1776, the case is well made that religious life improved. At a deeper level as well there is no doubt that the profound stirrings of religious aspirations before the war attained a generous measure of fulfillment by the close of the century. The different faith traditions of Christians, finally, grew out freely into those national configurations of ecclesiastical life each one chose from inner force and outward need.

Perhaps more bold than this in the revolutionary generation was their venture into the subtleties of church-state relations. Although not congenial to the twentieth century in all of its ideological elements, the adjustment for their times was truly creative. For they dared to say that the state must respond to the total life of its people without fear for the difficult adjustment of its religious ingredient. Marylanders acted, so they believed, without damage to their fundamental laws of personal freedom drawn from the seventeenth century. The Christian state, to their mind, emerged most naturally from the travail of revolution. Equally important to posterity, they opened the door to revision and further growth of human freedom which became the dominant thrust of the twentieth century.

In retrospect the eighteenth century Marylanders might appear disturbing in their conception of a Christian state as an alternative to a confessional state. Upon reflection, however, the conception's deeper significance in the long reach of history is an unrecognized challenge for today: How will other eras in America better succeed with Maryland's inspiration, with its desire that religion and the total life of its people be embodied in the vital organism of the state?

REFERENCES

[1]Hanley, *Theological Studies*, XXVI, 390.
[2]Max Farrand, ed., *Records of the Federal Convention of 1787* (4 vols.; New Haven, Conn., 1911-17), III, 227.
[3]*Maryland Historical Magazine*, L, 282-91.
[4]Werline, pp. 200-01.
[5]Claggett to Duke, Sep. 26, 1796 (Maryland Diocesan Archives).
[6]Duke, Journal, Aug. 8, 1789.
[7]Ralph to Claggett, Dec. 24, 1796 (printed circular letter, Maryland Diocesan Archives).
[8]West to Barr, July 23, 1789 (*ibid.*).
[9]Claggett to Duke, Nov. 24, 1794 (*ibid.*).
[10]Claggett to Washington Gentlemen, Spring, 1797 [1798 ?] (*ibid.*).
[11]? to Waring, Sep. 26, 1777 (*ibid.*).
[12]West-Vestry Claims, 1787-1788 (*ibid.*).
[13]Duke, Journal, Jan. 4, 1787.
[14]Kilty, *Laws of Maryland* (Nov. 1796), Chaps. LXXX, LXXIII; (Nov. 1791), Chap. XVIII.
[15]St. George's Parish Vestry Minutes (Maryland Historical Society), Apr. 31, 1776; June 7, 1779; Mar. 11, 1787; Aug. 5, 1790; Apr. 4, 1796; Apr. 6, 1795; Feb. 1, 1796.
[16]Bisset to Claggett, Oct. 11, 1792 (Maryland Diocesan Archives).
[17]Hawkes, pp. 321, 334.
[18]St. George's Parish Vestry Minutes, Apr. 4, 1796 (Maryland Historical Society).
[19]Jackson to Duke, Nov. 18, 1796; Duke to Kemp, Dc. 3, 1796 (Maryland Diocesan Archives).
[20]Hawkes, p. 314.

[21]Utley, p. 87.

[22]Hawkes, p. 320.

[23]Bend to Claggett, May 1796; Utley, p. 95.

[24]Bend to Claggett, June 7, 1797, and June 1, 1798; Utley, p. 98; St. James Parish Vestry Records, June 5, 1797 (Maryland Historical Society).

[25]Bend to Claggett, June 7, 1797; June 1, 1798; May, 1796. See Utley, pp. 94-97.

[26]Bend to Claggett, May and June 7, 1796; Utley, 97-100.

[27]St. George's Parish Vestry Records (Maryland Historical Society), June 5, 1797. Jackson to Duke, Aug. 21, 1796; St. Peter's Parish Report, June 5, 1797 and two undated reports and for 1801 (all in Maryland Diocesan Archives). See Utley, p. 102 for 1801 report.

[28]Duke, Journal, June 2, July 4, Aug. 29, 1774; and July 2, 1789.

[29]Read to Claggett, June 2, 1800; Utley, pp. 103-04; Report of St. Peter's Parish (Western Counties), 1898; and Bower to Claggett, July 11, 1797 (Maryland Diocesan Archives).

[30]Report of 1807, St. Mary's County (Maryland Diocesan Archive); Keith to Kemp, Sep. 30, 1793 (*ibid.*); Bend to Claggett, May 1796 (Utley, p. 97); Visiting Committee Report, 1797 (*ibid.*, p. 102); April 4, 1790 Report (*ibid.*, p. 35); Rumsey to Tilghman, Oct. 24, 1776, *Archives of Maryland*, XII, 399; Asbury, I, 106 (Feb. 7, 1774); Duke, Journal, Feb. 14, 1791, and Dec. 19, 1790; Kilty, *Laws of Maryland*, Chaps. LXII, XXX (Nov. 1796).

[31]Duke, *State of Religion*, p. 17. Duke, Journal, Aug. 29, 1789; Nov. 24, 1793; June 12, 1791; July 25-26, 1789.

[32]*Ibid.*, Mar. 20, 1791; Jan. 19, 1787; May 25, 1793; Duke, *State of Religion*, p. 12; Eddis, p. 146.

[33]Ferguson, Sermon for May 9, 1798 (Maryland Diocesan Archive); Cameron, p. 93; Lewes Minutes, Oct. 15, 1782 (p. 116) (Presbyterian Historical Society); Qualben, pp. 246-47.

[34]Cameron, p. 93.

[35]Lewes Minutes, Oct. 5, 1782 (Presbyterian Historical Society).

[36]Qualben, 246-47.

[37]Rush to Carroll, July 18, 1798 (John Carroll Papers).

[38]Davis to Council of Safety, July 1776, *Archives of Maryland*, XII, 23.

[39]Eddis, pp. 81-82.

[40]Kilty, *Laws of Maryland*, Chaps. LII (Nov. 1785), XV (Nov. 1785), LVI (Nov. 1785), XV (Nov. 1785). *Laws of Maryland* (Nov. 1787), Chaps. XI, XVI (Nov. 1788), Chaps. XXXVI, XIV, XV, XXVI (May 1788), Chap. VI.

[41]Kilty, *Laws of Maryland* (April 1787), Chap. XIV; (Nov. 1793), Chap. LI; (Nov. 1794), Chap. XXII; (Nov. 1785), Chap. XLVII; (Nov. 1796), Chaps. LXVII, IX. *Laws of Maryland* (Nov. 1799), Chaps. LXXXII, LXV; (Nov. 1789), Chap. XX.

[42]Garrettson, Journal, Mar. 28, 1779 (p. 99).

[43]Asbury, I, 497 (Oct. 10, 1785).

[44]Haskins, Journal, Oct. 28, 1783. Duke, Journal, Oct. 19, 1792; April 5, December 13, 1793; February 7, 1794.

[45]*Laws of Maryland*, May 13, 1788.

[46]Chester Parish Vestry Records, Mar. 6, 1780 (Maryland Historical Society).

[47]Kilty, *Laws of Maryland* (Nov. 1784), LXXVIII, LXXVIII.

[48]Hooker, Chap. 2, and pp. 248-50, 194-98.

[49]Bridenbaugh, pp. 209-10, *et passim*.

[50]*Baptists Association*, p. 239 (1788).

[51]Asbury, I, 697 (Dec. 5, 1791) and 497 (Oct. 10, 1785); Cameron, p. 104; Garrettson, Journal, I, 42 (Sep. 1776).

[52]Kent Monthly Meeting Minutes, Jan. 10, 1776 (Maryland Historical Society).

[53]Kilty, *Laws of Maryland* (Nov. 1795), Chap. II; (Nov. 1796), Chap. CII. Duke, Journal, Nov. 17, 1790.

[54]Boucher, pp. 57-58; Eddis, pp. 65, 326-27.

[55]Kilty, *Laws of Maryland* (Apr. 1787), Chap. XXXIII; (Nov. 1795), Chap. LXVII; (Nov. 1796), Chaps. LXVII, VII; (Nov. 1798), Chap. LXXVIII.

⁵⁶*Ibid.* (Nov. 1793), Chap. LXII; (Nov. 1795), Chaps. LXVII, XLVII; (Nov. 1796), Chaps. LXVII, LXXV. *Laws of Maryland* (Nov. 1789) and (Nov. 1791), Chap. LXXX and elsewhere has laws regarding slavery.

⁵⁷Drake, pp. 96-97.

⁵⁸St. George and Cecil County minutes (Maryland Historical Society), Nov. 9, 1774; Jan. 14, 1778; Nov. - Dec. 1784. Kent County Monthly Meetings (*ibid.*), Sep. 10, 1777; Jan. 24, and Feb. 11, 1778; Mar. 10, 1779.

⁵⁹Cameron, pp. 98-100.

⁶⁰Asbury, I, Dec. 7-8, 1772; 89 (Aug. 2, 1773) 469 (Oct. 14, 1784) 655-56 (Nov. 4, 1790); II, 193 (May 9, 1799).

⁶¹Haskins, Journal, Jan. 26, Apr. 2, 1785; Garrettson, Journal, II, 52 (Sep. 21, 1778).

⁶²*Records of the Presbyterian Church,* pp. 527 (May 24, 1786), 539-40 (May 26, 28, 1787).

⁶³*Baptist Association,* p. 247 (1789).

⁶⁴Wentz, pp. 56-57.

⁶⁵John Carroll to Thayer, July 15, 1794 (John Carroll Papers); Mosley to sister, Oct. 3, 1774, *Woodstock Letters,* XXV, 235.

⁶⁶Bend to Claggett, Jan. 21, 1797 (Maryland Diocesan Archives).

⁶⁷St. Peter's Parish Report to Claggett, 1797 (*ibid.*).

⁶⁸*Archives of Maryland: Assembly Proceedings* (1666-1676, pp. 262-64; Steiner, p. 8; Fell, p. 8.

⁶⁹*Proceedings of the Convention,* p. 148 (May 23, 1776).

⁷⁰Cubberly, E. P., *Public Education in the United States* (Boston, 1934), p. 93; Max Savelle, *The Seeds of Liberty* (New York, 1948), pp. 264-65.

⁷¹John Carroll to Plowden, Mar. 16, 1790, and to Francis Neale, Jan. 19, 1790 (John Carroll Papers).

⁷²Duke, *State of Religion,* pp. 51-53.

⁷³Kilty, *Laws of Maryland* (April, 1782), Chaps. VIII; (Nov. 1784), Chap. VII.

⁷⁴Smith to West [?], 1784, and May 5, 1790 (Maryland Diocesan Archives).

⁷⁵Kilty, *Laws of Maryland* (Nov. 1784), Chap. XXXVII; Philip A. Crowl, *Maryland During and After the Revolution: A Political and Economic Study* (Baltimore, 1942), pp. 85-86.

⁷⁶Kilty, *Laws of Maryland* (Nov. 1796), Chap. XL.

⁷⁷Carroll to Antonelli, Mar. 1, 1784, and to Thorpe, Feb. 17, 1785 (John Carroll Papers); Minutes of the Board of Directors of Georgetown College from 1797 to 1815, entry for April 24, 1799 (Georgetown University Archives).

⁷⁸Asbury, I, 584 (Dec. 9, 1788); 597 (May 3, 1789); (Oct. 1, 1790); 657 (Nov. 21, 1790).

⁷⁹Kilty, *Laws of Maryland* (Nov. 1795), Chaps. XXIII, LXVI, LXVI; (Nov. 1798), Chaps. XXXIII, LXXVIII, LVIII; (Nov. 1799), Chap. LVI.

⁸⁰*Ibid.* (Nov. 1785), Chap. XXXIX; (Nov. 1796), Chaps. XXIII, LXVII, XXXV; (Nov. 1799), Chap. LIV. Asbury, II, 90 (June 22, 1796).

BIBLIOGRAPHY

Manuscript Collections

American Baptist Historical Society, Rochester, N. Y. (Minutes of Second Baptist Church, Baltimore; and George's Hill Church).

Archives of the Moravian Church, Bethlehem, Pa. (Graceham Diary, and Correspondence).

Baltimore Cathedral Archives, Baltimore, Md. (Manuscripts, Letters, and Administration of Archbishop Carroll).

Catholic University Archives, Washington, D. C. (John Carroll Papers in photoduplicates from all sources).

Drew University, Rose Library, Madison, N. J. (Journal of Freeborn Garrettson).

Duke University Library, Durham, N. C. (Protestant Episcopal Church, Diocese of Maryland Papers, 1770-1800).

General Theological Seminary Library of the Protestant Episcopal Church, New York, N. Y. (Howard Chandler Robbins Collection of Bishops' Papers; Thomas Claggett, and other Maryland Papers).

Georgetown University Archives, Washington, D. C. (Shea Manuscript and Transcript Collection; College Records).

Historical Society of Pennsylvania, Philadelphia, Pa. (Miscellaneous Collection of Letters of Clergymen; Records of the Society for the Relief of Widows and Orphans of Clergymen).

Homewood Friends Meeting Library, Baltimore, Md. (Minutes of Yearly Meetings for Period).

Kauth Memorial Library, Philadelphia, Pa. (Archives of the Lutheran Ministerium of Pennsylvania; Protocols).

Kent Monthly Meeting of Friends, Cecil County, Md. Minutes.

Library of Congress, Washington, D. C. (Journals of Thomas Haskins, and Richard Whatcoat).

Lovely Lane Museum, Baltimore, Md. (Journal of Nelson Reed; and Letter Collection on Period).

Maryland Hall of Records, Annapolis, Md. (Parish Vestry Records of the Protestant Episcopal Church of Maryland; Miscellaneous Correspondence).

Maryland Historical Society Library, Baltimore, Md. (Callister Papers [Letters of Anglican Clergy]. Ethan Allen Collection [Reports and Letters of Claggett, Bend, Duke, *et al.*];[1] Maryland Diocesan Archives, Miscellaneous Letters, Sermons, etc.; Moravian, Lutheran, Quaker, and other Church Records in photoduplicate or transcript; Parish Vestry Records of the Protestant Episcopal Church of Maryland. Maryland Diocesan Archives [formerly at the Peabody Library, Baltimore, Md.]).

North Carolina University Library, Chapel Hill, N. C. (Edward Dromgoole Papers; Diaries of Joshua Evans and Jeremiah Norman).

Presbyterian Historical Society Library, Philadelphia, Pa. (Allison, Patrick, "The Rise and Progress of the Presbyterian Church in Baltimore Town, 1761-1793 and the Rise and Progress of a Small Presbyterian Society in Soldiers' Delight, 1766-1793". Anon. "The Rise & Progress of the Presbyterian Congregation in

---

[1] In the last century the Rev. Ethan Allen brought together a large amount of manuscript material on the Protestant Episcopal Church in Maryland. It has since been distributed to at least the two libraries indicated here. There is some evidence that the Duke University Library and General Theological Library have other portions of this original collection.

George Town and of Frederick Town, April 19, 1793"; McMaster, Samuel, Memoir; Minutes of the Presbytery of Baltimore, 1786-1853; Minutes of the Lewistown [Lewes] Presbytery, 1758-1788; Muir, James. "A Brief History of the Presbytery of Baltimore, 1786-1803"; Sessional [Records] of the Presbyterian Church [of Snow Hill], Maryland, 1745-1799; "Statistics of the Presbytery of Baltimore").

[Allison, Patrick]. *Vindex Candid Animadversions on a Petition, Presented to the General Assembly of Maryland by the Rev. Dr. William Smith and the Rev. Gates; First Published in 1783: Together with a Fully [sic] Display of the Assembly's Gross Partiality, Flagrant Injustice, and Scandalous Waste of Public Treasure, in Favor of a Particular Denomination of Christians.* Baltimore, 1793.

Carroll, Charles (of Carrollton) and Daniel Dulany, Jr. *Correspondence of "First Citizen" — Charles Carroll of Carrollton and "Atilon" — Daniel Dulany, Jr., 1773, with a History of Governor Eden's Administration in Maryland 1769-1776.* Edited by Elihu S. Riley. Baltimore, 1902.

Coke, Thomas. *The Substance of a Sermon on the Godhead of Christ, Preached at Baltimore, in the State of Maryland, on the 26th Day of December, 1784, Before the General Conference of the Methodist Episcopal Church.* New York, 1815.

Duke, William. *Observations on the Present State of Religion in Maryland: By a Clergyman.* Baltimore, 1795.

Moore, Jeremiah. *An Inquiry into the Nature and Propriety of Ecclesiastical Establishments, in a Letter to Howard Griffith, Esq.* Baltimore, 1808.

Semple, Robert, B. *A History of the Rise and Progress of the Baptists in Virginia* [1810]. Edited by G. W. Beale. Richmond, 1894.

Smith, William. *Four Dissertations on the Reciprocal Advantages of a Perpetual Union Between Great-Britain and Her American College.* Philadelphia, 1766.

—————————. [*Candidus*] *Plain Truth; Addressed to the Inhabitants of America, Containing Remarks on a Late Pamphlet Entitled Common Sense.* Philadelphia, 1776.

Vans Murray, William. *Political Sketches, Inscribed to His Excellency John Adams, Minister Plenipotentiary from the United States to the Court of Great Britain, by a Citizen of the United States.* London, 1787.

—————————. "William Vans Murray on Freedom of Religion in the United States, 1787." *Maryland Historical Magazine,* L (December, 1955), 282-291. Edited by Alexander DeConde.

Ware, Thomas. "The Christmas Conference of 1784," *The Methodist Magazine and Quarterly Review,* XIV (New Series, III) (January, 1823), 97-104.

White, William. *The Case of the Episcopal Churches in the United States Considered.* Philadelphia, 1782.

Published Journal, Diaries, Letters, etc.

Asbury, Francis. *The Journal and Letters of Francis Asbury.* Edited by Elmer T. Clarke *et al.* 3 vols.; Nashville, 1958.

Boucher, Jonathan. *Reminiscences of an American Loyalist, 1738-1789.* Boston, 1925.

Carroll, John.[2] *The Life and Times of John Carroll: Archbishop of Baltimore (1735-1815).* By Peter Guilday. New York, 1922.

Claggett, Thomas J. *The Life and Times of Thomas J. Claggett: First Bishop of Maryland and the First Bishop Consecrated in America.* By George B. Utley. Chicago, 1913.

Coke, Thomas. *Extracts from the Journals of the Rev. Dr. Coke's Five Visits to America.* London, 1793.

---

[2]This and similarly published books mentioned under Claggett, Ettwein, and William Smith, were used as primary sources since they contained letters, etc. not readily available elsewhere.

Eddis, William. *Letters from America, Historical and Descriptive; Comprising Occurrences from 1769-1777, Inclusive.* London, 1792.

Ettwein, John. *John Ettwein and the Moravian Church During the Revolutionary Period.* By Kenneth G. Hamilton. Bethlehem, Pa., 1940.

Garrettson, Freeborn. *The Experiences and Travels of the Rev. Freeborn Garrettson, Minister of the Methodist Episcopal Church in North-America.* Philadelphia, 1791.

Hicks, Elias. *The Letters of Elias Hicks, Including Also Observations on the Slavery of the Africans and Their Descendents, and in the Use of Produce of Their Labor.* Philadelphia, 1861.

Mosley, Joseph. "Letters of Father Joseph Mosley, 1757-1786" ed. by E. I. Devitt, *Woodstock Letters,* XXXV No. 1 (1906).

Muhlenburg, Henry M. *The Journals of Henry Melchior Muhlenburg.* Translated and edited by Theodore G. Tappert and John W. Doberstein. Philadelphia, 1942.

Purviance, Robert. *A Narrative of Events which occurred in Baltimore Town During the Revolutionary War to Which are Appended Various Documents and Letters, the Greater Part of Which Have Never Been Heretofore Published.* Baltimore, 1849.

Smith, Horace W. *The Life and Correspondence of Rev. William Smith.* 2 vols. Philadelphia, 1880.

Sweet, William W. (ed.). *The Methodists, a Collection of Source Materials.* Chicago, 1946.

——————. *The Presbyterians: 1783-1840: A Collection of Source Materials.* New York, 1936.

Published Documents

American Constitutions and Religion: Religious References in the Charters of the Thirteen Colonies and the Constitutions of the Forty-Eight States. Edited by Conrad H. Moehlman. Berne, Ind., 1938.

Baptists. *Minutes of the Philadelphia Baptist Association, 1707-1807.* Edited by A. D. Gillette. Philadelphia, 1851.

——————. *The Universal Annual Register of the Baptist Denomination of North America.* Edited by John Asplund. Hanover, N. H., 1796.

Catholic Church. "Documents Relative to the Adjustment of the Roman Catholic Organization in the United States to the Conditions of National Independence, 1783-1789." Edited by Carl R. Fish. *American Historical Review,* XV (July, 1910), 801-829.

Friends, Society of. *The Revised Discipline Approved by the Yearly Meeting of Friends, Held in Baltimore, for the Western-Shore of Maryland and the Adjacent Parts of Pennsylvania and Virginia, in the Year One Thousand Seven Hundred and Ninety Three.* Baltimore, 1794.

Jewry, American. *American Jewry: Documents of the Eighteenth Century.* ("Publications of the American Jewish Archives, No. III). Edited by Jacob R. Marcus. Cincinnati, 1959.

Lutheran, Evangelical Ministerium. *Documentary History of the Evangelical Lutheran Ministerium of Pennsylvania and Adjacent States. Proceedings of the Annual Conventions from 1748 to 1821. Compiled and Translated from Records in the Archives and from the Written Protocols.* Philadelphia, 1898.

Maryland Historical Society Archives of Maryland. 68 vols. Edited by William H. Browne, *et al.* Baltimore, 1883.

Maryland, State of. *Laws of Maryland Made and Passed at a Session of the Assembly.* Annapolis, 1776.

——————. *The Laws of Maryland to Which are Prefixed the Original Charter, with an English Translation, The Bill of Rights and Constitution of the State, as Originally Adopted by the Convention, with Several Alterations by Acts of Assembly, the Declaration of Independence, the Articles of Confederation, the Constitution of the General Government, and the Amendments*

Made Thereto, With an Index to the Laws, the Bill of Rights and the Constitution. 2 vols. Revised and collected under the Authority of the Legislature, by William Kilty, Attorney at Law. Annapolis, 1799.

—————————.*Proceedings of the Convention of the Province of Maryland, Held at Annapolis, in 1774, 1775, & 1776.* Annapolis, 1836.

Methodist Episcopal Church. *Minutes of the Annual Conferences of the Methodist Episcopal Church for the Years 1773-1828.* New York, 1840.

—————————. *Minutes of Several Conversations Between the Rev. Thomas Coke, LL. D., the Rev. Francis Asbury and Others, at a Conference, Begun in Baltimore in the State of Maryland, on Monday the 27th of December, in the Year 1784; Composing a Form of Discipline for the Ministers, Preachers and Other Members of the Methodist Episcopal Church in America.* Philadelphia, 1785.

Oerter, A. L. "Graceham, Frederick County, Md. An Historical Sketch," *Transactions of the Moravian Historical Society,* IX, Pts. I and II (1913), 119-305.[3]

Presbyterian Church. "First Presbyterian Church Membership, 1766-1783." *Maryland Historical Magazine,* XXXV (September, 1940), 256-261.

—————————. *Records of the Presbyterian Church in the United States.* Philadelphia, 1841.

Protestant Episcopal Church. *Historical Collections Relating to the American Colonial Church.* 4 vols. Edited by William S. Perry. Hartford, Conn., 1870-1873.

—————————. *Journals of the General Conventions of the Protestant Episcopal Church in the United States of America: From the Year 1784 to the Year 1814, Inclusive; Also First Appendix Containing the Constitution and Canons; and Second Appendix Containing Three Pastoral Letters.* Philadelphia, 1817.

—————————. *Notices and Journals and Remains of Journals of the Two Preliminary Conventions of the Clergy, and of the First Five Annual Conventions and Two Adjourned Conventions of the Clergy and Laity of the Protestant Episcopal Church in the Diocese of Maryland in the Years 1783, 1784, 1785, 1786, 1787, 1788: Together with the Ratifications of the Constitutions and Canons of the Diocese by the Several Parishes in 1788; and the Returns of Property to Sundry Parishes by the Vestries Thereof in 1789, to the Convention of that Year: From the Papers of the Convention. (Never Before Published.)* Bound collection of pamphlets from 1783-1789, Rare Book Room, Library of Congress, Washington, D. C.

—————————. *Historical Collections Relating to the American Colonial Church.* 4 vols.; Hartford, Conn., 1870-78, Ed. by William S. Perry.

Special Studies on Maryland

Allen, Ethan. *The Clergy in Maryland of the Protestant Episcopal Church Since the Independence of 1783.* Baltimore, 1860.

Bangs, Nathan. *The Life of Freeborn Garrettson.* New York, 1829.

Barker, Charles A. *The Background of the Revolution in Maryland.* New Haven, 1940.

Breed, William P. *Presbyterians and the Revolution.* Philadelphia, 1776.

Buck, Emory S., ed. *The History of American Methodism.* 3 vols.; New York, 1964.

Cameron, Richard M., ed. *The Rise of Methodism, a Source Book.* New York, 1954.

Cross, Arthur L. *The Anglican Episcopate and the American Colonies.* Cambridge, 1902.

Crowl, Philip A. *Maryland During and After the Revolution: A Political and Economic Study* ("The Johns Hopkins University Studies in Historical and

---

[3]This work is a calendar and translation of much of the official Church diary.

Political Science," Ser. LXI, No. 1). Baltimore, 1942.

Cunz, Dieter. *The Maryland Germans: A History.* Princeton, N. J., 1948.

Daley, John M. *Georgetown University: Origin and Early Years.* Washington, D. C., 1957.

Dole, Esther M. *Maryland During the American Revolution.* Baltimore, 1941.

Drake, Thomas E. *Quakers and Slavery in America.* New Haven, 1950.

Fell, Thomas. *Some Historical Accounts of the Founding of King William's School and Its Subsequent Establishment as St. John's College.* Baltimore, 1894.

Gambrall, Thomas C. *Church Life in Colonial Maryland.* Baltimore, 1885.

Gegenheimer, Albert F. *William Smith, Educator and Churchman.* Philadelphia, 1943.

Guttmacher, Adolf. *History of the Baltimore Hebrew Congregation.* Baltimore, 1907.

Hanley, Thomas O'Brien. *Charles Carroll of Carrollton: The Making of a Revolutionary Gentleman.* Washington, D. C., 1970.

—————————. *Their Rights and Liberties: The Beginnings of Religious and Political Freedom in Maryland.* Westminster, Md., 1959.

Hawks, Francis L. *Contributions to the Ecclesiastical History of the United States.* Vol. I: Maryland. New York, 1839.

Jones, Joseph H. *History of the Baltimore Baptist Association.* Baltimore, 1892.

Lee, Jesse. *A Short History of the Methodists in the United States of America.* Baltimore, 1811.

Loveland, Clare O. *The Critical Years: The Reconstruction of the Anglican Church in the United States of America: 1780-1789.* Greenwich, Conn., 1956.

McCormick, Leo J. *Church-State Relationships in Education in Maryland.* Washington, D. C., 1942.

McCulloh, Gerald O., ed. *The Ministry in the Methodist Heritage.* Nashville, Tenn., 1960.

McIlvain, James W. *First Presbyterian Church in Baltimore, Md.* Baltimore, 1906.

Melville, Annabelle M. *John Carroll of Baltimore: Founder of the American Catholic Hierarchy.* New York, 1955.

Metzger, Charles H. *Catholics and the American Revolution: A Study in Religious Climate.* Chicago, 1962.

Moore, William C. *Jeremiah Moore, 1746-1815.* Richmond, 1933.

Niles, Alfred S. *Analysis of the Constitution of Maryland: For Use in Constitutional Law Class, University of Maryland.* Baltimore, 1924.

Pfatteicher, Helen E. *The Ministerium of Pennsylvania: Oldest Lutheran Synod, Founded in Colony Days.* Philadelphia, 1938.

Rightmyer, Nelson Waite. *Maryland's Established Church.* Baltimore, 1956.

—————————. *Parishes of the Diocese of Maryland.* Reistertown, Md., 1960.

Shoemaker, Robert W. *The Origin and Meaning of the Name "Protestant Episcopal".* New York, 1959.

Silver, John A. *The Provisional Government of Maryland (1774-1777).* ("Johns Hopkins University Studies in Historical and Political Science," Ser. 16, No. 10.) Baltimore, 1895.

Simpson, John F. *Monocacy Valley Maryland Presbiterianism: A History of the Frederick, Emmitsburg, Piney Creek, Taneytown and New Winsdor Presbyterian Congregations.* Frederick, Md., 1936.

Smith, Ellen H. *Charles Carroll of Carrollton.* Cambridge, Mass., 1942.

Smith, Joseph T. *Eighty Years: Embracing a History of Presbyterianism in Baltimore, With an Appendix.* Philadelphia, 1899.

Steiner, Bernard C. *History of Education in Maryland.* Washington, D. C., 1894.

Stowe, Walter H. *The Life and Letters of Bishop William White.* New York, 1937.

Trinterud, Leonard J. *The Forming of an American Tradition.* New York, 1949.

Wallace, Paul A. W. *The Muhlenbergs of Pennsylvania.* Philadelphia, 1950.

Weishampel, J. F. *History of the Baptist Churches of Maryland Connected with the Maryland Baptist Union Association.* Baltimore, 1885.

Werline, Albert W. *Problems of Church and State in Maryland During the Seventeenth and Eighteenth Centuries (1632-1789)*. South Lancaster, Mass., 1948.
Wilbur, Henry W. *The Life and Labors of Elias Hicks*. Philadelphia, 1910.

Selected General Studies

Alden, John R. *The American Revolution, 1775-1783*. New York, 1954.
Andrews, Matthew P. *History of Maryland: Province and State*. Garden City, N. J., 1929.
Baldwin, Alice M. *The New England Clergy and the American Revolution*. Durham, N. C., 1928.
Berger, Daniel. *History of the Church of the United Brethern in Christ*. ("The American Church History Series," Vol. XII.) New York, 1894.
Bibbins, Ruthella M. *How Methodism Came, the Beginnings of Methodism in England and America*. Baltimore, 1945.
Bracket, J. R. *Negro in Maryland*. 1889.
Bridenbaugh, Carl. *Mitre and Sceptre*. New York, 1962.
Burr, Nelson R. *A Critical Bibliography of Religion in America*. 2 vols.; Princeton, N. J., 1961.
Cobb, Sanford H. *The Rise of Religious Liberty in America*. New York, 1902.
East, Robert A. *Business Enterprise in the American Revolutionary Era*. ("Columbia University Studies in History, Economics, and Public Law," No. 439.) New York, 1938.
Eller, Paul H. *These Evangelical United Brethren*. Dayton, O., 1950.
Ellis, John Tracy. *Catholics in Colonial America*. Baltimore, Md., 1963.
Greene, Evarts B. *The Revolutionary Generation, 1763-1790*. Vol. IV of *A History of America Life*. Edited by Arthur M. Schlesinger and Dixon R. Fox. 12 vols. New York, 1943.
Hamilton, John T. *A History of the Church Known as the Moravian Church, or the Unitas Fratrum, or the Brethren, During the Eighteenth and Nineteenth Centuries*. Bethlehem, Penna., 1900.
Hardon, John A. *The Protestant Churches of America*. Westminster, Md., 1958.
Heimert, Alan. *Religion and the American Mind: From the Great Awakening to the Revolution*. Cambridge, Mass., 1966.
Humphrey, Edward F. *Nationalism and Religion in America*. Boston, 1924.
James, Sidney V. *A People Among Peoples*. Cambridge, Mass., 1963.
James, William. *The Will to Believe and Other Essays in Popular Philosophy*. New York, 1927.
Jameson, John F. *American Revolution Considered as a Social Movement*. Princeton, N. J., 1926.
Koch, G. Adolf. *Republican Religion: The American Revolution and the Cult of Reason*. ("Studies in Religion and Culture, American Religion Series, VII.") New York, 1933.
Marty, Martin. *The Infidel: Freethought and American Religion*. New York, 1961.
Maxson, Charles H. *The Great Awakening in the Middle Colonies*. Chicago, 1920.
Morais, Herbert M. *Deism in Eighteenth Century America*. New York, 1960.
Nevins, Allan. *The American States During and After the Revolution, 1775-1789*. New York, 1924.
Pourrat, Pierre. *Christian Spirituality: Later Developments: Part. II: From Jansenism to Modern Times*. Trans. by Donald Attwater. 4 vols., Westminster, Md., 1955.
Qualben, Lars P. *The Lutheran Church in Colonial America*. New York, 1940.
Ray, Sister Mary Augustina. *American Opinion of Roman Catholicism in the Eighteenth Century*. New York, 1936.
Shea, John G. *A History of the Catholic Church in the United States*. 4 vols. New York, 1886-1892.

Schimberg, Andre. *L'education morale dans les colléges de la Companie de Jésus en France sous l'Ancien Régime* (XVe, XVIe, XVIIe, XVIIIe siècles). Paris, 1913.

Simpson, Matthew (ed.). *Cyclopaedia of Methodism: Embracing Sketches of its Rise, Progress and Present Condition, with Biographical Notices and Numerous Illustrations.* Philadelphia, 1881.

Smith, H. Shelton, Handy, Robert T., and Loetscher, Lefferts A. *American Christianity: An Historical Interpretation with Representative Documents.* 2 vols. New York, 1960.

Sweet, William W. *Methodism in American History.* New York, 1933.

——————. *Religion in the Development of American Culture, 1765-1840.* New York, 1952.

Thomas, Allen C. and Richard H. *A History of the Friends in America.* Philadelphia, 1894.

Trappes-Lovax, Michael. *Bishop Challoner: A Biographical Study Derived from Dr. Edwin Burton's Life and Times of Bishop Challoner.* New York, 1936.

U. S. Congress, House. *Biographical Directory of the American Congress, September 5, 1774, to October 21, 1788; The Congress of the United States From the First to the Eightieth Congress, March 4, 1789, to January 3, 1949, Inclusive.* Washington, D. C., 1950.

Wentz, Abdel R. *A Basic History of Lutheranism in America.* Philadelphia, 1955.

Articles

Barroll, L. Wethered. "Washington College, 1783," *Maryland Historical Magazine,* VI (June, 1911), 164-79.

Bowie, Lucy L. "Maryland Troops at the Battle of Harlem Heights," *Maryland Historical Magazine,* XLIII (March, 1948), 1-27.

Gardner, John H. "Presbyterians in Old Baltimore, 1729-1859," *Maryland Historical Magazine,* XXXV (September, 1940), 224-61.

Hamilton, William. "Some Accounts of Cokesbury College," *Methodist Quarterly Review,* XLI (April, 1859), 173-87.

Hanley, Thomas O'Brien. "Church and State in the Maryland Ordinance of 1639," *Church History,* XXVI (Dec. 1957), 325-41.

——————. "His Excellency's Council: Maryland, 1715-1720." *Records of the American Catholic Historical Society of Philadelphia,* LXXIV (1963), 137-50.

——————. "The Catholic and Anglican Gentry in Maryland Politics," *Historical Magazine of the Protestant Episcopal Church,* XXXVIII (June, 1969), 143-52.

——————. "The Emergence of Pluralism in the United States," *Theological Studies,* XXIII (June, 1962), 207-32.

——————. "Reluctant Witness to Pluralism in Early America." *Theological Studies,* XXVI (Sep., 1965), 375-92.

——————. *In The New Catholic Encyclopedia* (15 vols.; New York, 1967): "Church and State in the U. S. Colonial Period," III, 743-46; "Toleration Acts of 1639 and 1649, Maryland," XIV, 193-94; "Missions in Colonial America," IX, 471-74.

——————. "The State and Dissenters in the Revolution," *Maryland Historical Magazine,* LVIII (Dec., 1963), 325-32.

——————. "Young Mr. Carroll and Montesquieu," *Maryland Historical Magazine,* LXII (Dec., 1967), 394-418.

Hortogensis, Benjamin H. "Unequal Rights in Maryland Since 1776," *Publications of the American Jewish Historical Society,* No. 25 (1917), pp. 93-107.

Hughes, Nathaniel C. "The Methodist Christmas Conference: Dec. 24, 1784 - Jan. 2, 1785," *Maryland Historical Magazine,* LIV (September, 1959), 272-92.

Matthews, Donald G. "The Great Awakening as an Organizing Process," *American Quarterly*, XXI (Spring, 1969), 25-43.

Monk, Robert C. "Unity and Diversity Among Eighteenth Century Colonial Anglicans and Methodists," *Historical Magazine of the Protestant Episcopal Church*, XXXVIII (Mar., 1969), 63-67.

Skaggs, David C. "Maryland's Impulse Toward Social Revolution: 1750-1776," *The Journal of American History*, LIV (Mar., 1968), 771-85.

——————. "Thomas Cradock's Sermon on the Governance of Maryland's Established Church," *The William and Mary Quarterly*, Third Series, XXVII (Oct., 1970), 630-53.

Tolles, Frederick B. "The American Revolution Considered as a Social Movement: A Re-Evaluation," *American Historical Review*, LX (1954), 1-12.

Unpublished Material

Davis, Robert P. "Beginnings of Presbyterianism in Makemieland to 1788: A Study of the Early History of the Presbyterian Church in Somerset, Worcester, and Wicomico Counties, Maryland" (M. A. Thesis, Union Theological Seminary, Richmond, Va., 1941).

Hanley, Thomas O'Brien. "The Impact of the American Revolution on Religion in Maryland: 1776-1800" (Ph. D. Diss., Georgetown Univ., 1961).

Hartdgen, Harold E. "The Anglican Vestry in Colonial Maryland" (Ph. D. Diss., Northwestern Univ., 1965).

Hooker, Richard. "The Anglican Church and the American Revolution" (Ph. D. Diss., University of Chicago, 1943).

Maring, Norman H. "A Denominational History of the Maryland Baptists: 1742-1882" (Ph. D. Diss., University of Maryland, 1948).

Simpson, Robert D. "Freeborn Garrettson, American Methodist Pioneer" (Ph. D. Diss., Drew University, 1955).

INDEX